Foundations of 3D Graphics Programming

Jim X. Chen
Edward J. Wegman

Foundations of 3D Graphics Programming

Using JOGL and Java3D

With 139 Figures

 Springer

Jim X. Chen, PhD
Computer Science Department
George Mason University
Fairfax, VA 22030
USA
jchen@cs.gmu.edu

Edward J. Wegman, PhD
Center for Computational Statistics
George Mason University
Fairfax, VA 22030
USA
ewegman@gmu.edu

British Library Cataloguing in Publication Data
A catalogue record for this book is available from the British Library

Library of Congress Control Number: 2005937739

ISBN-10: 1-84628-185-7
ISBN-13: 978-1-84628-185-3

Printed on acid-free paper

Printed in the United States of America.   (MVY)

9 8 7 6 5 4 3 2 1

Springer Science+Business Media

springer.com

Preface

OpenGL, which has been bound in C, is a seasoned graphics library for scientists and engineers. As we know, Java is a rapidly growing language becoming the de facto standard of Computer Science learning and application development platform as many undergraduate computer science programs are adopting Java in place of C/C++. Released by Sun Microsystems in June 2003, the recent OpenGL binding with Java, JOGL, provides students, scientists, and engineers a new venue of graphics learning, research, and applications.

Overview

This book aims to be a shortcut to graphics theory and programming in JOGL. Specifically, it covers OpenGL programming in Java, using JOGL, along with concise computer graphics theories. It covers all graphics basics and several advanced topics without including some implementation details that are not necessary in graphics applications. It also covers some basic concepts in Java programming for C/C++ programmers. It is designed as a textbook for students who know programming basics already. It is an excellent shortcut to learn 3D graphics for scientists and engineers who understand Java programming. It is also a good reference for C/C++ graphics programmers to learn Java and JOGL. This book is a companion to *Guide to Graphics Software Tools* (Springer-Verlag, New York, ISBN 0-387-95049-4), which covers a smaller graphics area with similar examples in C but has a comprehensive list of graphics software tools.

Organization and Features

This book concisely introduces graphics theory and programming in Java with JOGL. A top-down approach is used to lead the audience into programming and applications up front. The theory provides a high-level understanding of all basic graphics principles without some detailed low-level implementations. The emphasis is on understanding graphics and using JOGL instead of implementing a graphics system. The contents of the book are integrated with the sample programs, which are specifically designed for learning and accompany this book. To keep the book's conciseness and clarity as a high priority, the sample programs are not production-quality code in some perspectives. For example, error handling, GUI, controls, and exiting are mostly simplified or omitted.

Chapter 1 introduces OpenGL, Java, JOGL, and basic graphics concepts including object, model, image, frame buffer, scan-conversion, clipping, and antialiasing. Chapter 2 discusses transformation theory, viewing theory, and OpenGL programming in detail. 3D models, hidden-surface removal, and collision detection are also covered. Chapter 3 overviews color in hardware, eye characteristics, gamma correction, interpolation, OpenGL lighting, and surface shading models. The emphasis is on OpenGL lighting. Chapter 4 surveys OpenGL blending, image rendering, and texture mapping. Chapter 5 introduces solid models, curves, and curved surfaces. Chapter 6 discusses scene graph and Java3D programming with concise examples. Chapter 7 wraps up basic computer graphics principles and programming with some advanced concepts and methods.

Web Resources

JOGL and Java3D sample programs (their sources and executables) are available online. The following Web address contains all the updates and additional information, including setting up the OpenGL programming environment and accompanying Microsoft PowerPoint course notes for learners and instructors:

http://cs.gmu.edu/~jchen/graphics/jogl/

Audience

The book is intended for a very wide range of readers, including scientists in different disciplines, undergraduates in Computer Science, and Ph.D. students and advanced researchers who are interested in learning and using computer graphics on Java and JOGL platform.

Chapters 1 through 4 are suitable for a one-semester graphics course or self-learning. These chapters should be covered in order. Prerequisites are preliminary programming skills and basic knowledge of linear algebra and trigonometry. Chapters 5 and 6 are independent introductions suitable for additional advanced graphics courses.

Acknowledgments

As a class project in CS 652 at George Mason University, Danny Han initially coded some examples for this book. We acknowledge the anonymous reviewers and the whole production team at Springer. Their precious comments, editings, and help have significantly improved the quality and value of the book.

Jim X. Chen and Edward J. Wegman
May 2006

Contents

Chapter 2

Transformation and Viewing   37

Chapter 3

Color and Lighting   117

Chapter 4

Blending and Texture Mapping   *159*

Chapter 7

Advanced Topics   *257*

1
Introduction

Chapter Objectives:

- Introduce basic graphics concepts — object, model, image, graphics library, frame buffer, scan-conversion, clipping, and antialiasing

- Set up Java, JOGL programming environments

- Understand simple JOGL programs

1.1 Graphics Models and Libraries

A graphics *display* is a drawing area composed of an array of fine points called *pixels*. At the heart of a graphics system there is a magic pen, which can move at lightning speed to a specific pixel and draw the pixel with a specific color — a red, green, and blue (RGB) vector value. This pen can be controlled directly by hand through an input device (mouse or keyboard) like a simple paintbrush. In this case, we can draw whatever we imagine, but it takes a real artist to come up with a good painting. Computer graphics, however, is about using this pen automatically through programming.

A real or imaginary *object* is represented in a computer as a model and is displayed as an image. A *model* is an abstract description of the object's shape (vertices) and attributes (colors), which can be used to find all the points and their colors on the object corresponding to the pixels in the drawing area. Given a model, the application program will control the pen through a graphics library to generate the corresponding image. An *image* is simply a 2D array of pixels.

A *graphics library* provides a set of graphics commands or functions. These commands can be bound in *C, C++, Java,* or other programming languages on different platforms. Graphics commands can specify primitive 2D and 3D geometric models to be digitized and displayed. Here *primitive* means that only certain simple shapes (such as points, lines, and polygons) can be accepted by a graphics library. To draw a complex shape, we need an application program to assemble or construct it by displaying pieces of simple shapes (primitives). We have the magic pen that draws a pixel. If we can draw a pixel, we can draw a line, a polygon, a curve, a block, a building, an airplane, and so forth. A general application program can be included into a graphics library as a command to draw a complex shape. Because our pen is magically fast, we can draw a complex object, clear the drawing area, draw the object at a slightly different location or shape, and repeat the above processes — the object is now *animated*.

OpenGL is a graphics library that we will integrate with the *Java programming language* to introduce graphics theory, programming, and applications. When we introduce program examples, we will succinctly discuss Java-specific concepts and programming as well for C/C++ programmers.

1.2 OpenGL Programming in Java: JOGL

OpenGL is the most widely used graphics library (GL) or application programming interface (API), and is supported across all popular desktop and workstation platforms, ensuring wide application deployment. *JOGL* implements Java bindings for OpenGL. It provides hardware-supported 3D graphics to applications written in Java. It is part of a suite of open-source technologies initiated by the Game Technology Group at Sun Microsystems. JOGL provides full access to OpenGL functions and integrates with the AWT and Swing widget sets.

First, let's spend some time to set up our working environment, compile J1_0_Point.java, and run the program. The following file contains links to all the example programs in this book and detailed information for setting up working environments on different platforms for the most recent version:

    http://cs.gmu.edu/~jchen/graphics/setup.html

1.2.1 Setting Up Working Environment

JOGL provides full access to the APIs in the OpenGL 1.4 specification as well as nearly all vendor extensions. To install and run JOGL, we need to install Java

Development Kit. In addition, a Java IDE is also preferred to help coding. The following steps will guide you through installing Java, JOGL, and Eclipse or JBuilder IDE.

1. Installing Java Development Kit 1.4 or Above

Java Development Kit (JDK) contains a compiler, interpreter, and debugger. If you have not installed JDK, it is freely available from Sun Microsystems. You can download the latest version from the download section at http://java.sun.com. Make sure you download the JDK (or SDK) not the JRE (runtime environment) that matches the platform you use. For example, version 1.5.0 can be downloaded from   Java2   Standard   Edition   (J2SE)   at http://java.sun.com/j2se/1.5.0/download.jsp. After downloading the JDK, you can run the installation executable file. During the installation, you will be asked the directory "Install to:". You need to put it somewhere you know. For example: "C:\j2sdk1.5.0\".

2. Installing JOGL

The first step required is to obtain the binaries that you will need in order to compile and run your applications. These pre-compiled binaries can be obtained from the project Web site (https://jogl.dev.java.net/) Precompiled binaries and documentation. Go to Release Builds 2005 and download "jogl.jar", and then download the binaries that match the platform you use. For Windows platform, for example,   it   is   named   "jogl-natives-win32.jar".   After   downloading "jogl-natives-win32.jar", you should extract "jogl.dll" and jogl_cg.dll" from it by the following command:

```
"C:\j2sdk1.5.0\bin\jar" -xvf jogl-natives-win32.jar
```

After that, you can put the three files (jogl.jar, jogl.dll, and jogl_cg.dll) in the directory with the Java (JOGL) examples and compile all them on the command line in the current directory with:

```
"C:\j2sdk1.5.0\bin\javac" -classpath jogl.jar *.java
```

After that, you can run the sample program with (the command in one line):

```
"C:\j2sdk1.5.0\bin\java" -classpath .;jogl.jar;
-Djava.library.path=. J1_0_Point
```

That is, you need to place the "jogl.jar" file in the CLASSPATH of your build environment in order to be able to compile an application with JOGL and run, and place "jogl.dll" and "jogl_cg.dll" in the directory listed in the "java.library.path" environment variable during execution. Java loads the native libraries (such as the dll file for Windows) from the directories listed in the "java.library.path" environment variable. For Windows, placing the dll files under "C:\WINDOWS\system32\" directory works. This approach gets you up running quickly without worrying about the "java.library.path" setting.

3. Installing a Java IDE (Eclipse, jGRASP, or JBuilder)

   Installing a Java IDE (Integrated Development Environment) is optional. Without an IDE, you can edit Java program files using any text editor, compile and run Java programs using the commands we introduced above after downloading JOGL.

   Java IDEs such as Eclipse, JBuilder, or jGRASP are development environments that make Java programming much faster and easier. If you use Eclipse, you can put "jogl.jar" in "C:\j2re1.5.0\lib\ext\" directory in the Java runtime environment.

   You can download from http://eclipse.org the latest version of Eclipse that matches the platform you use. Expand it into the folder where you would like Eclipse to run from, (e.g., "C:\eclipse\"). There is no installation to run. To remove Eclipse you simply delete the directory, because Eclipse does not alter the system registry.

   If you use jGRASP, in the project under "compiler->setting for workspace->PATH", you can add the directory of the *.dll files to the system PATH window, and add "jogl.jar" file with full path to the CLASSPATH window.

   As an alternative, you can download a free version of JBuilder from http://www.borland.com/jbuilder/. JBuilder comes with its own JDK. If you use JBuilder as the IDE and want to use your downloaded JDK, you need to start JBuilder, go to "Tools->Configue JDKs", and click "Change" to change the "JDK home path:" to where you install your JDK. For example, "C:\j2sdk1.5.0\". Also, under "Tools->Configue JDKs", you can click "Add" to add "jogl.jar" from wherever you save it to the JBuilder environment.

4. Creating a Sample Program in Eclipse

   As an example, here we introduce using Eclipse. After downloading it, you can run it to start programming. Now in Eclipse you click on "File->New->Project" to create a new *Java Project* at a name you prefer. Then, you click on

"File->New->Class" to create a new class with name: "J1_0_Point". After that, you can copy the following code into the space, and click on "Run->Run As->Java Application" to start compiling and running. You should see a window with a very tiny red pixel at the center. In the future, you can continue creating new classes, as we introduce each example as a new class.

/* draw a point */

```
/* Java's supplied classes are "imported". Here the awt
(Abstract Windowing Toolkit) is imported to provide "Frame"
class, which includes windowing functions */
import java.awt.*;

// JOGL: OpenGL functions
import net.java.games.jogl.*;

/* Java class definition: "extends" means "inherits". So
J1_0_Point is a subclass of Frame, and it inherits Frame's
variables and methods. "implements" means GLEventListener is
an interface, which only defines methods (init(), reshape(),
display(), and displaychanged()) without implementation.These
methods are actually callback functions handling events.
J1_0_Point will implement GLEventListener's methods and use
them for different events. */

public class J1_0_Point extends Frame implements
GLEventListener {
    static int HEIGHT = 400, WIDTH = 400;
    static GL gl; //interface to OpenGL
    static GLCanvas canvas; // drawable in a frame
    GLCapabilities capabilities; // OpenGL capabilities

    public J1_0_Point() { // constructor

        //1. specify a drawable: canvas
        capabilities = new GLCapabilities();
        canvas =
GLDrawableFactory.getFactory().createGLCanvas(capabilities);

        //2. listen to the events related to canvas: reshape
        canvas.addGLEventListener(this);

        //3. add the canvas to fill the Frame container
        add(canvas, BorderLayout.CENTER);
        /* In Java, a method belongs to a class object.
        Here the method "add" belongs to J1_0_Point's
        instantiation, which is frame in "main" function.
```

```
        It is equivalent to use "this.add(canvas, ...)" */
        //4. interface to OpenGL functions
        gl = canvas.getGL();
    }


public static void main(String[] args) {
    J1_0_Point frame = new J1_0_Point();

        //5. set the size of the frame and make it visible
        frame.setSize(WIDTH, HEIGHT);
        frame.setVisible(true);
    }


// Called once for OpenGL initialization
public void init(GLDrawable drawable) {

        //6. specify a drawing color: red
        gl.glColor3f(1.0f, 0.0f, 0.0f);
    }


// Called for handling reshaped drawing area
public void reshape(GLDrawable drawable, int x, int y,
    int width, int height) {

        //7. specify the drawing area (frame) coordinates
        gl.glMatrixMode(GL.GL_PROJECTION);
        gl.glLoadIdentity();
        gl.glOrtho(0, width, 0, height, -1.0, 1.0);
    }


// Called for OpenGL rendering every reshape
public void display(GLDrawable drawable) {

        //8. specify to draw a point
        gl.glBegin(GL.GL_POINTS);
            gl.glVertex2i(WIDTH/2, HEIGHT/2);
        gl.glEnd();
    }


// called if display mode or device are changed
public void displayChanged(GLDrawable drawable,
    boolean modeChanged,boolean deviceChanged) {
    }
}
```

1.2.2 Drawing a Point

The above *J1_0_Point.java* is a Java application that draws a red point using JOGL. If you are a C/C++ programmer, you should read all the comments in the sample program carefully, because they include explanations about Java-specific terminologies and coding. Our future examples are built on top of this one. Here we explain in detail. The program is complex to us at this point of time. We only need to understand the following:

1. Class GLCanvas is an Abstract Window Toolkit (AWT) component that provides OpenGL rendering support. Therefore, the GLCanvas object, <u>canvas,</u> corresponds to the drawing area that will appear in the Frame object <u>frame</u>, which corresponds to the display window. Here *object* means an instance of a class in object-oriented programming, not a 3D object. In the future, we omit using a class name and underline its object name in our discussion. In many cases, object names are lowercases of the corresponding class names to facilitate understanding.

2. An *event* is a user input or a system state change, which is queued with other events to be handled. Event handling is to register an object to act as a listener for a particular type of event on a particular component. Here <u>frame</u> is a listener for the GL events on <u>canvas</u>. When a specific event happens, it sends <u>canvas</u> to the corresponding event handling method and invokes the method. GLEventListener has four event-handling methods:

   - *init()* is called immediately after the OpenGL context is initialized for the first time, which is a system event. It can be used to perform one-time OpenGL initialization;

   - *reshape()* is called if <u>canvas</u> has been resized, which happens when the user changes the size of the window. The listener also passes the drawable <u>canvas</u> and the display area's lower-left corner (*x, y*) and size (*width, height*) to the method. At this time, (*x, y*) is always (*0, 0*), and the <u>canvas</u>' size is the same as the display window's <u>frame</u>. The client can update the coordinates of the display corresponding to the resized window appropriately. *reshape()* is called at least once when program starts. Whenever *reshape()* is called, *display()* is called as well;

   - *display()* is called to initiate OpenGL rendering when program starts. It is called afterwards when reshape event happens;

- *displayChanged()* is called when the display mode or the display device has been changed. Currently we do not use this event handler.

3. canvas is added to frame to cover the whole display area. canvas will reshape with frame.

4. gl is an interface handle to OpenGL methods. All OpenGL commands are prefixed with "gl" as well, so you will see OpenGL method like ***gl.glColor()***. When we explain the OpenGL command, we often omit the interface handle.

5. Here we set the physical size of frame and make its contents visible. Here the physical size corresponds to the number of pixels in *x* and *y* direction. The actual physical size also depends on the *resolution* of the display, which is measured in number of pixels per inch. At this point, the window frame appears. Depending on the JOGL version, the physical size may include the boarders, which is a little larger than the visible area that is returned as *w* and *h* in *reshape()*.

6. The foreground drawing color is specified as a vector (red, green, blue). Here (1, 0, 0) represents a red color.

7. These methods specify the logical coordinates. For example, if we use the command *glOrtho(0, width, 0, height, −1.0, 1.0)*, then the coordinates in frame (or canvas) will be $0 \le x \le width$ from the left side to the right side of the window, $0 \le y \le height$ from the bottom side to the top side of the window, and $-1 \le z \le 1$ in the direction perpendicular to the window. The *z* direction is ignored in 2D applications. It is a coincidence that the logical coordinates correspond to the physical (pixel) coordinates, because *width* and *height* are initially from frame's WIDTH and HEIGHT. We can specify *glOrtho(0, 100*WIDTH, 0, 100*HEIGHT, −1.0, 1.0)* as well, then point (*WIDTH/2, HEIGHT/2*) will appear at the lower-left corner of the frame instead of the center of the frame.

8. These methods draw a point at (*WIDTH/2, HEIGHT/2*). The coordinates are logical coordinates not directly related to the canvas' size. The *width* and *height* in *glOrtho()* are actual window size. It is the same as WIDTH and HEIGHT at the beginning, but if you reshape the window, they will be different, respectively. Therefore, if we reshape the window, the red point moves.

In summary, when Frame is instantiated, constructor *J1_0_Point()* will create a drawable canvas, add event listener to it, attach the display to it, and get a handle to gl methods from it. *reshape()* will set up the display's logical coordinates in the window frame. *display()* will draw a point in the logical coordinates. When program starts, *main()* will be called, then <u>frame</u> instantiation, *J1_0_Point()*, *setSize()*, *setVisible()*, *init()*, *reshape()*, *and dsplay()*. *reshape()* and *dsplay()* will be called again and again if the user changes the display area. You may not find it, but a red point appears in the window.

1.2.3 Drawing Randomly Generated Points

J1_1_Point extends *J1_0_Point*, so it inherits all the methods from *J1_0_Point* that are not private. We can reuse the constructor and some of the methods.

/* draw randomly generated points */

```
import net.java.games.jogl.*;
import java.awt.event.*;


//built on J1_0_Point class
public class J1_1_Point extends J1_0_Point {
   static Animator animator; // drive display() in a loop

   public J1_1_Point() {
      // use super's constructor to initialize drawing

      //1. specify using only a single buffer
      capabilities.setDoubleBuffered(false);

      //2. add a listener for window closing
      addWindowListener(new WindowAdapter() {
        public void windowClosing(WindowEvent e) {
          animator.stop(); // stop animation
          System.exit(0);
        }
      });
   }


   // Called one-time for OpenGL initialization
   public void init(GLDrawable drawable) {
      // specify a drawing color: red
      gl.glColor3f(1.0f, 0.0f, 0.0f);

      //3. clear the background to black
      gl.glClearColor(0.0f, 0.0f, 0.0f, 0.0f);
      gl.glClear(GL.GL_COLOR_BUFFER_BIT);
```

```
    //4. drive the display() in a loop
    animator = new Animator(canvas);
    animator.start(); // start animator thread
}


// Called for OpenGL rendering every reshape
public void display(GLDrawable drawable) {

    //5. generate a random point
    double x = Math.random()*WIDTH;
    double y = Math.random()*HEIGHT;

    // specify to draw a point
    gl.glBegin(GL.GL_POINTS);
    gl.glVertex2d(x, y);
    gl.glEnd();
}


public static void main(String[] args) {
    J1_1_Point f = new J1_1_Point();

    //6. Add a title on the frame
    f.setTitle("JOGL J1_1_Point");
    f.setSize(WIDTH, HEIGHT);
    f.setVisible(true);
}
}
```

1. *J1_1_Point* is built on (extends) the super (previous) class, so we can reuse its methods. The super class's constructor is automatically called to initialize drawing and event handling. Here we specify using a single frame buffer. Frame buffer corresponds to the display, which will be discussed in the next section.

2. In order to avoid window hanging, we add a listener for window closing and stop animation before exit. Animation (<u>animator</u>) will be discussed later.

3. *glClearColor()* specifies the background color. OpenGL is a state machine, which means that if we specify the color, unless we change it, it will always be the same. Therefore, whenever we call *glClear()*, the background will be black unless we call *glCearClor()* to set it differently.

4. Object <u>animator</u> is attached to <u>canvas</u> to drive its *display()* method in a loop. When <u>animator</u> is started, it will generate a thread to call display repetitively. A thread is a process or task that runs with current program concurrently. Java is a multi-threaded programming language that allows starting multiple threads. <u>animator</u> is stopped before window closing.

5. A random point is generated. Because <u>animator</u> will run *display()* again and again in its thread, randomly generated points are displayed.

In summary, the super class' constructor, which is called implicitly, will create a drawable <u>canvas</u>, add event listener to it, and attach the display to it. *reshape()* will set up the display's logical coordinates in the window frame. *animator.start()* will call *display()* multiple times in a thread. *display()* will draw a point in logical coordinates. When program starts, *main()* will be called, then red points appear in the window.

1.3 Frame Buffer, Scan-conversion, and Clipping

The graphics system digitizes a specific model into a frame of discrete color points saved in a piece of memory called the *frame buffer*. This digitalization process is called *scan-conversion*. Sometimes *drawing* or *rendering* is used to mean scan-conversion. However, drawing and rendering are more general terms that do not focus on the digitalization process. The color points in the frame buffer will be sent to the corresponding pixels in the display device by a piece of hardware called the *video controller*. Therefore, whatever is in the frame buffer corresponds to the image on the screen. The application program accepts user input, manipulates the models (creates, stores, retrieves, and modifies the descriptions), and produces an image through the graphics system. The display is also a window for us to manipulate the model behind the image through the application program. A change on the display corresponds to a change in the model. A programmer's tasks concern mostly creating the model, changing the model, and handling user interaction. OpenGL (JOGL) and Java functions are the interfaces between the application program and the graphics hardware (Fig. 1.1).

Before using more JOGL primitive drawing functions directly, let's look at how these functions are implemented. Graphics libraries may be implemented quite differently, and many functions can be implemented in both software and hardware.

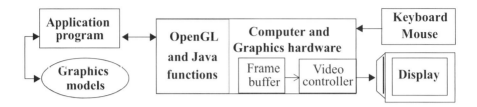

Fig. 1.1 A conceptual graphics system

1.3.1 Scan-converting Lines

A line object is described as an abstract model with two end points (x_0, y_0) and (x_n, y_n). It is scan-converted into the frame buffer by a graphics library function. The line equation is $y = mx + B$, where the slope $m = (y_n - y_0)/(x_n - x_0)$ and B is the y interception, a constant. Let's assume $-1 \leq m \leq 1$. For the pixels on the line, $x_{i+1} = x_i + 1$, and $y_{i+1} = mx_{i+1} + B = m(x_i + 1) + B = (mx_i + B) + m$. That is, $y_{i+1} - y_i + m$. To scan-convert the line, we need only to draw all the pixels at $(x_i,$ Round$(y_i))$ for $i = 0$ to n. If $1 \leq m$ or $m \leq -1$, we can call the same function with x and y switched. The following line scan-conversion program is built on rounding y and drawing a point.

/* draw randomly generated lines with -1<m<1 */

```
import net.java.games.jogl.*;


//built on J1_0_Point class
public class J1_2_Line extends J1_1_Point {

  // use super's constructor to initialize drawing

  // Called for OpenGL rendering every reshape
  public void display(GLDrawable drawable) {

    int x0, y0, xn, yn, dx, dy;
```

```
//1. generate a random line with -1<m<1;
do {
  x0 = (int) (Math.random()*WIDTH);
  y0 = (int) (Math.random()*HEIGHT);
  xn = (int) (Math.random()*WIDTH);
  yn = (int) (Math.random()*HEIGHT);
  dx = xn-x0;
  dy = yn-y0;

  if (x0>xn) {
    dx = -dx;
  }
  if (y0>yn) {
    dy = -dy;
  }
} while (dy>dx);

//2. draw a green line
gl.glColor3f(0, 1, 0);
line(x0, y0, xn, yn);
}


// scan-convert an integer line with slope -1<m<1
void line(int x0, int y0, int xn, int yn) {
  int x;
  float m, y;

  m = (float) (yn-y0)/(xn-x0);

  x = x0;
  y = y0;

  while (x<xn+1) {

    //3. write a pixel into frame buffer
    gl.glBegin(GL.GL_POINTS);
    gl.glVertex2i(x, (int) y);
    gl.glEnd();

    x++;
    y += m; /* next pixel's position */
  }
}


public static void main(String[] args) {
  J1_2_Line f = new J1_2_Line();
```

```
    f.setTitle("JOGL J1_2_Line");
    f.setSize(WIDTH, HEIGHT);
    f.setVisible(true);
  }
}
```

Because this program is a subclass of *J1_1_Point*, it inherits all the methods of *J1_1_Point*. The constructor function, *init()*, *reshape()*, and some other methods are all inherited. In other words, although we don't have these methods in this program, they are available from its superclass *J1_1_Point*, and can be called (executed) accordingly. For example, at initialization "J1_2_Line f = new J1_2_Line();", *J1_1_Point*'s constructor will be called, then in turn *J1_0_Point*'s constructor will be called, which initializes <u>canvas</u>, <u>gl</u> handle, and so on. In any case, constructing an instance of a class invokes all the superclasses along the inheritance chain. For any other methods, there is no chaining. For example, after the above initialization, *J1_1_Point*'s *init()* will be called. That is, subclass *J1_1_Point*'s *init()* overrides its superclass *J1_0_Point*'s *init()*.

Bresenham[1] developed a line scan-conversion algorithm using only integer operations, which can be implemented very efficiently in hardware. Let's assume pixel (x_p, y_p) is on the line and $0 \leq m \leq 1$ (Fig. 1.2). Which pixel should we choose next: E or NE? The line equation is $y = mx + B$, i.e. $F(x, y) = ax + by + c = 0$, where $a = dy = (y_n - y_0)$, $b = -dx = -(x_n - x_0) < 0$, and $c = B*dx$. Because $b < 0$, if y increases, $F(x, y)$ decreases, and vice versa. Therefore,

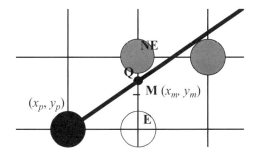

Fig. 1.2 Find the next pixel: E or NE

if the midpoint $M(x_m, y_m)$ between pixels NE and E is on the line, $F(x_m, y_m) = 0$; if $M(x_m, y_m)$ is below the line, $F(x_m, y_m) > 0$; and if $M(x_m, y_m)$ is above the line, $F(x_m, y_m) < 0$.

1. Bresenham, J. E., "Algorithm for Computer Control of Digital Plotter," *IBM Systems Journal*, 4 (1), 1965, 25–30.

If $F(x_m, y_m) > 0$, Q is above $M(x_m, y_m)$, we choose NE; otherwise we choose E. Therefore, $F(x_m, y_m)$ is a *decision factor*: d_{old}. From d_{old}, we can derive the decision factor d_{new} for the next pixel. We can see that $x_m = x_p + 1$ *and* $y_m = y_p + 1/2$. Therefore we have:

$$d_{old} = F(x_m, y_m) = F(x_p + 1, y_p + 1/2) = F(x_p, y_p) + a + b/2 = a + b/2. \qquad \text{(EQ 1)}$$

If $d_{old} \le 0$, E is chosen, the next middle point is at $(x_p + 2, y_p + 1/2)$:

$$d_{new} = F(x_p + 2, y_p + 1/2) = d_{old} + a. \qquad \text{(EQ 2)}$$

If $d_{old} > 0$, NE is chosen, the next middle point is at $(x_p + 2, y_p + 3/2)$:

$$d_{new} = F(x_p + 2, y_p + 3/2) = d_{old} + a + b. \qquad \text{(EQ 3)}$$

We can see that only the initial d_{old} is not an integer. If we multiply by 2 on both sides of Equations 1, 2, and 3, all decision factors are integers. Note that if a decision factor is greater/smaller than zero, multiplying it by 2 does not change the fact that it is still greater/smaller than zero. So the decision remains the same. Let $dE = 2dy$, $dNE = 2(dy - dx)$, and $d_{old} = 2dy - dx$:

$$\text{If E is chosen, } d_{new} = d_{old} + dE; \qquad \text{(EQ 4)}$$

$$\text{If NE is chosen, } d_{new} = d_{old} + dNE. \qquad \text{(EQ 5)}$$

Therefore, in the line scan-conversion algorithm, the arithmetic needed to evaluate d_{new} for any step is a simple integer addition.

```
// Bresenham's midpoint line algorithm for m<1
  void line(int x0, int y0, int xn, int yn) {
      int dx, dy, incrE, incrNE, d, x, y;

      x = x0; y = y0; d = 2 * dy - dx;
      incrE = 2 * dy; incrNE = 2 * (dy - dx);

      while (x < xn + 1) {
          writepixel(x, y); /* write frame buffer */
```

```
            x++; /* consider next pixel */
            if (d <= 0) {
                d += incrE;
            } else {
                y++;
                d += incrNE;
            }
        }
    }
}
```

We need to consider the cases in which the line's slope is in an arbitrary orientation. Fortunately, an arbitrary line can be mapped into the case above through a mirror around x axis, y axis, or the diagonal line ($m = 1$). The following is an implementation of Bresenham's algorithm that handles all these cases.

/* use Bresenham's algorithm to draw lines */

```
import net.java.games.jogl.*;


public class J1_3_Line extends J1_2_Line {

  // Called for OpenGL rendering every reshape
  public void display(GLDrawable drawable) {

    //generate a random line;
    int x0 = (int) (Math.random()*WIDTH);
    int y0 = (int) (Math.random()*HEIGHT);
    int xn = (int) ((Math.random()*WIDTH));
    int yn = (int) (Math.random()*HEIGHT);

    // draw a white line using Bresenham's algorithm
    gl.glColor3f(1, 1, 1);
    bresenhamLine(x0, y0, xn, yn);
  }


  // Bresenham's midpoint line algorithm
  void bresenhamLine(int x0, int y0, int xn, int yn) {
    int dx, dy, incrE, incrNE, d, x, y, flag = 0;

    if (xn<x0) {
      //swapd(&x0,&xn);swapd(&y0,&yn);
      int temp = x0;
```

```
    x0 = xn; xn = temp;
    temp = y0; y0 = yn; yn = temp;
  }
  if (yn<y0) {
    y0 = -y0; yn = -yn;
    flag = 10;
  }
  dy = yn-y0; dx = xn-x0;

  if (dx<dy) {
    //swapd(&x0,&y0);
    int temp = x0;
    x0 = y0; y0 = temp;

    //swapd(&xn,&yn);
    temp = xn; xn = yn; yn = temp;

    //swapd(&dy,&dx);
    temp = dy; dy = dx; dx = temp;
    flag++;
  }

  x = x0; y = y0; d = 2*dy-dx;
  incrE = 2*dy; incrNE = 2*(dy-dx);

  while (x<xn+1) {
    writepixel(x, y, flag); /* write frame buffer */

    x++; /* consider next pixel */
    if (d<=0) {
      d += incrE;
    } else {
      y++; d += incrNE;
    }
  }
}


void writepixel(int x, int y, int flag) {

  gl.glBegin(GL.GL_POINTS);
  if (flag==0) {
    gl.glVertex2i(x, y);
  } else if (flag==1) {
    gl.glVertex2i(y, x);
  } else if (flag==10) {
    gl.glVertex2i(x, -y);
  } else if (flag==11) {
    gl.glVertex2i(y, -x);
```

```
        }
      gl.glEnd();
   }

   public static void main(String[] args) {
      J1_3_Line f = new J1_3_Line();

      f.setTitle("JOGL J1_3_Line");
      f.setSize(WIDTH, HEIGHT);
      f.setVisible(true);
   }
}
```

Of course, OpenGL has a line scan-conversion function. To draw a line, we can simply call

```
gl.glBegin(GL.GL_LINES);
   gl.glVertex2i(x0,y0);
   gl.glVertex2i(xn,yn);
glEnd();
```

1.3.2 Scan-converting Curves, Triangles, and Polygons

Although the above example (*J1_3_Line.java*) is really a simulation, because the program does not directly manipulate the frame buffer, it does help us understand the scan-conversion process. Given a line equation, we can scan-convert the line by calculating and drawing all the pixels corresponding to the equation in the frame buffer. Similarly, given a circle equation, we can calculate and draw all the pixels of the circle into the frame buffer. This applies to all different types of curves. To speed up the scan-conversion process, we often use short lines to approximate short curve segments. Therefore, a curve can be approximated by a sequence of short lines.

A wireframe object is an object composed of only lines and curves without filled surfaces. Because a wireframe polygon is composed of line segments, we extend to discuss scan-converting filled triangles and polygons. Given three vertices corresponding to a triangle, we have three lines (edges). Because we can find all the pixels on the lines, we can scan-convert the triangle by drawing all pixels between the pixel pairs on different edges that have the same *y* coordinates. In other words, we can find the intersections of each horizontal line (called a scan-line) on the edges of the triangle and fill the pixels between the intersections that lie in the interior of the triangle. If we can scan-convert a triangle, we can scan-convert a polygon because a polygon can be divided into triangles. The emphasis of this book is more on using the implemented scan-conversion functions through programming.

We can develop a general polygon scan-conversion algorithm as follows. For each y from the bottom to the top of the display window, we can find all the pixels on the polygon edges that have the same y coordinates. Then we order the edge pixels from left to right according to their current x coordinates. If we draw a horizontal scan-line, the first (third, fifth, etc.) edge pixel is where we enter the polygon, the second (fourth, sixth, etc.) edge pixel is where we leave the polygon, and so on. We can scan-convert the polygon by drawing all pixels between the odd-even pixel pairs on different edges that have the same y coordinates. In other words, we can find the intersections of each scan-line with the edges of the polygon and fill the pixels between the intersections that lie in the interior of the polygon. The general concept of polygon scan-conversion is important because many other functions are related to its operations. For example, when we talk about hidden-surface removal or lighting later in the book, we need to calculate each pixel's depth or color information during scan-converting a pixel into the frame buffer.

A graphics library provides basic primitive functions. For example, OpenGL draws a convex polygon with the following commands:

```
gl.glBegin(GL.GL_POLYGON);
    // a list of vertices
    ...
gl.glEnd();
```

A *convex* polygon means that all the angles inside the polygon formed by the edges are smaller than 180 degrees. If a polygon is not convex, it is *concave*. Convex polygons can be scan-converted faster than concave polygons.

In summary, different scan-conversion algorithms for a graphics primitive (line, polygon, etc.) have their own merits. If a primitive scan-conversion function is not provided in a graphics library, we know now that we can create one or implement an existing one.

1.3.3 Scan-converting Characters

Characters are polygons. However, they are used so often that we prefer saving the polygon shapes in a library called the *font library*. The polygons in the font library are not represented by vertices. Instead, they are represented by *bitmap font* images — each character is saved in a rectangular binary array of pixels, called a *bitmap*. The shapes in small bitmaps do not scale well. Therefore, more than one bitmap must be defined for a given character for different sizes and type faces. Bitmap fonts are loaded into a font cache (fast memory) to allow quick retrieval. Displaying a character is simply copying its image from the font cache into the frame buffer at the desired position. During the copying process, colors may be used to draw into the frame buffer replacing the 1s and 0s in the bitmap font images.

Another method of describing character shapes is using straight lines and curve sections. These fonts are called *outline font*s. Outline fonts require less storage because each variation does not require a distinct font cache. However, the scaled shapes for different font sizes may not be pleasing to our eyes, and it takes more time to scan-convert the characters into the frame buffer.

Although the idea is simple, accessing fonts is often platform-dependent. JOGL's Class GLUT provides a simple platform-independent subset of bitmap and stroke font methods in 3D environment. *glutBitmapCharacter()* will draw a bitmap character at the current raster position. The current raster position is a point (*x, y, z*) in the viewing volume, which is specified by *glRasterPos3f(x, y, z)*. *glutBitmapString()* will draw a string of bitmap characters at the current raster position. *glutStrokeCharacter()* will draw a stroke character at the current raster position. *glutStrokeString()* will draw a string of stroke characters at the current raster position. The *stroke fonts* are simple outline fonts, which are transformed like 3D objects. Transformation will be discussed in the next chapter.

/*draw bitmap and stroke characters and strings */

```
import net.java.games.jogl.*;
import net.java.games.jogl.util.*;


public class J1_3_xFont extends J1_3_Triangle {
  GLUT glut = new GLUT();
```

```
// Called for OpenGL rendering every reshape
public void display(GLDrawable drawable) {
  //generate a random line;
  int x0 = (int)(Math.random()*WIDTH);
  int y0 = (int)(Math.random()*HEIGHT);
  int xn = (int)((Math.random()*WIDTH));
  int yn = (int)(Math.random()*HEIGHT);

  // draw a white line
  gl.glColor3f(1, 1, 1);
  bresenhamLine(x0, y0, xn, yn);

  gl.glRasterPos3f(x0, y0, 0); // start position

  glut.glutBitmapCharacter(gl,
                      GLUT.BITMAP_HELVETICA_12, 's');
  glut.glutBitmapString(gl,
                    GLUT.BITMAP_HELVETICA_12, "tart");

  gl.glPushMatrix();
  gl.glTranslatef(xn, yn, 0); // end position
  gl.glScalef(0.2f, 0.2f, 0.2f);
  glut.glutStrokeCharacter(gl, GLUT.STROKE_ROMAN, 'e');
  glut.glutStrokeString(gl, GLUT.STROKE_ROMAN, "nd");
  gl.glPopMatrix();

  // Display() thread sleeps to slow down the rendering
  try {
    Thread.sleep(100);
  } catch (Exception ignore) {}
}

public static void main(String[] args) {
  J1_3_xFont f = new J1_3_xFont();

  f.setTitle("JOGL J1_3_xFont");
  f.setSize(WIDTH, HEIGHT);
  f.setVisible(true);
}
}
```

1.3.4 Clipping

When a graphics system scan-converts a model, the model may be much larger than the display area. The display is a window used to look at a portion of a large model.

Clipping algorithms are necessary to clip the model and display only the portion that fits the window. For line clipping, if a line's two end points are inside the clipping window, then the clipping is trivially done. Otherwise, we can cut the line into sections at the edges of the clipping window, and keep only the section that lies inside the window. For polygon clipping, we can walk around the vertices of the polygon. If a polygon's edge lies inside the clipping window, the vertices are accepted for the new polygon. Otherwise, we can throw out all vertices outside the window, cut two edges that go out of or into the window at the window boundary, and generate new vertices along the window boundary between the two edges to replace the vertices that are outside the window. The clipped polygon has all vertices in the window.

Clipping algorithms for lines, polygons, and other 2D primitives have been developed. In addition to primitive 2D rectangular clipping, clipping algorithms have also been developed to cut models in other 2D shapes or 3D volumes. We will further discuss clipping against 3D volumes in Chapter 2.

1.4 Attributes and Antialiasing

In general, any parameter that affects the way a primitive is to be displayed is referred to as an attribute parameter. For example, a line's attributes include color, intensity (or brightness), type (solid, dashed, dotted), width, cap (shape of the end points: butt, round, etc.), join (miter, round, etc.), and so forth.

The display and the corresponding frame buffer are discrete. Therefore, a line, curve, or an edge of a polygon is often like a zigzag staircase. This is called *aliasing*. We can display the pixels at different intensities to relieve the aliasing problem. Methods to relieve aliasing are called *antialiasing* methods, and we introduce several below. In order to simplify the discussion, we only consider line antialiasing. Polygon antialiasing is similar to line antialiasing, except it deals with only one side of the lines (edges) of polygons.

1.4.1 Area Sampling

A displayed line has a width. Here we simply consider a line as a rectangular area overlapping with the pixels (Fig. 1.3a). We may display the pixels with different intensities or colors to achieve the effect of antialiasing. For example, if we display those pixels that are partially inside the rectangular line area with colors between the line color and the background color, the line looks less jaggy. Fig. 1.3b shows parallel lines that are drawn with or without antialiasing. Area sampling determines a pixel intensity by calculating the overlap area of the pixel with the line.

Unweighted area sampling determines the pixel intensity by the overlap area only. For unweighted area sampling, if a pixel is not completely inside or outside the line, it is cut into two or more areas by the boundaries of the rectangular line area. The portion inside the line determines the pixel intensity.

Similarly, weighted area sampling allows equal areas within a pixel to contribute unequally: an area closer to the pixel's center has greater influence on the pixel's intensity than an equal area further away from the pixel's center. Let's assume the drawing area is a flat surface tiled with pixels. For weighted area sampling, we assume each pixel is sat by a 3D solid cone (called a *cone filter*) or a bun-shaped volume (*Gaussian filter*) with the flat bottom occupying the pixel. The bottom of the cone may even be bigger than the pixel itself, so the cones or bun-shaped volumes are overlapping one another. The boundaries of the rectangular line area cut through the cone in the direction perpendicular to the display, and the portion (volume) of the cone inside the line area determines the corresponding pixel's intensity. The center area in the pixel is thicker (higher) than the boundary area of the pixel and thus has more influence on the pixel's intensity. Also, you can see that if the bottom of the cone is bigger than the pixel, the pixel's intensity is affected even though the line only passes by without touching the pixel.

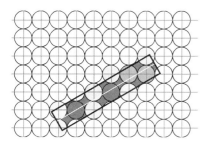

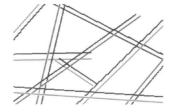

(a) A line is a rectangular area   *(b) Parallel lines with or without antialiasing*

Fig. 1.3 Antialiasing: area sampling

1.4.2 Antialiasing a Line with Weighted Area Sampling

For weighted area sampling, calculating a pixel's intensity according to the cone filter or Gaussian filter takes time. Instead, we can build up an intensity table and use the distance from the center of the pixel to the center of the line as an index to find the intensity for the pixel directly from the table. The intensities in the table are precalculated according to the filter we use and the width of the line. The following is an implementation of scan-converting an antialiased line.

If we assume the distance from the current pixel to the line is D, then the distances from the E, S, N, and NE pixels can be calculated, respectively. The distances are shown in Fig. 1.4. (The distances from the pixels above the line are negatively labeled, which are useful for polygon edge antialiasing.) We can modify Bresenham's algorithm to scan-convert an antialiased line. The distances from the pixels closest to the line are calculated iteratively.

Given a point (x, y), the function *IntensifyPixel()* will look up the intensity level of the point according to the index D and draw the pixel (x, y) at its intensity into the frame buffer. In our example, instead of building up a filter table, we use a simple equation to calculate the intensity. Here we implement a three-pixel wide antialiased line algorithm as an example.

In Bresenham's algorithm, the distance from the center of the pixel to the center of the line is $|D| \leq 0.5$. Therefore, the distance from N (the pixel above the current pixel) is $|D - \cos\alpha| \leq 1.5$, and the distance from S is $|D + \cos\alpha| \leq 1.5$. Given the current pixel's color (r, g, b), we can modify the intensity by $(r1, g1, b1)$, where $r1 = r*(1 - D/1.5)$, $g1 = g*(1 - D/1.5)$, and $b1 = b*(1 - D/1.5)$. When a pixel is exactly on the line $(D = 0)$, the pixel's intensity is not changed. When a pixel is far away from the center of the line $(D = 1.5)$, the pixel's intensity is modified to $(0, 0, 0)$. Therefore, the pixels have different intensity levels depending on their distances from the center of the line. Here, we assume the background color to be black. If otherwise, we need to know the background color, and linearly blend the foreground with background: $r = r_f*(1 - D/1.5) + r_b*D/1.5$. Here r is the final red color component, r_f is the foreground color component, and r_b is the background color component. The equation is the same for green and blue color components. The background color can be read from the destination (frame buffer).

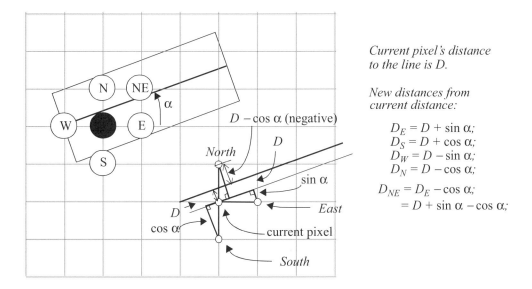

Current pixel's distance to the line is D.

New distances from current distance:

$$D_E = D + \sin \alpha;$$
$$D_S = D + \cos \alpha;$$
$$D_W = D - \sin \alpha;$$
$$D_N = D - \cos \alpha;$$

$$D_{NE} = D_E - \cos \alpha;$$
$$= D + \sin \alpha - \cos \alpha;$$

Fig. 1.4 **Iteratively calculate the distances from the pixels to the line**

The following example (*J1_4_Line.java*) implements Bresenham's algorithm with antialiasing. The program draws randomly generated lines of 3 pixel width, as shown in Fig. 1.5.

/* scan-convert randomly generated lines with antialiasing */

```
import net.java.games.jogl.*;


public class J1_4_Line extends J1_3_Line {
   private float r, g, b;

   // Called for OpenGL rendering every reshape
   public void display(GLDrawable drawable) {

      //generate a random line;
      int x0 = (int)(Math.random()*WIDTH);
      int y0 = (int)(Math.random()*HEIGHT);
      int xn = (int)((Math.random()*WIDTH));
      int yn = (int)(Math.random()*HEIGHT);
```

```java
  // generate a random color for this line
  r = (float)((Math.random()*9))/8;
  g = (float)((Math.random()*9))/8;
  b = (float)((Math.random()*9))/8;

  gl.glColor3f(r, g, b);
  // draw a three pixel antialiased line
  antialiasedLine(x0, y0, xn, yn);

  // sleep to slow down the rendering
  try {
    Thread.sleep(500);
  } catch (Exception ignore) {}
}


// draw pixel with intensity by its distance to the line
void IntensifyPixel(int x, int y, float D, int flag) {
  float d, r1, g1, b1;

  if (D<0) {
    d = -D; // negative if the pixel is above the line
  } else {
    d = D;
  }

  // calculate intensity according to the distance d
  r1 = (float)(r*(1-d/1.5));
  g1 = (float)(g*(1-d/1.5));
  b1 = (float)(b*(1-d/1.5));
  gl.glColor3f(r1, g1, b1);
  writepixel(x, y, flag);
}


//  scan-convert a 3 pixel wide antialiased line
void antialiasedLine(int x0, int y0, int xn, int yn) {
  int dx, dy, incrE, incrNE, d, x, y, flag = 0;
  float D = 0, sin_a, cos_a, sin_cos_a, Denom;

  if (xn<x0) {
    //swapd(& x0, & xn);
    int temp = x0; x0 = xn; xn = temp;
    //swapd(& y0, & yn);
    temp = y0; y0 = yn; yn = temp;
  }

  if (yn<y0) {
    y0 = -y0; yn = -yn;
```

```
      flag = 10;
    }

  dy = yn-y0; dx = xn-x0;
  if (dx<dy) {
    //swapd(& x0, & y0);
    int temp = x0; x0 = y0; y0 = temp;
    //swapd(& xn, & yn);
    temp = xn; xn = yn; yn = temp;
    //swapd(& dy, & dx);
    temp = dy; dy = dx; dx = temp;
    flag++;
  }

  x = x0; y = y0; d = 2*dy-dx; // decision factor
  incrE = 2*dy; incrNE = 2*(dy-dx);

  Denom = (float)Math.sqrt((double)(dx*dx+dy*dy));
  sin_a = dy/Denom; cos_a = dx/Denom;
  sin_cos_a = sin_a-cos_a;

  while (x<xn+1) {
    IntensifyPixel(x, y, D, flag);
    IntensifyPixel(x, y+1, D-cos_a, flag); // N
    IntensifyPixel(x, y-1, D+cos_a, flag); // S

    x++;
    // consider the next pixel
    if (d<=0) {
      D += sin_a; // distance to the line from E
      d += incrE;
    } else {
      D += sin_cos_a; // distance to the line: NE
      y++;
      d += incrNE;
    }
  }
}


public static void main(String[] args) {
  J1_4_Line f = new J1_4_Line();

  f.setTitle("JOGL J1_4_Line");
  f.setSize(WIDTH, HEIGHT);
  f.setVisible(true);
}
}
```

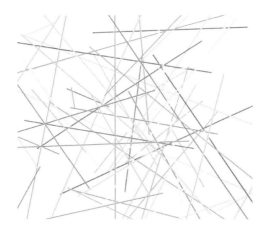

Fig. 1.5 Draw randomly generated lines with antialiasing [*See* Color Plate 1]

1.5 Double-buffering for Animation

A motion picture effect can be achieved by projecting images at 24 frames per second on a screen. Animation on a computer can be achieved by drawing or refreshing frames of different images. Here, the display *refresh rate* is the speed of reading from the frame buffer and sending the pixels to the display by the video controller. A refresh rate at 60 (frames per second) is smoother than one at 30, and 120 is marginally better than 60. Refresh rates faster than 120 frames per second are not necessary, because the human eye cannot tell the difference. Let's assume that the refresh rate is 60 frames per second. We can then build an animation program as follows:

```
open_window_with_single_buffer_mode();

for (i = 0; i < 100; i++) {
    clear_buffer();
    draw_frame(i);
    wait_until_1/60_of_a_second_is_over();
}
```

Items drawn first are visible for the full 1/60 second; items drawn toward the end are instantly cleared as the program starts on the next frame. This causes the display to present a blurred or jittered animation.

To solve this problem, we can have two frame buffers instead of one, which is known as double-buffering. One frame buffer named the *front buffer* is being displayed while the other, named the *back buffer,* is being drawn for scan-converting models. When the drawing of a frame is complete, the two buffers are swapped. That is, the back buffer becomes the front buffer for display, and the front buffer becomes the back buffer for scan-conversion. The animation program looks as follows:

```
open_window_with_double_buffer_mode();

for (i = 0; i < 100; i++) {
   clear_back_buffer();
   draw_frame_into_back_buffer(i);
   wait_until_1/60_of_a_second_is_over();
   swap_buffers();
}
```

JOGL uses *capabilities.setDoubleBuffered(true)* to specify the display with double buffers. Animator drives the *display()* method in a loop. When it is running in double buffer mode, it swaps the front and back buffers automatically by default, displaying the results of the rendering. You can turn automatic swapping off by the following method: *drawable.setAutoSwapBufferMode(false)*. Then, the programmer is responsible for calling *drawable.swapBuffers()* manually.

What often happens is that a frame is too complicated to draw in 1/60 second. If this happens, each frame in the frame buffer is displayed more than once and the display refresh rate is still 1/60. However, the image frame rate is much lower, and the animation could be jittering. The image frame rate depends on how fast frames of images are scan-converted, which corresponds to the rate of finishing drawing in the frame buffer. To achieve smooth animation, we need high-performance algorithms as well as graphics hardware to carry out many graphics functions efficiently.

J1_5_Circle.java is an example that demonstrates animation: drawing a circle with a radius that is changing every frame in double-buffer mode. It also helps us review vector operations. The circle is approximated by a set of triangles, as shown in Fig. 1.6. At the beginning, *v1, v2, v3, v4,* and the center of the coordinate *v0* are provided. When the variable *depth* = *0*, we draw four triangles, and the circle is approximated by a square.

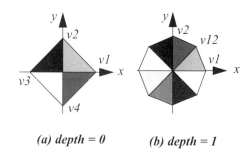

(a) depth = 0   *(b) depth = 1*

Fig. 1.6 Draw a circle by subdivision

When *depth* = *1*, each triangle is subdivided into two and we draw eight triangles. Given *v1* and *v2*, how do we find *v12*? Let's consider *v1, v2,* and *v12* as vectors. Then, *v12* is in the direction of $(v1 + v2) = (v1_x+v2_x, v1_y+v2_y, v1_z+v2_z)$ and the lengths of the vectors are equal: $|v1| = |v2| = |v12|$. If the radius of the circle is one, then *v12* = *normalize(v1 + v2)*. Normalizing a vector is equivalent to scaling the vector to a unit vector. In general, *v12* = *cRadius*normalize(v1 + v2)*, and for every frame the program changes the value of *cRadius* to achieve animation. We can find all other unknown vertices in Fig. 1.6b similarly through vector additions and normalizations. This subdivision process goes on depending on the value of the *depth*. Given a triangle with two vertices and the coordinate center, *subdivideCircle()* recursively subdivides the triangle *depth* times and draws 2^{depth} triangles. A snapshot of running *J1_5_Circle.java* is shown in Fig. 1.7.

The above method to draw a circle is quite cumbersome. We can draw a circle by just drawing a polygon that has many vertices around the circle. The reason we design and discuss the above method is that we will build other objects, such as cone and cylinder, on top of this method very easily. This will support easy learning and fast development.

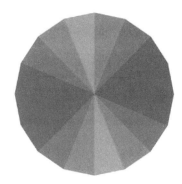

Fig. 1.7 A circle in animation [*See* Color Plate 1]

/* animate a circle */

```java
import net.java.games.jogl.*;

public class J1_5_Circle extends J1_4_Line {
    static int depth = 0; // number of subdivisions
    static int cRadius = 2, flip = 1;

    // vertex data for the triangles
    static float cVdata[][] = { {1.0f,  0.0f,  0.0f}
                              , {0.0f,  1.0f,  0.0f}
                              , {-1.0f, 0.0f,  0.0f}
                              , {0.0f, -1.0f,  0.0f}
    };

    public J1_5_Circle() {
        // use super's constructor to initialize drawing

        //1. specify using double buffers
        capabilities.setDoubleBuffered(true);
    }


    public void reshape(GLDrawable drawable, int x,
                        int y, int w, int h) {
        //2. the width and height of the new drawing area
        WIDTH = w;
        HEIGHT = h;

        //3. origin at the center of the drawing area
        gl.glMatrixMode(GL.GL_PROJECTION);
        gl.glLoadIdentity();
        gl.glOrtho(-w/2, w/2, -h/2, h/2, -1, 1);
    }


    public void display(GLDrawable drawable) {

        // when the circle is too big or small, change
        // the direction (growing or shrinking)
        if (cRadius>=(HEIGHT/2)|| cRadius==1) {
            flip = -flip;
            depth++; // number of subdivisions
            depth = depth%7;
        }
        cRadius += flip; // circle's radius change
```

```
  //4. clear the frame buffer and draw a new circle
  gl.glClear(GL.GL_COLOR_BUFFER_BIT);
  drawCircle(cRadius, depth);

 // sleep to slow down the rendering
  try {
    Thread.sleep(15);
  } catch (Exception ignore) {}
}


// draw a circle with center at the origin in xy plane
public void drawCircle(int cRadius, int depth) {

  subdivideCircle(cRadius, cVdata[0], cVdata[1], depth);
  subdivideCircle(cRadius, cVdata[1], cVdata[2], depth);
  subdivideCircle(cRadius, cVdata[2], cVdata[3], depth);
  subdivideCircle(cRadius, cVdata[3], cVdata[0], depth);
}


// subdivide a triangle recursively, and draw them
private void subdivideCircle(int radius, float[] v1,
                             float[] v2, int depth) {
  float v11[] = new float[3];
  float v22[] = new float[3];
  float v00[] = {0, 0, 0};
  float v12[] = new float[3];

  if (depth==0) {

    //5. specify a color related to triangle location
    gl.glColor3f(v1[0]*v1[0], v1[1]*v1[1], v1[2]*v1[2]);

    for (int i = 0; i<3; i++) {
      v11[i] = v1[i]*radius;
      v22[i] = v2[i]*radius;
    }
    drawtriangle(v11, v22, v00);
    return;
  }

  v12[0] = v1[0]+v2[0];
  v12[1] = v1[1]+v2[1];
  v12[2] = v1[2]+v2[2];

  normalize(v12);
```

```
    // subdivide a triangle recursively, and draw them
    subdivideCircle(radius, v1, v12, depth-1);
    subdivideCircle(radius, v12, v2, depth-1);
  }


  // normalize a 3D vector
  public void normalize(float vector[]) {
    float d = (float)Math.sqrt(vector[0]*vector[0]
      +vector[1]*vector[1] + vector[2]*vector[2]);

    if (d==0) {
      System.out.println("0 length vector: normalize().");
      return;
    }
    vector[0] /= d;
    vector[1] /= d;
    vector[2] /= d;
  }


  public void drawtriangle(float[] v1,
                           float[] v2, float[] v3) {
    gl.glBegin(GL.GL_TRIANGLES);
    gl.glVertex3fv(v1);
    gl.glVertex3fv(v2);
    gl.glVertex3fv(v3);
    gl.glEnd();
  }


  public static void main(String[] args) {
    J1_5_Circle f = new J1_5_Circle();

    f.setTitle("JOGL J1_5_Circle");
    f.setSize(WIDTH, HEIGHT);
    f.setVisible(true);
  }
}
```

The above program animates a circle by drawing a circle repetitively with growing or shrinking radius. There are a couple of things that need to be emphasized, as highlighted in the code:

1. For animation, we turn on double-buffering mode.

2. The new *w* and *h* of the returned Drawable in *reshape()* are saved in global *WIDTH* and *HEIGHT*. They are used to assign new drawing area coordinates as well as control the radius of the circle later.

3. The coordinates for the new drawing area are specified. Here the origin is at the center of the new drawing area. Therefore, if the drawing area is reshaped, the origin will change accordingly to the new center.

4. The frame buffer is cleared every time we redraw the circle.

5. A vertex of a triangle in the circle is different from other triangle's vertices, so we specify each triangle's color according to one of its vertex coordinates. Here because each vertex is a unit vector, and each color component is specified as a value between 0 and 1, we use square to avoid negative vector values.

1.6 Review Questions

1. $A(a_1,a_2,a_3)$ **and** $B(b_1,b_2,b_3)$ **are two vectors; please calculate the following:**

    a. $|A|$ b. $A - B$ c. $A \bullet B$ d. $A \times B$ e. θ between A and B

2. Please fill in the blanks between the two sides to connect the closest relations:

a. frame buffer	(___)	1. animation
b. double-buffering	(___)	2. pixmap for display
c. event	(___)	3. user input
d. graphics library	(___)	4. distance between pixels
e. scan-conversion	(___)	5. description of an object
f. resolution	(___)	6. basic graphics functions
g. 3D model	(___)	7. drawing

3. What is provided by the Animator class in JOGL?

    a. calling reshape()   b. implementing interface functions
    c. calling display() repetitively   d. transforming the objects

4. Which of the following is a graphics model?

    a. a picture on the paper   b. a pixmap in the frame buffer
    c. a data structure in the memory   d. an image on the display

5. What's the difference between bitmap fonts and outline fonts?

    a. Outline fonts are represented as 3D models   b. They have different sizes
    c. Bitmap fonts are represented as 3D models   d. They have different colors

6. **What are provided by the JOGL's GLUT class?**

a. bitmap and stroke font methods

b. antialiasing

c. calling reshape() or display()

d. handling display area

7. **The Cohen-Sutherland line-clipping algorithm works as follows: (a) At a clipping edge, if both end points are on the clipping window side, they are accepted. If both end points are not, they are rejected; (b) if not accepted or rejected, the line is divided into two segments at the clipping edge; (c) repeat (a) and (b) for the segment that is not rejected on the other three clipping edges. For an arbitrary line, what is the maximum number of comparisons and intersection calculations?**

Comparisons_____; Intersections _____.

8. **The Sutherland-Hodgman's polygon-clipping algorithm works as follows: we walk around the polygon boundary to generated a new clipped polygon represented by a list of vertices. For each boundary edge, (a) At a clipping edge, if both end points are on the clipping window side, they are accepted. If both end points are not, they are rejected. If accepted, the vertices are in the new polygon. If rejected, they are discarded; (b) if non-trivial, the intersection on the clipping edge is a generated vertex in the new polygon replacing the vertex outside; (c) repeat (a) and (b) until all of the polygon's edges are considered; (d) repeat (a), (b), and (c) for the other three clipping edges to have a final clipped polygon. For a triangle, what is the maximum number of comparisons and intersection calculations?**

Maximum_____; Minimum_____.

9. *Supersampling* **is to achieve antialiasing by**

a. increasing sampling rate

b. decreasing the sampling rate

c. using OpenGL antialiasing function

d. calculating the areas of overlap

10. **In the antialiased line algorithm, D is the distance from the center of the current pixel to the center of the line. Given D, please calculate the distances from NE and X pixels (D_X and D_{NE}).**

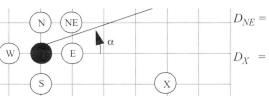

$D_{NE} =$

$D_X =$

11. **In the antialiased line algorithm, d is the decision factor for choosing East or Northeast, and D is the distance from the center of the current pixel to the center of the line. Given the line starting (0,0) as in the figure, please calculate d and D for the dark pixel.**

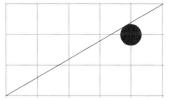

$d =$ _____ $D =$ _____

12. **In drawing a filled circle in the book, we start with 4 triangles. Please calculate if we subdivide n times, how many triangles we will have in the final circle.**

_____

1.7 Programming Assignments

1. Draw a point that moves slowly along a circle. You may want to draw a circle first, and a point that moves on the circle with a different color.

2. Draw a point that bounces slowly in a square or circle.

3. Draw a star in a circle that rotates, as shown on the right. You can only use glBegin(GL_POINTS) to draw the star.

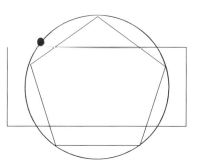

4. Write down "Bitmap" using Glut bitmap font function and "Stroke" using Glut stroke font function in the center of the display.

5. With the star rotating in the circle, implement the clipping of a window as shown on the right.

6. Implement an antialiasing line algorithm that works with the background that has a texture. The method is to blend the background color with the foreground color. You can get the current pixel color in the frame buffer using glGet() with GL_CURRENT_RASTER_COLOR.

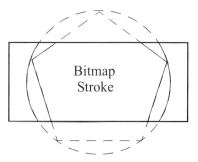

7. Implement a triangle filling algorithm for J1_3_Triangle class that draws a randomly generated triangle. Here you can only use glBegin(GL_POINTS) to draw the triangle.

8. Draw (and animate) the star with antialiasing and clipping. Add a filled circle inside the star using the subdivision method discussed in this chapter. You should use your own triangle filling algorithm. Also, clipping can be trickily done by checking the point to be drawn against the clipping window.

2
Transformation and Viewing

Chapter Objectives:

- Understand basic transformation and viewing methods

- Understand 3D hidden-surface removal and collision detection

- Design and implement 3D models (cone, cylinder, and sphere) and their animations in OpenGL

2.1 Geometric Transformation

In Chapter 1, we discussed creating and scan-converting primitive models. After a computer-based model is generated, it can be moved around or even transformed into a completely different shape. To do this, we need to specify the rotation axis and angle, translation vector, scaling vector, or other manipulations to the model. The ordinary *geometric transformation* is a process of mathematical manipulations of all the vertices of the model through matrix multiplications, where the graphics system then displays the final transformed model. The transformation can be predefined, such as moving along a planned trajectory; or interactive, depending on the user input. The transformation can be permanent — the coordinates of the vertices are changed and we have a new model replacing the original one; or just temporary — the vertices return to their original coordinates. In many cases a model is transformed in order to be displayed at a different position or orientation, and the graphics system discards the transformed model after scan-conversion. Sometimes all the vertices of a model go through the same transformation, and the shape of the model is preserved; sometimes different vertices go through different transformations, and the shape is dynamic.

A model can be displayed repetitively with each frame going through a small transformation step. This causes the model to be animated on display.

2.2 2D Transformation

Translation, *rotation*, and *scaling* are the basic and essential transformations. They can be combined to achieve most transformations in many applications. To simplify the discussion, we will first introduce 2D transformation and then generalize it into 3D.

2.2.1 2D Translation

A point (x, y) is translated to (x', y') by a distance vector (d_x, d_y):

$$x' = x + d_x,$$

(EQ 6)

$$y' = y + d_y.$$

(EQ 7)

In the homogeneous coordinates, we represent a point (x, y) by a column vector $P = \begin{bmatrix} x \\ y \\ 1 \end{bmatrix}$. Similarly, $P = \begin{bmatrix} x' \\ y' \\ 1 \end{bmatrix}$. Then, translation can be achieved by matrix multiplication:

$$\begin{bmatrix} x' \\ y' \\ 1 \end{bmatrix} = \begin{bmatrix} 1 & 0 & d_x \\ 0 & 1 & d_y \\ 0 & 0 & 1 \end{bmatrix} \begin{bmatrix} x \\ y \\ 1 \end{bmatrix}.$$

(EQ 8)

Let's assume $T(d_x, d_y) = \begin{bmatrix} 1 & 0 & d_x \\ 0 & 1 & d_y \\ 0 & 0 & 1 \end{bmatrix}$. We can denote the translation matrix equation as:

$$P = T(d_x, d_y)P.$$

(EQ 9)

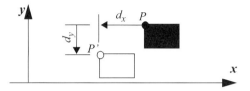

Fig. 2.1 Basic transformation: translation

If a model is a set of vertices, all vertices of the model can be translated as points by the same translation vector (Fig. 2.1). Note that translation moves a model through a distance without changing its orientation.

2.2.2 2D Rotation

A point $P(x, y)$ is rotated counter-clockwise to $P'(x', y')$ by an angle θ around the origin $(0,0)$. Let us assume that the distance from the origin to point P is $r = OP$, and the angle between OP and x axis is α. If the rotation is clockwise, the rotation angle θ is then negative. The rotation axis is perpendicular to the 2D plane at the origin:

$$x' = r\cos(\alpha + \theta), \qquad \text{(EQ 10)}$$

$$y' = r\sin(\alpha + \theta), \qquad \text{(EQ 11)}$$

$$x' = r(\cos\alpha\cos\theta - \sin\alpha\sin\theta), \qquad \text{(EQ 12)}$$

$$x' = r(\sin\alpha\cos\theta + \cos\alpha\sin\theta), \qquad \text{(EQ 13)}$$

$$x' = x\cos\theta - y\sin\theta, \qquad \text{(EQ 14)}$$

$$y' = x\sin\theta + y\cos\theta. \qquad \text{(EQ 15)}$$

In the homogeneous coordinates, rotation can be achieved by matrix multiplication:

$$\begin{bmatrix} x' \\ y' \\ 1 \end{bmatrix} = \begin{bmatrix} \cos\theta & -\sin\theta & 0 \\ \sin\theta & \cos\theta & 0 \\ 0 & 0 & 1 \end{bmatrix} \begin{bmatrix} x \\ y \\ 1 \end{bmatrix}.$$ (EQ 16)

Let's assume $R(\theta) = \begin{bmatrix} \cos\theta & -\sin\theta & 0 \\ \sin\theta & \cos\theta & 0 \\ 0 & 0 & 1 \end{bmatrix}$. The simplified rotation matrix equation is

$$P = R(\theta)P.$$ (EQ 17)

If a model is a set of vertices, all vertices of the model can be rotated as points by the same angle around the same rotation axis (Fig. 2.2). Rotation moves a model around the origin of the coordinates. The distance of each vertex to the origin is not changed during rotation.

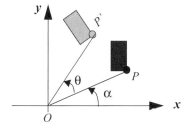

2.2.3 2D Scaling

Fig. 2.2 Basic transformation: rotation

A point $P(x, y)$ is scaled to $P(x', y')$ by a scaling vector (s_x, s_y):

$$x' = s_x x,$$ (EQ 18)

$$y' = s_y y.$$ (EQ 19)

In the homogeneous coordinates, again, scaling can be achieved by matrix multiplication:

$$\begin{bmatrix} x' \\ y' \\ 1 \end{bmatrix} = \begin{bmatrix} s_x & 0 & 0 \\ 0 & s_y & 0 \\ 0 & 0 & 1 \end{bmatrix} \begin{bmatrix} x \\ y \\ 1 \end{bmatrix}.$$ (EQ 20)

Let's assume $S(s_x, s_y) = \begin{bmatrix} s_x & 0 & 0 \\ 0 & s_y & 0 \\ 0 & 0 & 1 \end{bmatrix}$. We can denote the scaling matrix equation as:

$$P = S(s_x, s_y)P.$$ (EQ 21)

If a model is a set of vertices, all vertices of the model can be scaled as points by the same scaling vector (Fig. 2.3). Scaling amplifies or shrinks a model around the origin of the coordinates. Note that a scaled vertex will move unless it is at the origin.

2.2.4 Simulating OpenGL Implementation

OpenGL actually implements 3D transformations, which we will discuss later. Here, we implement 2D transformations in our own code in *J2_0_2DTransform.java*, which corresponds to the OpenGL implementation in hardware.

OpenGL has a MODELVIEW matrix stack that saves the current matrices for transformation. Let us define a matrix stack as follows:

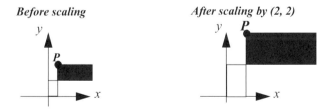

Fig. 2.3 Basic transformation: scaling

/* 2D transformation OpenGL style implementation */

```
import net.java.games.jogl.*;

public class J2_0_2DTransform extends J1_5_Circle {
   private static float my2dMatStack[][][] =
      new float[24][3][3];
   private static int stackPtr = 0;

      . . .
}
```

The identity matrix for 2D homogeneous coordinates is $I = \begin{bmatrix} 1 & 0 & 0 \\ 0 & 1 & 0 \\ 0 & 0 & 1 \end{bmatrix}$. Any matrix

multiplied with identity matrix does not change.

The stackPtr points to the current matrix on the matrix stack (*my2dMatrixStack[stackPtr]*) that is in use. Transformations are then achieved by the following methods: *my2dLoadIdentity()*, *my2dMultMatrix(float mat[][])*, *my2dTranslatef(float x, float y)*, *my2dRotatef(float angle)*, *my2dScalef(float x, float y)*, and *my2dTransformf(float vertex[], float vertex1[])* (or *my2dTransVertex(float vertex[], float vertex1[])* for vertices already in homogeneous form).

1. *my2dLoadIdentity()* loads the current matrix on the matrix stack with the identity matrix:

```
// initialize a 3*3 matrix to all zeros
   private void my2dClearMatrix(float mat[][]) {

      for (int i = 0; i<3; i++) {
        for (int j = 0; j<3; j++) {
          mat[i][j] = 0.0f;
        }
      }
   }


   // initialize a matrix to Identity matrix
   private void my2dIdentity(float mat[][]) {
```

```
      my2dClearMatrix(mat);
      for (int i = 0; i<3; i++) {
        mat[i][i] = 1.0f;
      }
    }


    // initialize the current matrix to Identity matrix
    public void my2dLoadIdentity() {
      my2dIdentity(my2dMatStack[stackPtr]);
    }
```

2. *my2dMultMatrix(float mat[][])* multiplies the current matrix on the matrix stack with the matrix *mat*: CurrentMatrix = currentMatrix*Mat.

```
  // multiply the current matrix with mat
    public void my2dMultMatrix(float mat[][]) {
      float matTmp[][] = new float[3][3];

      my2dClearMatrix(matTmp);

      for (int i = 0; i<3; i++) {
        for (int j = 0; j<3; j++) {
          for (int k = 0; k<3; k++) {
            matTmp[i][j] +=
                my2dMatStack[stackPtr][i][k]*mat[k][j];
          }
        }
      }
      // save the result on the current matrix
      for (int i = 0; i<3; i++) {
        for (int j = 0; j<3; j++) {
          my2dMatStack[stackPtr][i][j] = matTmp[i][j];
        }
      }
    }
```

3. *my2dTranslatef(float x, float y)* multiplies the current matrix on the matrix stack with the translation matrix *T(x, y)*:

```
  // multiply the current matrix with a translation matrix
    public void my2dTranslatef(float x, float y) {
```

```
    float T[][] = new float[3][3];

    my2dIdentity(T);

    T[0][2] = x;
    T[1][2] = y;

    my2dMultMatrix(T);
}
```

4. *my2dRotatef(float angle)* multiplies the current matrix on the matrix stack with the rotation matrix *R(angle)*:

```
// multiply the current matrix with a rotation matrix
public void my2dRotatef(float angle) {
    float R[][] = new float[3][3];

    my2dIdentity(R);

    R[0][0] = (float)Math.cos(angle);
    R[0][1] = (float)-Math.sin(angle);
    R[1][0] = (float)Math.sin(angle);
    R[1][1] = (float)Math.cos(angle);

    my2dMultMatrix(R);
}
```

5. *my2dScalef(float x, float y)* multiplies the current matrix on the matrix stack with the scaling matrix *S(x, y)*:

```
// multiply the current matrix with a scale matrix
public void my2dScalef(float x, float y) {
    float S[][] = new float[3][3];

    my2dIdentity(S);

    S[0][0] = x;
    S[1][1] = y;

    my2dMultMatrix(S);
}
```

6. *my2dTransformf(float vertex[]; vertex1[])* multiplies the current matrix on the matrix stack with *vertex*, and save the result in *vertex1*. Here *vertex* is first extended to homogeneous coordinates before matrix multiplication.

```
// v1 = (the current matrix) * v
// here v and v1 are vertices in homogeneous coord.
public void my2dTransHomoVertex(float v[], float v1[]) {
   int i, j;

   for (i = 0; i<3; i++) {
     v1[i] = 0.0f;

   }
   for (i = 0; i<3; i++) {
      for (j = 0; j<3; j++) {
        v1[i] +=
            my2dMatStack[stackPtr][i][j]*v[j];
      }
   }
}


// vertex = (the current matrix) * vertex
// here vertex is in homogeneous coord.
public void my2dTransHomoVertex(float vertex[]) {
      float vertex1[] = new float[3];

   my2dTransHomoVertex(vertex, vertex1);
   for (int i = 0; i<3; i++) {
     vertex[i] = vertex1[i];
   }
}


// transform v to v1 by the current matrix
// here v and v1 are not in homogeneous coordinates
public void my2dTransformf(float v[], float v1[]) {
   float vertex[] = new float[3];

   // extend to homogenous coord
    vertex[0] = v[0];
   vertex[1] = v[1];
   vertex[2] = 1;

   // multiply the vertex by the current matrix
   my2dTransHomoVertex(vertex);
```

```
// return to 3D coord
v1[0] = vertex[0]/vertex[2];
v1[1] = vertex[1]/vertex[2];
}


// transform v by the current matrix
 // here v is not in homogeneous coordinates
public void my2dTransformf(float[] v) {
   float vertex[] = new float[3];

   // extend to homogenous coord
   vertex[0] = v[0];
   vertex[1] = v[1];
   vertex[2] = 1;

   // multiply the vertex by the current matrix
   my2dTransHomoVertex(vertex);

   // return to 3D coord
   v[0] = vertex[0]/vertex[2];
   v[1] = vertex[1]/vertex[2];
}
```

7. In addition to the above methods, *my2dPushMatrix()* and *my2dPopMatrix()* are a powerful mechanism to change the current matrix on the matrix stack, which we will discuss in more detail later. PushMatrix will increase the stack pointer and make a copy of the previous matrix to the current matrix. Therefore, the matrix remains the same, but we are using a different set of memory locations on the matrix stack. PopMatrix will decrease the stack pointer, so we return to the previous matrix that was saved at PushMatrix.

```
// move the stack pointer up, and copy the previous
// matrix to the current matrix
public void my2dPushMatrix() {
   int tmp = stackPtr+1;

   for (int i = 0; i<3; i++) {
     for (int j = 0; j<3; j++) {
       my2dMatStack[tmp][i][j] =
           my2dMatStack[stackPtr][i][j];
     }
   }
   stackPtr++;
}
```

```
// move the stack pointer down
public void my2dPopMatrix() {

    stackPtr--;
}
```

With the above 2D transformation methods, the following example (*J2_0_2DTransform.java*) achieves different transformations using the implemented methods, as shown in Fig. 2.4.

/* 2D transformation: OpenGL style implementatoin */

```
import net.java.games.jogl.*;


public    class    J2_0_2DTransform
extends J1_5_Circle {

    ....// the matrix stack

    static float vdata[][] = { {1.0f,  0.0f,  0.0f}
                             , {0.0f,  1.0f,  0.0f}
                             , {-1.0f,  0.0f,  0.0f}
                             , {0.0f, -1.0f,  0.0f}
    };
    static int cnt = 1;

    // called for OpenGL rendering every reshape
    public void display(GLDrawable drawable) {

        if (cnt<1||cnt>200) {
            flip = -flip;
        }
        cnt = cnt+flip;

        gl.glClear(GL.GL_COLOR_BUFFER_BIT);

        // white triangle is scaled
        gl.glColor3f(1, 1, 1);
        my2dLoadIdentity();
```

Fig. 2.4 Transformations of triangles [*See* Color Plate 1]

```
    my2dScalef(cnt, cnt);
    transDrawTriangle(vdata[0], vdata[1], vdata[2]);

    // red triangle is rotated and scaled
    gl.glColor3f(1, 0, 0);
    my2dRotatef((float)cnt/15);
    transDrawTriangle(vdata[0], vdata[1], vdata[2]);

    // green triangle is translated, rotated, and scaled
    gl.glColor3f(0, 1, 0);
    my2dTranslatef((float)cnt/100, 0.0f);
    transDrawTriangle(vdata[0], vdata[1], vdata[2]);

    try {
      Thread.sleep(20);
    } catch (InterruptedException e) {}
  }


// the vertices are transformed first then drawn
public void transDrawTriangle(float[] v1,
                              float[] v2, float[] v3) {
    float v[][] = new float[3][3];

    my2dTransformf(v1, v[0]);
    my2dTransformf(v2, v[1]);
    my2dTransformf(v3, v[2]);

    gl.glBegin(GL.GL_TRIANGLES);
    gl.glVertex3fv(v[0]);
    gl.glVertex3fv(v[1]);
    gl.glVertex3fv(v[2]);
    gl.glEnd();
  }

  ... // the transformation methods

public static void main(String[] args) {
    J2_0_2DTransform f = new J2_0_2DTransform();

    f.setTitle("JOGL J2_0_2DTransform");
    f.setSize(500, 500);
    f.setVisible(true);
  }
}
```

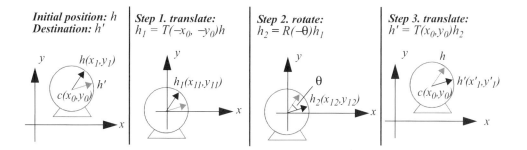

Initial position: h Destination: h'	Step 1. translate: $h_1 = T(-x_0, -y_0)h$	Step 2. rotate: $h_2 = R(-\theta)h_1$	Step 3. translate: $h' = T(x_0,y_0)h_2$

Fig. 2.5 Moving the clock hand by matrix multiplications

2.2.5 Composition of 2D Transformations

A complex transformation is often achieved by a series of simple transformation steps. The result is a composition of translations, rotations, and scalings. We will study this through the following three examples.

Example 1: Find the coordinates of a moving clock hand in 2D. Consider a single clock hand. The center of rotation is given at $c(x_0, y_0)$, and the end rotation point is at $h(x_1, y_1)$. If we know the rotation angle is θ, can we find the new end point h' after the rotation? As shown in Fig. 2.5, we can achieve this by a series of transformations.

1. Translate the hand so that the center of rotation is at the origin. Note that we only need to find the new coordinates of the end point h:

$$\begin{bmatrix} x_{11} \\ y_{11} \\ 1 \end{bmatrix} = \begin{bmatrix} 1 & 0 & -x_0 \\ 0 & 1 & -y_0 \\ 0 & 0 & 1 \end{bmatrix} \begin{bmatrix} x_1 \\ y_1 \\ 1 \end{bmatrix}.$$

(EQ 22)

That is, $h_1 = T(-x_0, -y_0)h$.

(EQ 23)

2. Rotate θ degrees around the origin. Note that the positive direction of rotation is counter-clockwise:

$$h_2 = R(-\theta)h_1. \tag{EQ 24}$$

3. After the rotation. We translate again to move the clock back to its original position:

$$h' = T(x_0, y_0)h_2. \tag{EQ 25}$$

Therefore, putting Equations 23, 24, and 25 together, the combination of transformations to achieve the clock hand movement is

$$h' = T(x_0, y_0)R(-\theta)T(-x_0, -y_0)h. \tag{EQ 26}$$

That is,
$$\begin{bmatrix} x'_1 \\ y'_1 \\ 1 \end{bmatrix} = \begin{bmatrix} 1 & 0 & x_0 \\ 0 & 1 & y_0 \\ 0 & 0 & 1 \end{bmatrix} \begin{bmatrix} \cos\theta & \sin\theta & 0 \\ -\sin\theta & \cos\theta & 0 \\ 0 & 0 & 1 \end{bmatrix} \begin{bmatrix} 1 & 0 & -x_0 \\ 0 & 1 & -y_0 \\ 0 & 0 & 1 \end{bmatrix} \begin{bmatrix} x_1 \\ y_1 \\ 1 \end{bmatrix}. \tag{EQ 27}$$

In the future, we will write matrix equations concisely using only symbol notations instead of full matrix expressions. However, we should always remember that the symbols represent the corresponding matrices.

Let's assume $M=T(x_0,y_0)R(-\theta)T(-x_0, -y_0)$. We can further simplify the equation:

$$h' = Mh. \tag{EQ 28}$$

The order of the matrices in a matrix expression matters. The sequence represents the order of the transformations. For example, although matrix M in Equation 28 can be calculated by multiplying the first two matrices first $[T(x_0, y_0)R(-\theta)]T(-x_0, -y_0)$ or by multiplying the last two matrices first $T(x_0, y_0)[R(-\theta)T(-x_0, -y_0)]$, the order of the matrices cannot be changed.

When we analyze a model's transformations, we should remember that, logically speaking, the order of transformation steps are from right to left in the matrix expression. In this example, the first logical step is $T(-x_0, -y_0)h$; the second step is $R(-\theta)[T(-x_0, -y_0)h]$; and the last step is $T(x_0, y_0)[R(-\theta)[T(-x_0, -y_0)]]$. In the actual OpenGL style implementation, the matrix multiplication is from left to right, and there

is always a final matrix on the matrix stack. The following is a segment of
J2_1_Clock2d.java that simulates a real-time clock.

```
my2dLoadIdentity();
my2dTranslate(c[0], c[1]); // x0=c[0], y0=c[1];
my2dRotate(-a);
my2dTranslate(-c[0], -c[1]);
transDrawClock(c, h);
```

In the above code, first the current matrix on the matrix stack is loaded with the
identity matrix I, then it is multiplied by a translation matrix $T(x_0, y_0)$, after that it is
multiplied by a rotation matrix $R(-\theta)$, and finally it is multiplied by a translation
matrix $T(-x_0, -y_0)$. Written in an expression, it is $[[[I]T(x_0, y_0)]R(-\theta)]T(-x_0, -y_0)$. In
transDrawClock(), the clock center c and end h are both transformed by the current
matrix, and then scan converted to display. In OpenGL, transformation is implied. In
other words, the vertices are first transformed by the system before they are sent to the
scan-conversion. The following is the complete program.

/* 2D clock hand transformation */

```
public class J2_1_Clock2d extends J2_0_2DTransform {
    static final float PI = 3.1415926f;

  public void display(GLDrawable glDrawable) {
      // homogeneous coordinates
      float c[] = {0, 0, 1};
      float h[] = {0, WIDTH/6, 1};

      long curTime;
      float ang, second, minute, hour;

      gl.glClear(GL.GL_COLOR_BUFFER_BIT);

      curTime = System.currentTimeMillis()/1000;
      // returns the current time in milliseconds
      hsecond = curTime%60;
      curTime = curTime/60;
      hminute = curTime%60+hsecond/60;
      curTime = curTime/60;
      hhour = (curTime%12)+8+hminute/60;
      // Eastern Standard Time
```

```
ang = PI*second/30; // arc angle

gl.glColor3f(1, 0, 0); // second hand in red
my2dLoadIdentity();
my2dTranslatef(c[0], c[1]);
my2dRotatef(-ang);
my2dTranslatef(-c[0], -c[1]);
gl.glLineWidth(1);
transDrawClock(c, h);

gl.glColor3f(0, 1, 0); // minute hand in green
my2dLoadIdentity();
ang = PI*minute/30; // arc angle
my2dTranslatef(c[0], c[1]);
my2dScalef(0.8f, 0.8f); // minute hand shorter
my2dRotatef(-ang);
my2dTranslatef(-c[0], -c[1]);
gl.glLineWidth(2);
transDrawClock(c, h);

gl.glColor3f(0, 0, 1); // hour hand in blue
my2dLoadIdentity();
ang = PI*hour/6; // arc angle
my2dTranslatef(c[0], c[1]);
my2dScalef(0.5f, 0.5f); // hour hand shortest
my2dRotatef(-ang);
my2dTranslatef(-c[0], -c[1]);
gl.glLineWidth(3);
transDrawClock(c, h);
}


public void transDrawClock(float C[], float H[]) {
  float End1[] = new float[3];
  float End2[] = new float[3];

  my2dTransHomoVertex(C, End1);
  // Transform the center by the current matrix
  my2dTransHomoVertex(H, End2);
  // Transform the end by the current matrix

  // assuming z = w = 1;
  gl.glBegin(GL.GL_LINES);
  gl.glVertex3fv(End1);
  gl.glVertex3fv(End2);
  gl.glEnd();
}
```

```
public static void main(String[] args) {

    J2_1_Clock2d f = new J2_1_Clock2d();

    f.setTitle("JOGL J2_1_Clock2d");
    f.setSize(500, 500);
    f.setVisible(true);
  }
}
```

Example 2: Reshaping a rectangular area. In OpenGL, we can use the mouse to reshape the display area. In the Reshape callback function, we can use *glViewport()* to adjust the size of the drawing area accordingly. The system makes corresponding adjustments to the models through the same transformation matrix. Viewport transformation will be discussed later in the section "Viewing".

Here, we discuss a similar problem: a transformation that allows reshaping a rectangular area. Let's assume the coordinate system of the screen is as in Fig. 2.6. After reshaping, the rectangular area and all the vertices of the model inside the rectangular area go through the following transformations: translate so that the lower-left corner of the area is at the origin, scale to the size of the new area, and then translate to the scaled area location. The corresponding matrix expression is

$$T(P_2)S(s_x, s_y)T(-P_1).$$ (EQ 29)

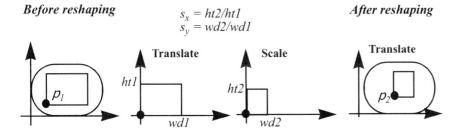

Before reshaping $s_x = ht2/ht1$ *After reshaping*
                            $s_y = wd2/wd1$

Fig. 2.6 Scaling an arbitrary rectangular area

P_1 is the starting point for scaling, and P_2 is the destination. We can use the mouse to interactively drag P_1 to P_2 in order to reshape the corresponding rectangular area. In the following example (*J2_2_Reshape.java*), we use the mouse to drag the lower-left vertex P_1 of the rectangular area to a new location. The rectangle and the clock inside are reshaped accordingly. A snapshot is shown in Fig. 2.7.

Fig. 2.7 **Reshape a drawing area with a clock inside**

/* reshape the rectangular drawing area */

```
import net.java.games.jogl.*;
import java.awt.event.*;


public class J2_2_Reshape extends J2_1_Clock2d implements
    MouseMotionListener {

  // the point to be dragged as the lower-left corner
  private static float P1[] = {-WIDTH/4, -HEIGHT/4};

  // reshape scale value
  private float sx = 1, sy = 1;

  // when mouse is dragged, a new lower-left point
  // and scale value for the rectangular area
  public void mouseDragged(MouseEvent e) {
    float wd1 = WIDTH/2;
    float ht1 = HEIGHT/2;

    // The mouse location, new lower-left corner
    P1[0] = e.getX()-WIDTH/2;
    P1[1] = HEIGHT/2-e.getY();
    float wd2 = WIDTH/4-P1[0];
    float ht2 = HEIGHT/4-P1[1];
```

```
   // scale value of the current rectangular area
   sx = wd2/wd1;
   sy = ht2/ht1;
}


public void mouseMoved(MouseEvent e) {
}


public void init(GLDrawable drawable) {

   super.init(drawable);
   // listen to mouse motion
   drawable.addMouseMotionListener(this);
}


public void display(GLDrawable glDrawable) {
   // the rectangle lower-left and upper-right corners
   float v0[] = {-WIDTH/4, -HEIGHT/4};
   float v1[] = {WIDTH/4, HEIGHT/4};

   // reshape according to the current scale
   my2dLoadIdentity();
   my2dTranslatef(P1[0], P1[1]);
   my2dScalef(sx, sy);
   my2dTranslatef(-v0[0], -v0[1]);

   gl.glClear(GL.GL_COLOR_BUFFER_BIT);
   gl.glColor3f(1, 1, 1);  // the rectangle is white

   // rectangle area
   float v00[] = new float[2], v11[] = new float[2];
   my2dTransformf(v0, v00);
   my2dTransformf(v1, v11);
   gl.glBegin(GL.GL_LINE_LOOP);
   gl.glVertex3f(v00[0], v00[1], 0);
   gl.glVertex3f(v11[0], v00[1], 0);
   gl.glVertex3f(v11[0], v11[1], 0);
   gl.glVertex3f(v00[0], v11[1], 0);
   gl.glEnd();

   // the clock hands go through the same transformation
   curTime = System.currentTimeMillis()/1000;
   hsecond = curTime%60;
   curTime = curTime/60;
   hminute = curTime%60+hsecond/60;
   curTime = curTime/60;
```

```
    hhour = (curTime%12)+8+hminute/60;
    // Eastern Standard Time

    hAngle = PI*hsecond/30; // arc angle

    gl.glColor3f(1, 0, 0); // second hand in red
    my2dTranslatef(c[0], c[1]);
    my2dRotatef(-hAngle);
    my2dTranslatef(-c[0], -c[1]);
    gl.glLineWidth(3);
    transDrawClock(c, h);

    gl.glColor3f(0, 1, 0); // minute hand in green
    my2dLoadIdentity();
    my2dTranslatef(P1[0], P1[1]);
    my2dScalef(sx, sy);
    my2dTranslatef(-v0[0], -v0[1]);
    hAngle = PI*hminute/30; // arc angle
    my2dTranslatef(c[0], c[1]);
    my2dScalef(0.8f, 0.8f); // minute hand shorter
    my2dRotatef(-hAngle);
    my2dTranslatef(-c[0], -c[1]);
    gl.glLineWidth(5);
    transDrawClock(c, h);

    gl.glColor3f(0, 0, 1); // hour hand in blue
    my2dLoadIdentity();
    my2dTranslatef(P1[0], P1[1]);
    my2dScalef(sx, sy);
    my2dTranslatef(-v0[0], -v0[1]);
    hAngle = PI*hhour/6; // arc angle
    my2dTranslatef(c[0], c[1]);
    my2dScalef(0.5f, 0.5f); // hour hand shortest
    my2dRotatef(-hAngle);
    my2dTranslatef(-c[0], -c[1]);
    gl.glLineWidth(7);
    transDrawClock(c, h);
  }


  public static void main(String[] args) {
    J2_2_Reshape f = new J2_2_Reshape();

    f.setTitle("JOGL J2_2_Reshape");
    f.setSize(500, 500);
    f.setVisible(true);
  }
}
```

Example 3: Drawing a 2D robot arm with three moving segments. A 2D robot arm has 3 segments rotating at the joints in a 2D plane (Fig. 2.8). Given an arbitrary initial posture (A, B, C), let's find the transformation matrix expressions for another posture (A_f, B_f, C_f) with respective rotations (α, β, γ) around the joints. Here we specify (A, B, C) on the x axis, which is used to simplify the visualization. (A, B, C) can be initialized arbitrarily. There are many different methods to achieve the same goal. Here, we elaborate three methods for the same goal.

Method I.

1. Rotate $oABC$ around the origin by α degrees:

$$A_f = R(\alpha)A; \; B' = R(\alpha)B; \; C' = R(\alpha)C. \qquad \textbf{(EQ 30)}$$

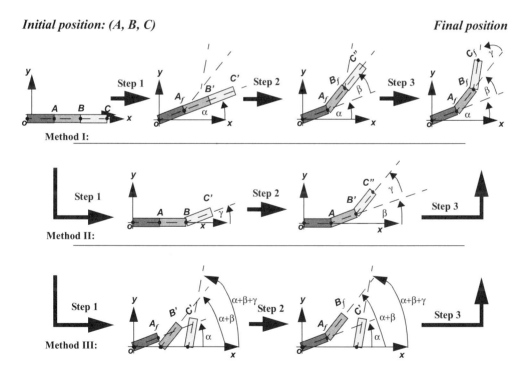

Fig. 2.8 A 2D robot arm rotates (α, β, γ) degrees at the 3 joints, respectively

2. Consider $A_f B'C'$ to be a clock hand like the example in Fig. 2.5. Rotate $A_f B'C'$ around A_f by β degrees. This is achieved by first translating the hand to the origin, rotating, then translating back:

$$B_f = T(A_f)R(\beta)T(-A_f)B'; \quad C'' = T(A_f)R(\beta)T(-A_f)C'. \qquad \text{(EQ 31)}$$

3. Again, consider $B_f C''$ to be a clock hand. Rotate $B_f C''$ around B_f by γ degrees:

$$C_f = T(B_f)R(\gamma)T(-B_f)C''. \qquad \text{(EQ 32)}$$

The corresponding code is as follows. Here *my2dTransHomoVertex(v1, v2)* will multiply the current matrix on the matrix stack with *v1*, and save the results in *v2*. *drawArm()* is just drawing a line segment.

```
// Method I: 2D robot arm transformations
public void transDrawArm1(float a, float b, float g) {
    float Af[] = new float[3];
    float B1[] = new float[3];
    float C1[] = new float[3];
    float Bf[] = ncw float[3];
    float C2[] = new float[3];
    float Cf[] = new float[3];

    my2dLoadIdentity();
    my2dRotatef(a);
    my2dTransHomoVertex(A, Af);
    my2dTransHomoVertex(B, B1);
    my2dTransHomoVertex(C, C1);

    drawArm(O, Af);

    my2dLoadIdentity();
    my2dTranslatef(Af[0], Af[1]);
    my2dRotatef(b);
    my2dTranslatef( -Af[0], -Af[1]);
    my2dTransHomoVertex(B1, Bf);
    my2dTransHomoVertex(C1, C2);
    drawArm(Af, Bf);

    my2dLoadIdentity();
    my2dTranslatef(Bf[0], Bf[1]);
    my2dRotatef(g);
    my2dTranslatef( -Bf[0], -Bf[1]);
```

```
      my2dTransHomoVertex(C2, Cf);
      drawArm(Bf, Cf);
   }
```

Method II.

1. Consider *BC* to be a clock hand. Rotate *BC* around *B* by γ degrees:

$$C' = T(B)R(\gamma)T(-B)C. \qquad\qquad \text{(EQ 33)}$$

2. Consider *ABC'* to be a clock hand. Rotate *ABC'* around *A* by β degrees:

$$B' = T(A)R(\beta)T(-A)B; \ C'' = T(A)R(\beta)T(-A)C'. \qquad\qquad \text{(EQ 34)}$$

3. Again, consider *oAB'C''* to be a clock hand. Rotate *oAB'C''* around the origin by α degrees:

$$A_f = R(\alpha)A; \qquad\qquad \text{(EQ 35)}$$

$$B_f = R(\alpha)B' = R(\alpha)T(A)R(\beta)T(-A)B; \qquad\qquad \text{(EQ 36)}$$

$$C_f = R(\alpha)C'' = R(\alpha)T(A)R(\beta)T(-A)T(B)R(\gamma)T(-B)C. \qquad\qquad \text{(EQ 37)}$$

The corresponding code is as follows. Here *transDraw()* will first transform the vertices, and then draw the transformed vertices as a line segment.

```
   // Method II: 2D robot arm transformations
   public void transDrawArm2(float a, float b, float g) {

      my2dLoadIdentity();
      my2dRotatef(a);
      transDrawArm(O, A);
      my2dTranslatef(A[0], A[1]);
      my2dRotatef(b);
      my2dTranslatef( -A[0], -A[1]);
```

```
    transDrawArm(A, B);
    my2dTranslatef(B[0], B[1]);
    my2dRotatef(g);
    my2dTranslatef( -B[0], -B[1]);
    transDrawArm(B, C);
}
```

Method III.

1. Consider oA, AB, and BC as clock hands with the rotation axes at o, A, and B, respectively. Rotate oA by α degrees, AB by $(\alpha+\beta)$ degrees, and BC by $(\alpha+\beta+\gamma)$ degrees:

$$A_f = R(\alpha)A; \; B' = T(A)R(\alpha+\beta)T(-A)B; \; C' = T(B)R(\alpha+\beta+\gamma)T(-B)C. \qquad \textbf{(EQ 38)}$$

2. Translate AB' to A_fB_f:

$$B_f = T(A_f)T(-A)B' = T(A_f)R(\alpha+\beta)T(-A)B. \qquad \textbf{(EQ 39)}$$

Note that $T(-A)T(A) = I$, which is the identity matrix: $I = \begin{bmatrix} 1 & 0 & 0 \\ 0 & 1 & 0 \\ 0 & 0 & 1 \end{bmatrix}$. Any matrix multiplied by the identity matrix does not change. The vertex is translated by vector A, and then reversed back to its original position by translation vector $-A$.

3. Translate BC' to B_fC_f:

$$C_f = T(B_f)T(-B)C' = T(B_f)R(\alpha+\beta+\gamma)T(-B)C. \qquad \textbf{(EQ 40)}$$

The corresponding code is as follows.

```
// Method III: 2D robot arm transformations
public void transDrawArm3(float a, float b, float g) {
    float Af[] = new float[3];
    float Bf[] = new float[3];
    float Cf[] = new float[3];
```

```
        my2dLoadIdentity();
        my2dRotatef(a);
        my2dTransHomoVertex(A, Af);
        drawArm(O, Af);
        my2dLoadIdentity();
        my2dTranslatef(Af[0], Af[1]);
        my2dRotatef(a + b);
        my2dTranslatef( -A[0], -A[1]);
        my2dTransHomoVertex(B, Bf);
        drawArm(Af, Bf);
        my2dLoadIdentity();
        my2dTranslatef(Bf[0], Bf[1]);
        my2dRotatef(a + b + g);
        my2dTranslatef( -B[0], -B[1]);
        my2dTransHomoVertex(C, Cf);
        drawArm(Bf, Cf);
    }
```

In the above examples, we use *Draw()* and *transDraw()*, which are implemented ourselves. The difference between the two functions are that *Draw()* will draw the two vertices as a line directly, whereas *transDraw()* will first transform the two vertices by the current matrix on the matrix stack, and then draw a line according to the transformed vertices. In OpenGL implementation, as we will see, *transDraw* is implied. That is, whenever we draw a primitive, the vertices of the primitive are always transformed by the current matrix on the MODELVIEW matrix stack, even though the transformation matrix multiplication is unseen. We will discuss this in detail later. The three different transformation are demonstrated in the following sample program (*J2_3_Robot2d.java*).

/* three different methods for 2D robot arm transformations */

```
import net.java.games.jogl.*;


public class J2_3_Robot2d extends J2_0_2DTransform {
    // homogeneous coordinates
    float O[] = {0, 0, 1};
    float A[] = {100, 0, 1};
    float B[] = {160, 0, 1};
    float C[] = {200, 0, 1};
    float a, b, g;
```

```
public void display(GLDrawable glDrawable) {

  gl.glClear(GL.GL_COLOR_BUFFER_BIT);

  a = a + 0.01f;
  b = b - 0.02f;
  g = g + 0.03f;

  gl.glColor3f(0, 1, 1);
  transDrawArm1(a, b, g);

  gl.glColor3f(1, 1, 0);
  transDrawArm2(-b, -g, a);

  gl.glColor3f(1, 0, 1);
  transDrawArm3(g, -a, -b);

  try {
    Thread.sleep(10);
  } catch (Exception ignore) {}
}


...; // Method I: 2D robot arm transformations
...; // Method II: 2D robot arm transformations
...; // Method III: 2D robot arm transformations


// transform the coordinates and then draw
private void transDrawArm(float C[], float H[]) {

  float End1[] = new float[3];
  float End2[] = new float[3];

  my2dTransHomoVertex(C, End1);
  // multiply the point with the matrix on the stack
  my2dTransHomoVertex(H, End2);

  // assuming z = w = 1;
  drawArm(End1, End2);
}


// draw the coordinates directly
public void drawArm(float C[], float H[]) {

  gl.glLineWidth(5);

  // assuming z = w = 1;
```

```
    gl.glBegin(GL.GL_LINES);
    gl.glVertex3fv(C);
    gl.glVertex3fv(H);
    gl.glEnd();
  }

  public static void main(String[] args) {
    J2_3_Robot2d f = new J2_3_Robot2d();

    f.setTitle("JOGL J2_3_Robot2d");
    f.setSize(500, 500);
    f.setVisible(true);
  }
}
```

2.3 3D Transformation and Hidden-Surface Removal

2D transformation is a special case of 3D transformation where $z=0$. For example, a 2D point (x, y) is $(x, y, 0)$ in 3D, and a 2D rotation around the origin $R(\theta)$ is a 3D rotation around the z axis $R_z(\theta)$ (Fig. 2.9). The z axis is perpendicular to the display with the arrow pointing toward the viewer. We can assume the display to be a view of a 3D drawing box, which is projected along the z axis direction onto the 2D drawing area at $z=0$.

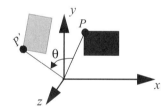

Fig. 2.9 A 3D rotation around z axis

2.3.1 3D Translation, Rotation, and Scaling

In 3D, for translation and scaling, we can translate or scale not only along the x and the y axis but also along the z axis. For rotation, in addition to rotating around the z axis, we can also rotate around the x axis and the y axis. In the homogeneous coordinates, the 3D transformation matrices for translation, rotation, and scaling are as follows:

$$\text{Translation: } T(d_x, d_y, d_z) = \begin{bmatrix} 1 & 0 & 0 & d_x \\ 0 & 1 & 0 & d_y \\ 0 & 0 & 1 & d_z \\ 0 & 0 & 0 & 1 \end{bmatrix} ; \qquad \text{(FQ 41)}$$

$$\text{Scaling: } S(s_x, s_y, s_z) = \begin{bmatrix} s_x & 0 & 0 & 0 \\ 0 & s_y & 0 & 0 \\ 0 & 0 & s_z & 0 \\ 0 & 0 & 0 & 1 \end{bmatrix} ; \qquad \text{(EQ 42)}$$

$$\text{Rotation around x axis: } R_x(\theta) = \begin{bmatrix} 1 & 0 & 0 & 0 \\ 0 & \cos\theta & -\sin\theta & 0 \\ 0 & \sin\theta & \cos\theta & 0 \\ 0 & 0 & 0 & 1 \end{bmatrix} ; \qquad \text{(EQ 43)}$$

$$\text{Rotation around y axis: } R_y(\theta) = \begin{bmatrix} \cos\theta & 0 & \sin\theta & 0 \\ 0 & 1 & 0 & 0 \\ -\sin\theta & 0 & \cos\theta & 0 \\ 0 & 0 & 0 & 1 \end{bmatrix} ; \qquad \text{(EQ 44)}$$

$$\text{Rotation around z axis: } R_z(\theta) = \begin{bmatrix} \cos\theta & -\sin\theta & 0 & 0 \\ \sin\theta & \cos\theta & 0 & 0 \\ 0 & 0 & 1 & 0 \\ 0 & 0 & 0 & 1 \end{bmatrix} . \qquad \text{(EQ 45)}$$

For example, the 2D transformation Equation 35 can be replaced by the corresponding 3D matrices:

$$A_f = R_z(\alpha)A, \qquad \text{(EQ 46)}$$

$$\text{where } A = \begin{bmatrix} A_x \\ A_y \\ A_z \\ 1 \end{bmatrix}, A_f = \begin{bmatrix} A_{fx} \\ A_{fy} \\ A_{fz} \\ 1 \end{bmatrix}, \text{ and } A_z{=}0. \text{ We can show that } A_{fz}{=}0 \text{ as well.}$$

2.3.2 Transformation in OpenGL

As an example, we will again implement in OpenGL the robot arm transformation MODELVIEW matrix stack to achieve the transformation. We consider the transformation to be a special case of 3D at $z{=}0$.

In OpenGL, all the vertices of a model are multiplied by the matrix on the top of the MODELVIEW matrix stack and then by the matrix on the top of the PROJECTION matrix stack before the model is scan-converted. Matrix multiplications are carried out on the top of the matrix stack automatically in the graphics system. The MODELVIEW matrix stack is used for geometric transformation. The PROJECTION matrix stack is used for viewing, which will be discussed later. Here, we explain how OpenGL handles the geometric transformations in the following example (*J2_4_Robot.java*, which implements *Method II* in Fig. 2.8.)

1. Specify that current matrix multiplications are carried out on the top of the MOD-ELVIEW matrix stack:

   ```
   gl.glMatrixMode (GL.GL_MODELVIEW);
   ```

2. Load the current matrix on the matrix stack with the identity matrix:

   ```
   gl.glLoadIdentity ();
   ```

   The identity matrix for 3D homogeneous coordinates is $I = \begin{bmatrix} 1 & 0 & 0 & 0 \\ 0 & 1 & 0 & 0 \\ 0 & 0 & 1 & 0 \\ 0 & 0 & 0 & 1 \end{bmatrix}$.

3. Specify the rotation matrix $R_z(\alpha)$, which will be multiplied by whatever on the current matrix stack already. The result replaces the matrix currently on the top of the stack. If the identity matrix is on the stack, then $IR_z(\alpha)=R_z(\alpha)$:

```
gl.glRotatef (alpha, 0.0, 0.0, 1.0);
```

4. Draw a robot arm — a line segment between point O and A. Before the model is scan-converted into the frame buffer, O and A will first be transformed by the matrix on the top of the MODELVIEW matrix stack, which is $R_z(\alpha)$. That is, $R_z(\alpha)O$ and $R_z(\alpha)A$ will be used to scan-convert the line (Equation 35):

```
drawArm (O, A);
```

5. In the following code section, we specify a series of transformation matrices, which in turn will be multiplied by whatever is already on the current matrix stack: I, $[I]R(\alpha)$, $[[I]R(\alpha)]T(A)$, $[[[I]R(\alpha)]T(A)]R(\beta)$, $[[[[I]R(\alpha)]T(A)]R(\beta)]T(-A)$. Before $drawArm\ (A,\ B)$, we have $M = R(\alpha)T(A)R(\beta)T(-A)$ on the matrix stack, which corresponds to Equation 36:

```
gl.glPushMatrix();
    gl.glLoadIdentity ();
    gl.glRotatef (alpha, 0.0, 0.0, 1.0);
    drawArm (O, A);

    gl.glTranslatef (A[0], A[1], 0.0);
    gl.glRotatef (beta, 0.0, 0.0, 1.0);
    gl.glTranslatef (-A[0], -A[1], 0.0);
    drawArm (A, B);
gl.glPopMatrix();
```

The matrix multiplication is always carried out on the top of the matrix stack. *glPushMatrix()* will move the stack pointer up one slot and duplicate the previous matrix so that the current matrix is the same as the matrix immediately below it on the stack. *glPopMatrix()* will move the stack pointer down one slot. The advantage of this mechanism is to separate the transformations of the current model between *glPushMatrix()* and *glPopMatrix()* from other transformations of models later.

Status of the OpenGL MODELVIEW matrix stack

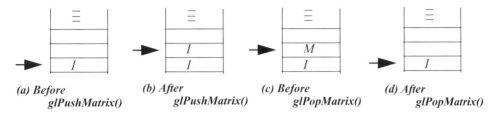

(a) Before   *(b) After*   *(c) Before*   *(d) After*
    glPushMatrix()   *glPushMatrix()*   *glPopMatrix()*   *glPopMatrix()*

Fig. 2.10 Matrix stack operations with *glPushMatrix()* and *glPopMatrix()*

Let's look at the function *drawRobot()* in *J2_4_Robot.java* below. Fig. 2.10 shows what is on the top of the matrix stack, when *drawRobot()* is called once and then again. At *drawArm(B, C)* right before *glPopMatrix()*, the matrix on top of the stack is $M = R(\alpha)T(A)R(\beta)T(-A)T(B)R(\gamma)T(-B)$, which corresponds to Equation 37.

6. Suppose we remove *glPushMatrix()* and *glPopMatrix()* from *drawRobot()*, if we call *drawRobot()* once, it appears fine. If we call it again, you will see that the matrix on the matrix stack is not an identity matrix. It is the previous matrix on the stack already (Fig. 2.11).

For beginners, it is a good idea to draw the state of the current matrix stack while you are reading the sample programs or writing your own programs. This will help you clearly understand what the transformation matrices are at different stages.

Status of the OpenGL MODELVIEW matrix stack

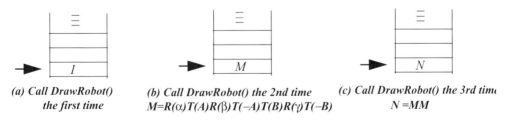

(a) Call DrawRobot()   *(b) Call DrawRobot() the 2nd time*   *(c) Call DrawRobot() the 3rd time*
   the first time $M=R(\alpha)T(A)R(\beta)T(-A)T(B)R(\gamma)T(-B)$ *N =MM*

Fig. 2.11 Matrix stack operations without *glPushMatrix()* and *glPopMatrix()*

Methods I and III (Fig. 2.8) cannot be achieved using OpenGL transformations directly, because OpenGL provides matrix multiplications, but not the vertex coordinates after a vertex is transformed by the matrix. This means that all vertices are always fixed at their original locations. This method avoids floating point accumulation errors. We can use *glGetDoublev(GL.GL_MODELVIEW_MATRIX, M[])* to get the current 16 values of the matrix on the top of the MODELVIEW stack, and multiply the coordinates by the current matrix to achieve the transformations for Methods I and III. Of course, you may implement your own matrix multiplications to achieve all the different transformation methods as well.

/* 2D robot transformation in OpenGL */

```
import net.java.games.jogl.*;

public class J2_4_Robot extends J2_3_Robot2d {

  public void display(GLDrawable glDrawable) {

    gl.glClear(GL.GL_COLOR_BUFFER_BIT);

    a = a+0.1f;
    b = b-0.2f;
    g = g+0.3f;

    gl.glLineWidth(7f); // draw a wide line for arm
    drawRobot(A, B, C, a, b, g);

    try {
      Thread.sleep(10);
    } catch (Exception ignore) {}
  }

  void drawRobot(
      float A[],
      float B[],
      float C[],
      float alpha,
      float beta,
      float gama) {

    gl.glPushMatrix();

    gl.glColor3f(1, 1, 0);
```

```
    gl.glRotatef(alpha, 0.0f, 0.0f, 1.0f);
    // R_z(alpha) is on top of the matrix stack
    drawArm(O, A);

    gl.glColor3f(0, 1, 1);
    gl.glTranslatef(A[0], A[1], 0.0f);
    gl.glRotatef(beta, 0.0f, 0.0f, 1.0f);
    gl.glTranslatef(-A[0], -A[1], 0.0f);
    // R_z(alpha)T(A)R_z(beta)T(-A) is on top
    drawArm(A, B);

    gl.glColor3f(1, 0, 1);
    gl.glTranslatef(B[0], B[1], 0.0f);
    gl.glRotatef(gama, 0.0f, 0.0f, 1.0f);
    gl.glTranslatef(-B[0], -B[1], 0.0f);
    // R_z(alpha)T(A)R_z(beta)T(-A) is on top
    drawArm(B, C);

    gl.glPopMatrix();
  }


  public static void main(String[] args) {
    J2_4_Robot f = new J2_4_Robot();

    f.setTitle("JOGL J2_4_Robot");
    f.setSize(WIDTH, HEIGHT);
    f.setVisible(true);
  }
}
```

2.3.3 Hidden-Surface Removal

Bounding volumes. We first introduce a simple method, called *bounding volume* or *minmax testing*, to determine visible 3D models without using a time-consuming hidden-surface removal algorithm. Here we assume that the viewpoint of our eye is at the origin and the models are in the negative z axis. If we render the models in the order of their distances to the viewpoint of the eye along z axis from the farthest to the closest, we will have correct overlapping of the models. We can build up a rectangular box (bounding volume) with the faces perpendicular to the x, y, or z axis to bound a 3D model and compare the minimum and maximum bounds in the z direction between boxes to decide which model should be rendered first. Using bounding volumes to decide the priority of rendering is also known as *minmax testing*. In addition to visible-model determination, bounding volumes are also used for *collision detection*, which will be discussed later in this chapter.

The z-buffer (depth-buffer) algorithm. In OpenGL, to enable the hidden-surface removal (or visible surface determination) mechanism, we need to enable the depth test once and then clear the depth buffer whenever we redraw a frame:

```
// enable zbuffer (depthbuffer) once
gl.glEnable(GL.GL_DEPTH_TEST);

// clear both frame buffer and zbuffer
gl.glClear(GL.GL_COLOR_BUFFER_BIT|GL.GL_DEPTH_BUFFER_BIT);
```

Corresponding to a frame buffer, the graphics system also has a z-buffer, or depth buffer, with the same number of entries. After *glClear()*, the z-buffer is initialized to the *z* value farthest from the viewpoint of our eye, and the frame buffer is initialized to the background color. When scan-converting a model (such as a polygon), before writing a pixel color into the frame buffer, the graphics system (the z-buffer algorithm) compares the pixel's *z* value to the corresponding *xy* coordinates' *z* value in the z-buffer. If the pixel is closer to the viewpoint, its *z* value is written into the z-buffer and its color is written into the frame buffer. Otherwise, the system moves on to considering the next pixel without writing into the buffers. The result is that, no matter what order the models are scan-converted, the image in the frame buffer only shows the pixels on the models that are not blocked by other pixels. In other words, the visible surfaces are saved in the frame buffer, and all the hidden surfaces are removed.

A pixel's *z* value is provided by the model at the corresponding *xy* coordinates. For example, given a polygon and the *xy* coordinates, we can calculate the *z* value according to the polygon's plane equation $z=f(x,y)$. Therefore, although scan-conversion is drawing in 2D, 3D calculations are needed to decide hidden-surface removal and others (as we will discuss in the future: lighting, texture mapping, etc.).

A plane equation in its general form is $ax + by + cz + 1 = 0$, where (*a, b, c*) corresponds to a vector perpendicular to the plane. A polygon is usually specified by a list of vertices. Given three vertices on the polygon, they all satisfy the plane equation and therefore we can find (*a, b, c*) and $z=-(ax + by + 1)/c$. By the way, because the cross-product of two edges of the polygon is perpendicular to the plane, it is proportional to (*a, b, c*) as well.

2.3.4 3D Models: Cone, Cylinder, and Sphere

Approximating a cone. In the example below (*J1_5_Circle.java*), we approximated a circle with subdividing triangles. If we raise the center of the circle along the *z* axis, we can approximate a cone, as shown in Fig. 2.12. Because the model is in 3D, we need to enable depth test to achieve hidden-surface removal. Also, we need to make sure that our model is contained within the defined coordinates (i.e., the viewing volume):

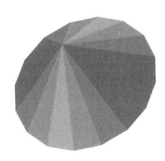

Fig. 2.12 A cone by subdivision [*See* **Color Plate 1**]

```
gl.glOrtho(-w/2, w/2,
           -h/2, h/2, -w, w);
```

/* draw a cone by subdivision */

```
import net.java.games.jogl.*;

public class J2_5_Cone extends J1_5_Circle {

  public void reshape(GLDrawable glDrawable,
       int x, int y, int w, int h) {

    WIDTH = w; HEIGHT = h;

    // enable depth buffer for hidden-surface removal
    gl.glEnable(GL.GL_DEPTH_TEST);

    gl.glMatrixMode(GL.GL_PROJECTION);
    gl.glLoadIdentity();

    // make sure the cone is within the viewing volume
    gl.glOrtho(-w/2, w/2, -h/2, h/2, -w, w);
```

```
  gl.glMatrixMode(GL.GL_MODELVIEW);
  gl.glLoadIdentity();
}

public void display(GLDrawable glDrawable) {

  if ((cRadius>(WIDTH/2))|| (cRadius==1)) {
    flip = -flip;
    depth++;
    depth = depth%5;
  }

  cRadius += flip;

  // clear both frame buffer and zbuffer
  gl.glClear(GL.GL_COLOR_BUFFER_BIT|
             GL.GL_DEPTH_BUFFER_BIT);

  gl.glRotatef(1, 1, 1, 1); // accumulated on matrix
  // rotate 1 degree alone vector (1, 1, 1)
  gl.glPushMatrix(); // not accumulated
  gl.glScaled(cRadius, cRadius, cRadius);
  drawCone();
  gl.glPopMatrix();

  try {
    Thread.sleep(10);
  } catch (Exception ignore) {}
}

private void subdivideCone(float v1[],
                           float v2[], int depth) {
  float v0[] = {0, 0, 0};
  float v12[] = new float[3];

  if (depth==0) {
    gl.glColor3f(v1[0]*v1[0], v1[1]*v1[1], v1[2]*v1[2]);

    drawtriangle(v1, v2, v0);
    // bottom cover of the cone

    v0[2] = 1; // height of the cone, the tip on z axis
    drawtriangle(v1, v2, v0); // side cover of the cone

    return;
  }
```

```
      for (int i = 0; i<3; i++) {
        v12[i] = v1[i]+v2[i];
      }
      normalize(v12);

      subdivideCone(v1, v12, depth-1);
      subdivideCone(v12, v2, depth-1);
    }

  public void drawCone() {
      subdivideCone(cVdata[0], cVdata[1], depth);
      subdivideCone(cVdata[1], cVdata[2], depth);
      subdivideCone(cVdata[2], cVdata[3], depth);
      subdivideCone(cVdata[3], cVdata[0], depth);
    }

  public static void main(String[] args) {
      J2_5_Cone f = new J2_5_Cone();

      f.setTitle("JOGL J2_5_Cone");
      f.setSize(WIDTH, HEIGHT);
      f.setVisible(true);
    }
}
```

Approximating a cylinder. If we can draw a circle at $z=0$, then draw another circle at $z=1$. If we connect the rectangles of the same vertices on the edges of the two circles, we have a cylinder, as shown in Fig. 2.13.

/* draw a cylinder by subdivision */

```
import net.java.games.jogl.*;


public      class      J2_6_Cylinder
extends J2_5_Cone {

  public void display(GLDrawable
glDrawable) {
```

Fig. 2.13 A cylinder by subdivision [*See* **Color Plate 1**]

```
if ((cRadius>(WIDTH/2))||(cRadius==1)) {
  flip = -flip;
  depth++;
  depth = depth%6;
}
cRadius += flip;

// clear both frame buffer and zbuffer
gl.glClear(GL.GL_COLOR_BUFFER_BIT|
           GL.GL_DEPTH_BUFFER_BIT);

gl.glRotatef(1, 1, 1, 1);
// rotate 1 degree alone vector (1, 1, 1)
gl.glPushMatrix();
gl.glScaled(cRadius, cRadius, cRadius);
drawCylinder();
gl.glPopMatrix();

try {
  Thread.sleep(20);
} catch (Exception ignore) {}
}


private void subdivideCylinder(float v1[],
                               float v2[], int depth) {
  float v11[] = {0, 0, 0};
  float v22[] = {0, 0, 0};
  float v0[] = {0, 0, 0};
  float v12[] = new float[3];
  int i;

  if (depth==0) {
    gl.glColor3f(v1[0]*v1[0],
                 v1[1]*v1[1], v1[2]*v1[2]);

    for (i = 0; i<3; i++) {
      v22[i] = v2[i];
      v11[i] = v1[i];
    }

    drawtriangle(v1, v2, v0);
    // draw sphere at the cylinder's bottom

    v11[2] = v22[2] = v0[2] = 1.0f;
    drawtriangle(v11, v22, v0);
    // draw sphere at the cylinder's bottom
```

```
        gl.glBegin(GL.GL_POLYGON);
        // draw the side rectangles of the cylinder
        gl.glVertex3fv(v11);
        gl.glVertex3fv(v22);
        gl.glVertex3fv(v2);
        gl.glVertex3fv(v1);
        gl.glEnd();

        return;
    }

    for (i = 0; i<3; i++) {
        v12[i] = v1[i]+v2[i];

    }
    normalize(v12);

    subdivideCylinder(v1, v12, depth-1);
    subdivideCylinder(v12, v2, depth-1);
}


public void drawCylinder() {
    subdivideCylinder(cVdata[0], cVdata[1], depth);
    subdivideCylinder(cVdata[1], cVdata[2], depth);
    subdivideCylinder(cVdata[2], cVdata[3], depth);
    subdivideCylinder(cVdata[3], cVdata[0], depth);
}


public static void main(String[] args) {
    J2_6_Cylinder f = new J2_6_Cylinder();

    f.setTitle("JOGL J2_6_Cylinder");
    f.setSize(WIDTH, HEIGHT);
    f.setVisible(true);
    }
}
```

Approximating a sphere. Let's assume that we have an equilateral triangle with its three vertices (v_1, v_2, v_3) on a sphere and $|v_1|=|v_2|=|v_3|=1$. That is, the three vertices are unit vectors from the origin. We can see that $v_{12} = normalize(v_1 + v_2)$ is also on the sphere. We can further subdivide the triangle into four equilateral triangles, as shown in Fig. 2.14a. Example *J2_7_Sphere.java* uses this method to subdivide an octahedron (Fig. 2.14b) into a sphere, as shown in Fig. 2.14c.

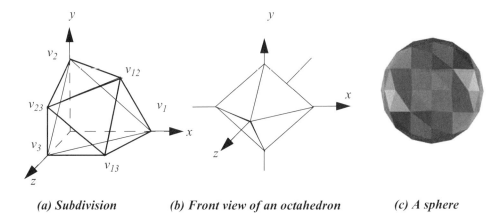

(a) Subdivision   *(b) Front view of an octahedron*   *(c) A sphere*

Fig. 2.14 Drawing a sphere through subdivision [*See* Color Plate 1]

/* draw a sphere by subdivision */

```
import net.java.games.jogl.*;

public class J2_7_Sphere extends J2_6_Cylinder {
   static float sVdata[][] = { {1.0f, 0.0f, 0.0f}
                             , {0.0f, 1.0f, 0.0f}
                             , {0.0f, 0.0f, 1.0f}
                             , { -1.0f, 0.0f, 0.0f}
                             , {0.0f, -1.0f, 0.0f}
                             , {0.0f, 0.0f, -1.0f}
   };

   public void display(GLDrawable glDrawable) {

      if ((cRadius > (WIDTH / 2)) || (cRadius == 1)) {
         flip = -flip;

         depth++;
         depth = depth % 5;
      }

      cRadius += flip;
```

```
  // clear both frame buffer and zbuffer
  gl.glClear(GL.GL_COLOR_BUFFER_BIT |
            GL.GL_DEPTH_BUFFER_BIT);

  gl.glRotatef(1, 1, 1, 1);
  // rotate 1 degree alone vector (1, 1, 1)
  gl.glPushMatrix();
  gl.glScalef(cRadius, cRadius, cRadius);
  drawSphere();
  gl.glPopMatrix();

  try {
    Thread.sleep(20);
  } catch (Exception ignore) {}
}


private void subdivideSphere(
    float v1[],
    float v2[],
    float v3[],
    long depth) {
  float v12[] = new float[3];
  float v23[] = new float[3];
  float v31[] = new float[3];
  int i;

  if (depth == 0) {
    gl.glColor3f(v1[0] * v1[0],
                v2[1] * v2[1], v3[2] * v3[2]);
    drawtriangle(v1, v2, v3);

    return;
  }
  for (i = 0; i < 3; i++) {
    v12[i] = v1[i] + v2[i];
    v23[i] = v2[i] + v3[i];
    v31[i] = v3[i] + v1[i];
  }
  normalize(v12);
  normalize(v23);
  normalize(v31);
  subdivideSphere(v1, v12, v31, depth - 1);
  subdivideSphere(v2, v23, v12, depth - 1);
  subdivideSphere(v3, v31, v23, depth - 1);
  subdivideSphere(v12, v23, v31, depth - 1);
}
```

```
public void drawSphere() {
  subdivideSphere(sVdata[0], sVdata[1], sVdata[2], depth);
  subdivideSphere(sVdata[0], sVdata[2], sVdata[4], depth);
  subdivideSphere(sVdata[0], sVdata[4], sVdata[5], depth);
  subdivideSphere(sVdata[0], sVdata[5], sVdata[1], depth);
  subdivideSphere(sVdata[3], sVdata[1], sVdata[5], depth);
  subdivideSphere(sVdata[3], sVdata[5], sVdata[4], depth);
  subdivideSphere(sVdata[3], sVdata[4], sVdata[2], depth);
  subdivideSphere(sVdata[3], sVdata[2], sVdata[1], depth);
}

public static void main(String[] args) {
  J2_7_Sphere f = new J2_7_Sphere();

  f.setTitle("JOGL J2_7_Sphere");
  f.setSize(WIDTH, HEIGHT);
  f.setVisible(true);
}
}
```

2.3.5 Composition of 3D Transformations

Example *J2_8_Robot3d.java* implements the robot arm in Example *J2_4_Robot.java* with 3D cylinders, as shown in Fig. 2.15. We also add one rotation around the *y* axis, so the robot arm moves in 3D.

/* 3D 3-segment arm transformation */

```
import net.java.games.jogl.*;

public class J2_8_Robot3d extends
J2_7_Sphere {

  static float alpha = -30;
  static float beta = -30;
  static float gama = 60;
  static float aalpha = 1;
  static float abeta = 1;
  static float agama = -2;
```

Fig. 2.15 A 3-segment robot arm [*See* Color Plate 2]

```
float O = 0;
float A = (float) WIDTH / 4;
float B = (float) 0.4 * WIDTH;
float C = (float) 0.5 * WIDTH;


public void display(GLDrawable glDrawable) {

   // for reshape purpose
   A = (float) WIDTH / 4;
   B = (float) 0.4 * WIDTH;
   C = (float) 0.5 * WIDTH;

   depth = 4;
   alpha += aalpha;
   beta += abeta;
   gama += agama;

   gl.glClear(GL.GL_COLOR_BUFFER_BIT |
            GL.GL_DEPTH_BUFFER_BIT);
   drawRobot(O, A, B, C, alpha, beta, gama);

void drawArm(float End1, float End2) {

   float scale;
   scale = End2 - End1;

   gl.glPushMatrix();

   // the cylinder lies in the z axis;
   // rotate it to lie in the x axis
   gl.glRotatef(90.0f, 0.0f, 1.0f, 0.0f);
   gl.glScalef(scale / 5.0f, scale / 5.0f, scale);
   drawCylinder();

   gl.glPopMatrix();
}


void drawRobot(float O, float A, float B, float C,
            float alpha, float beta, float gama) {
   // the robot arm is rotating around y axis
   gl.glRotatef(1.0f, 0.0f, 1.0f, 0.0f);
   gl.glPushMatrix();

   gl.glRotatef(alpha, 0.0f, 0.0f, 1.0f);
   // R_z(alpha) is on top of the matrix stack
   drawArm(O, A);
```

```
    gl.glTranslatef(A, 0.0f, 0.0f);
    gl.glRotatef(beta, 0.0f, 0.0f, 1.0f);
    // R_z(alpha)T_x(A)R_z(beta) is on top of the stack
    drawArm(A, B);

    gl.glTranslatef(B - A, 0.0f, 0.0f);
    gl.glRotatef(gama, 0.0f, 0.0f, 1.0f);
    // R_z(alpha)T_x(A)R_z(beta)T_x(B)R_z(gama) is on top
    drawArm(B, C);

    gl.glPopMatrix();
  }


  public static void main(String[] args) {
    J2_8_Robot3d f = new J2_8_Robot3d();

    f.setTitle("JOGL J2_8_Robot3d");
    f.setSize(WIDTH, HEIGHT);
    f.setVisible(true);
  }
}
```

Example *J2_9_Solar.java* is a simplified solar system. The earth rotates around the sun and the moon rotates around the earth in the *xz* plane. Given the center of the earth at $E(x_e, y_e, z_e)$ and the center of the moon at $M(x_m, y_m, z_m)$, let's find the new centers after the earth rotates around the sun *e* degrees, and the moon rotates around the earth *m* degrees. The moon also revolves around the sun with the earth (Fig. 2.16).

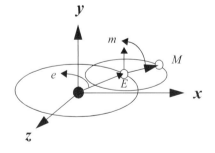

The moon rotates first:

$M' = T(E) R_y(m) T(-E) M;$

$E_f = R_y(e) E;$

$M_f = R_y(e) M';$

The earth-moon rotates first:

$E_f = R_y(e) E;$

$M' = R_y(e) M;$

$M_f = T(E_f) R_y(m) T(-E_f) M'$

Fig. 2.16 **Simplified solar system: a 2D problem in 3D**

This problem is exactly like the clock problem in Fig. 2.5, except that the center of the clock is revolving around *y* axis as well. We can consider the moon rotating around the earth first, and then the moon and the earth as one object rotating around the sun.

In OpenGL, because we can draw a sphere at the center of the coordinates, the transformation would be simpler.

/* draw a simplified solar system */

```
import net.java.games.jogl.*;
import net.java.games.jogl.util.*;

public class J2_9_Solar extends J2_8_Robot3d {

  public void display(GLDrawable glDrawable) {

    depth = (cnt/100)%6;
    cnt++;

    gl.glClear(GL.GL_COLOR_BUFFER_BIT|
               GL.GL_DEPTH_BUFFER_BIT);

    drawSolar(WIDTH/4, cnt, WIDTH/12, cnt);

    try {
      Thread.sleep(10);
    } catch (Exception ignore) {}
  }

  public void drawColorCoord(float xlen, float ylen,
                             float zlen) {
    GLUT glut = new GLUT();

    gl.glBegin(GL.GL_LINES);

    gl.glColor3f(1, 0, 0);

    gl.glVertex3f(0, 0, 0);
    gl.glVertex3f(0, 0, zlen);

    gl.glColor3f(0, 1, 0);

    gl.glVertex3f(0, 0, 0);
    gl.glVertex3f(0, ylen, 0);
```

```
gl.glColor3f(0, 0, 1);

gl.glVertex3f(0, 0, 0);
gl.glVertex3f(xlen, 0, 0);

gl.glEnd();

// coordinate labels: X, Y, Z
gl.glPushMatrix();
gl.glTranslatef(xlen, 0, 0);
gl.glScalef(xlen/WIDTH, xlen/WIDTH, 1);
glut.glutStrokeCharacter(gl, GLUT.STROKE_ROMAN, 'X');
gl.glPopMatrix();

gl.glPushMatrix();
gl.glColor3f(0, 1, 0);
gl.glTranslatef(0, ylen, 0);
gl.glScalef(ylen/WIDTH, ylen/WIDTH, 1);
glut.glutStrokeCharacter(gl, GLUT.STROKE_ROMAN, 'Y');
gl.glPopMatrix();

gl.glPushMatrix();
gl.glColor3f(1, 0, 0);
gl.glTranslatef(0, 0, zlen);
gl.glScalef(zlen/WIDTH, zlen/WIDTH, 1);
glut.glutStrokeCharacter(gl, GLUT.STROKE_ROMAN, 'Z');
gl.glPopMatrix();
}


void drawSolar(float E, float e, float M, float m) {

  drawColorCoord(WIDTH/4, WIDTH/4, WIDTH/4);

  gl.glPushMatrix();

  gl.glRotatef(e, 0.0f, 1.0f, 0.0f);
  // rotating around the "sun"; proceed angle

  gl.glTranslatef(E, 0.0f, 0.0f);

  gl.glPushMatrix();
  gl.glScalef(WIDTH/20f, WIDTH/20f, WIDTH/20f);
  drawSphere();
  gl.glPopMatrix();

  gl.glRotatef(m, 0.0f, 1.0f, 0.0f);
```

```
      // rotating around the "earth"
      gl.glTranslatef(M, 0.0f, 0.0f);
      drawColorCoord(WIDTH/8f, WIDTH/8f, WIDTH/8f);
      gl.glScalef(WIDTH/40f, WIDTH/40f, WIDTH/40f);
      drawSphere();

      gl.glPopMatrix();
   }


   public static void main(String[] args) {
      J2_9_Solar f = new J2_9_Solar();

      f.setTitle("JOGL J2_9_Solar");
      f.setSize(WIDTH, HEIGHT);
      f.setVisible(true);
   }
}
```

Next, we change the above solar system into a more complex system, which we call the *generalized solar system*. Now the earth is elevated along the y axis, and the moon is elevated along the axis from the origin toward the center of the earth, and the moon rotates around this axis as in Fig. 2.17. In other words, the moon rotates around the vector E. Given E and M and their rotation angles e and m, respectively, can we find the new coordinates of E_f and M_f?

We cannot come up with the rotation matrix for the moon, M, immediately. However, we can consider E and M as one object and create the rotation matrix by several steps. Note that for M's rotation around E, we do not really need to rotate E itself, but we use it as a reference to explain the rotation.

1. As shown in Fig. 2.17, the angle between the y axis and E is $\alpha = arc\ cos\ (y/r)$; the angle between the projection of E on the xz plane and the x axis is $\beta = arc\ tg\ (z/x)$; $r = sqrt(x^2 + y^2 + z^2)$.

2. Rotate M around the y axis by β degrees so that the new center of rotation E_1 is in the xy plane:

$$M_1 = R_y(\beta)M;\ E_1 = R_y(\beta)E. \hspace{3cm} \text{(EQ 47)}$$

$r = sqrt(x^2 + y^2 + z^2);$
$\alpha = arc\ cos\ (y/r);\ \beta = arc\ tg\ (z/x);$

$E_f = R_y(e)\ E;$ // the earth rotates around the y axis

$M_1 = R_y(\beta)\ M;$ // the center of rotation OE is in the xy plane
$M_2 = R_z(\alpha)\ M_1$ // OE is along the y axis
$M_3 = R_y(m)\ M_2;$ // the moon rotates along the y axis
$M_4 = R_z(-\alpha)\ M_3;$ //OE returns to the xy plane
$M_5 = R_y(-\beta)\ M_4;$ // OE returns to its original orientation
$M_f = R_y(e)\ M_5;$ // the moon proceeds with the earth

$$M_f = R_y(e)R_y(-\beta)\ R_z(-\alpha)\ R_y(m)\ R_z(\alpha)\ R_y(\beta)\ M;$$

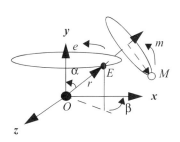

Fig. 2.17 Generalized solar system: a 3D problem

---

3. Rotate M_1 around the z axis by α degrees so that the new center of rotation E_2 is coincident with the y axis:

$$M_2 = R_z(\alpha)M_1;\ E_2 = R_z(\alpha)E_1. \hspace{2cm} \text{(EQ 48)}$$

4. Rotate M_2 around the y axis by m degree:

$$M_3 = R_y(m)M_2. \hspace{2cm} \text{(EQ 49)}$$

5. Rotate M_3 around the z axis by $-\alpha$ degree so that the center of rotation returns to the xz plane:

$$M_4 = R_z(-\alpha)M_3;\ E_1 = R_z(-\alpha)E_2. \hspace{2cm} \text{(EQ 50)}$$

6. Rotate M_4 around y axis by $-\beta$ degree so that the center of rotation returns to its original orientation:

$$M_5 = R_y(-\beta)M_4;\ E = R_y(-\beta)E_1. \hspace{2cm} \text{(EQ 51)}$$

7. Rotate M_5 around y axis e degree so that the moon proceeds with the earth around the y axis:

$$M_f = R_y(e)M_5;\ E_f = R_y(e)E. \qquad\qquad \text{(EQ 52)}$$

8. Putting the transformation matrices together, we have

$$M_f = R_y(e)R_y(-\beta)\ R_z(-\alpha)\ R_y(m)\ R_z(\alpha)\ R_y(\beta)\ M. \qquad\qquad \text{(EQ 53)}$$

Again, in OpenGL, we start with the sphere at the origin. The transformation is simpler. The following code demonstrates the generalized solar system. The result is shown in Fig. 2.18. Incidentally, *glRotatef(m, x, y, z)* specifies a single matrix that rotates a point along the vector $(x,\ y,\ z)$ by m degrees. Now, we know that the matrix is equal to $R_y(-\beta)\ R_z(-\alpha)\ R_y(m)$ $R_z(\alpha)\ R_y(\beta)$.

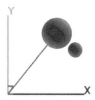

Fig. 2.18 Generalized solar system [*See* Color Plate 2]

/* draw a generalized solar system */

```
import net.java.games.jogl.*;


public class J2_10_GenSolar extends J2_9_Solar {
  static float tiltAngle = 40;

  void drawSolar(float earthDistance,
                 float earthAngle,
                 float moonDistance,
                 float moonAngle) {

    // Global coordinates
    gl.glLineWidth(6);
    drawColorCoord(WIDTH/4, WIDTH/4, WIDTH/4);

    gl.glPushMatrix();
```

```
        gl.glRotatef(earthAngle, 0.0f, 1.0f, 0.0f);
        // rotating around the "sun"; proceed angle
        gl.glRotatef(tiltAngle, 0.0f, 0.0f, 1.0f);
        // tilt angle, angle between the center line and y axis
        gl.glBegin(GL.GL_LINES);
        gl.glVertex3f(0.0f, 0.0f, 0.0f);
        gl.glVertex3f(0.0f, earthDistance, 0.0f);
        gl.glEnd();

        gl.glTranslatef(0.0f, earthDistance, 0.0f);
        gl.glLineWidth(2);

        gl.glPushMatrix();
        drawColorCoord(WIDTH/6, WIDTH/6, WIDTH/6);
        gl.glScalef(WIDTH/20, WIDTH/20, WIDTH/20);
        drawSphere();
        gl.glPopMatrix();

        gl.glRotatef(moonAngle, 0.0f, 1.0f, 0.0f);
        // rotating around the "earth"
        gl.glTranslatef(moonDistance, 0.0f, 0.0f);
        gl.glLineWidth(3);
        drawColorCoord(WIDTH/8, WIDTH/8, WIDTH/8);
        gl.glScalef(WIDTH/40, WIDTH/40, WIDTH/40);
        drawSphere();

        gl.glPopMatrix();
    }


    public static void main(String[] args) {

        J2_10_GenSolar f = new J2_10_GenSolar();

        f.setTitle("JOGL J2_10_GenSolar");
        f.setSize(WIDTH, HEIGHT);
        f.setVisible(true);
    }
}
```

The generalized solar system corresponds to a top that rotates and proceeds as shown in Fig. 2.19b. The rotating angle is m and the proceeding angle is e. The earth E is a point along the center of the top, and the moon M can be a point on the edge of the top. We learned to draw a cone in OpenGL. We can transform the cone to achieve the motion of a top. In the following example (*J2_11_ConeSolar.java*), we have a top that rotates and proceeds and a sphere that rotates around the top (Fig. 2.19c).

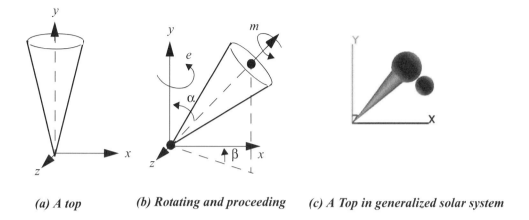

(a) A top   *(b) Rotating and proceeding*   *(c) A Top in generalized solar system*

Fig. 2.19 A top rotates and proceeds [*See* **Color Plate 2**]

/* draw a cone solar system */

```
public class J2_11_ConeSolar extends J2_10_GenSolar {

  void drawSolar(float E, float e, float M, float m) {

    // Global coordinates
    gl.glLineWidth(6);
    drawColorCoord(WIDTH / 4, WIDTH / 4, WIDTH / 4);

    gl.glPushMatrix();
    gl.glRotatef(e, 0.0f, 1.0f, 0.0f);
    // rotating around the "sun"; proceed angle
    gl.glRotatef(alpha, 0.0f, 0.0f, 1.0f); // tilt angle
    gl.glTranslatef(0.0f, E, 0.0f);
    gl.glPushMatrix();
    gl.glScalef(WIDTH / 20, WIDTH / 20, WIDTH / 20);
    drawSphere();
    gl.glPopMatrix();
    gl.glPushMatrix();
    gl.glScalef(E / 8, E, E / 8);
    gl.glRotatef(90, 1.0f, 0.0f, 0.0f); // orient the cone
    drawCone();
    gl.glPopMatrix();

    gl.glRotatef(m, 0.0f, 1.0f, 0.0f);
```

```
    // rotating around the "earth"
    gl.glTranslatef(M, 0.0f, 0.0f);
    gl.glLineWidth(4);
    drawColorCoord(WIDTH / 8, WIDTH / 8, WIDTH / 8);
    gl.glScalef(E / 8, E / 8, E / 8);
    drawSphere();
    gl.glPopMatrix();
  }

  public static void main(String[] args) {

    J2_11_ConeSolar f = new J2_11_ConeSolar();

    f.setTitle("JOGL J2_11_ConeSolar");
    f.setSize(WIDTH, HEIGHT);
    f.setVisible(true);
  }
}
```

2.3.6 Collision Detection

To avoid two models in an animation penetrating each other, we can use their bounding volumes to decide their physical distances and collision. Of course, the bounding volume can be in a different shape other than a box, such as a sphere. If the distance between the centers of the two spheres is bigger than the summation of the two radii of the spheres, we know that the two models do not collide with each other. We may use multiple spheres with different radii to more accurately bound a model, but the collision detection would be more complex. Of course, we may also detect collisions directly without using bounding volumes, which is likely much more complex and time consuming.

Fig. 2.20 **Collision detection**
[*See* **Color Plate 2**]

We can modify the above example to have three moons (a cylinder, a sphere, and a cone) that rotate around the earth in different directions and collide with one another changing the directions of rotation (Fig. 2.20). If we use a sphere as a bounding volume, the problem becomes how to find the centers of the bounding spheres. We know that each moon is transformed from the origin. If we know the current matrix on the matrix stack at the point we draw a moon, we can multiply the matrix with the origin $(0, 0, 0, 1)$ to find the center of the moon. Because at the origin x, y, and z are 0s, we only need to retrieve the last column in the matrix, which is shown in the following example (*J2_11_coneSolarCollision.java*). Collision detection is then decided by the distances among the moons' centers. If a distance is shorter than a predefined threshold, the two moons will change their directions of rotation around the earth.

/* draw a cone solar system with collisions of the moons */

```
import java.lang.Math;
import net.java.games.jogl.*;


public class J2_11_ConeSolarCollision extends
    J2_11_ConeSolar {
  //direction and speed of rotation
  static float coneD = WIDTH/110;
  static float sphereD = -WIDTH/64;
  static float cylinderD = WIDTH/300f;
  static float spherem = 120, cylinderm = 240;
  static float tmpD = 0, conem = 0;

  // centers of the objects
  static float[] coneC = new float[3];
  static float[] sphereC = new float[3];
  static float[] cylinderC = new float[3];

  // current matrix on the matrix stack
  static float[] currM = new float[16];


  void drawSolar(float E, float e, float M, float m) {

    // Global coordinates
    gl.glLineWidth(8);
    drawColorCoord(WIDTH/4, WIDTH/4, WIDTH/4);

    gl.glPushMatrix(); {
      gl.glRotatef(e, 0.0f, 1.0f, 0.0f);
      // rotating around the "sun"; proceed angle
      gl.glRotatef(alpha, 0.0f, 0.0f, 1.0f); // tilt angle
      gl.glTranslatef(0.0f, E, 0.0f);
```

```
gl.glPushMatrix();
gl.glScalef(WIDTH/20, WIDTH/20, WIDTH/20);
drawSphere();
gl.glPopMatrix();

gl.glPushMatrix();
gl.glScalef(E/8, E, E/8);
gl.glRotatef(90, 1.0f, 0.0f, 0.0f);

// orient the cone
drawCone();
gl.glPopMatrix();

gl.glPushMatrix();
cylinderm = cylinderm+cylinderD;
gl.glRotatef(cylinderm, 0.0f, 1.0f, 0.0f);
// rotating around the "earth"
gl.glTranslatef(M*2, 0.0f, 0.0f);
gl.glLineWidth(4);
drawColorCoord(WIDTH/8, WIDTH/8, WIDTH/8);
gl.glScalef(E/8, E/8, E/8);
drawCylinder();
// retrieve the center of the cylinder
// the matrix is stored column major left to right
gl.glGetFloatv(GL.GL_MODELVIEW_MATRIX, currM);
cylinderC[0] = currM[12];
cylinderC[1] = currM[13];
cylinderC[2] = currM[14];
gl.glPopMatrix();

gl.glPushMatrix();
spherem = spherem+sphereD;
gl.glRotatef(spherem, 0.0f, 1.0f, 0.0f);
// rotating around the "earth"
gl.glTranslatef(M*2, 0.0f, 0.0f);
drawColorCoord(WIDTH/8, WIDTH/8, WIDTH/8);
gl.glScalef(E/8, E/8, E/8);
drawSphere();
// retrieve the center of the sphere
gl.glGetFloatv(GL.GL_MODELVIEW_MATRIX, currM);
sphereC[0] = currM[12];
sphereC[1] = currM[13];
sphereC[2] = currM[14];
gl.glPopMatrix();

gl.glPushMatrix();
conem = conem+coneD;
gl.glRotatef(conem, 0.0f, 1.0f, 0.0f);
// rotating around the "earth"
```

```
    gl.glTranslatef(M*2, 0.0f, 0.0f);
    drawColorCoord(WIDTH/8, WIDTH/8, WIDTH/8);
    gl.glScalef(E/8, E/8, E/8);
    drawCone();
    // retrieve the center of the cone
    gl.glGetFloatv(GL.GL_MODELVIEW_MATRIX, currM);
    coneC[0] = currM[12];
    coneC[1] = currM[13];
    coneC[2] = currM[14];
    gl.glPopMatrix();
  }
  gl.glPopMatrix();

  if (distance(coneC, sphereC)<E/5) {
    // collision detected, swap the rotation directions
    tmpD = coneD;
    coneD = sphereD;
    sphereD = tmpD;
  }

  if (distance(coneC, cylinderC)<E/5) {
    // collision detected, swap the rotation directions
    tmpD = coneD;
    coneD = cylinderD;
    cylinderD = tmpD;
  }

  if (distance(cylinderC, sphereC)<E/5) {
    // collision detected, swap the rotation directions
    tmpD = cylinderD;
    cylinderD = sphereD;
    sphereD = tmpD;
  }
}


// distance between two points
float distance(float[] c1, float[] c2) {
  float tmp = (c2[0]-c1[0])*(c2[0]-c1[0])+
              (c2[1]-c1[1])*(c2[1]-c1[1])+
              (c2[2]-c1[2])*(c2[2]-c1[2]);

  return ((float)Math.sqrt(tmp));
}


public static void main(String[] args) {
  J2_11_ConeSolarCollision f =
      new J2_11_ConeSolarCollision();
```

```
        f.setTitle("JOGL J2_11_ConeSolarCollision");
        f.setSize(WIDTH, HEIGHT);
        f.setVisible(true);
    }
}
```

2.4 Viewing

The display has its device coordinate system in pixels, and our model has its (virtual) modeling coordinate system in which we specify and transform our model. We need to consider the relationship between the modeling coordinates and the device coordinates so that our virtual model will appear as an image on the display. Therefore, we need a *viewing* transformation — the mapping of an area or volume in the modeling coordinates to an area in the display device coordinates.

2.4.1 2D Viewing

In 2D viewing, we specify a rectangular area called the *modeling window* in the modeling coordinates and a display rectangular area called the *viewport* in the device coordinates (Fig. 2.21). The modeling window defines what is to be viewed; the viewport defines where the image appears. Instead of transforming a model in the modeling window to a model in the display viewport directly, we can first transform the modeling window into a square with the lower-left corner at (−1, −1) and the upper-right corner at (1, 1). The coordinates of the square are called the *normalized* coordinates. Clipping of the model is then calculated in the normalized coordinates against the square. After that, the normalized coordinates are scaled and translated to the device coordinates.

We should understand that the matrix that transforms the modeling window to the square will also transform the models in the modeling coordinates to the corresponding models in the normalized coordinates. Similarly, the matrix that transforms the square to the viewport will also transform the models accordingly. The process (or pipeline) in 2D viewing is shown in Fig. 2.21. Through normalization, the clipping algorithm avoid dealing with the changing sizes of the modeling window and the device viewport.

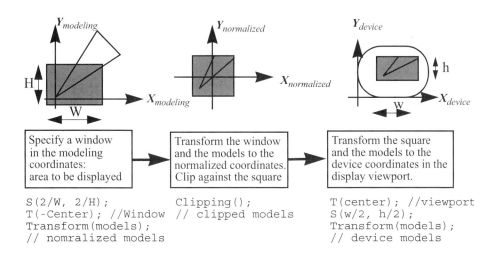

Specify a window in the modeling coordinates: area to be displayed

Transform the window and the models to the normalized coordinates. Clip against the square

Transform the square and the models to the device coordinates in the display viewport.

```
S(2/W, 2/H);
T(-Center); //Window
Transform(models);
// nomralized models
```

```
Clipping();
// clipped models
```

```
T(center); //viewport
S(w/2, h/2);
Transform(models);
// device models
```

Fig. 2.21 **2D viewing pipeline**

2.4.2 3D Viewing

The display is a 2D viewport, and our model can be in 3D. In 3D viewing, we need to specify a viewing volume, which determines a projection method (*parallel* or *perspective*) — for how 3D models are projected into 2D. The projection lines go from the vertices in the 3D models to the projected vertices in the projection plane — a 2D *view plane* that corresponds to the viewport. A parallel projection has all the projection lines parallel. A perspective projection has all the projection lines converging to a point named the *center of projection*. The center of projection is also called the *viewpoint*. You may consider that your eye is at the viewpoint looking into the viewing volume. Viewing is analogous to taking a photograph with a camera. The object in the outside world has its own 3D coordinate system, the film in the camera has its own 2D coordinate system. We specify a viewing volume and a projection method by pointing and adjusting the zoom.

As shown in Fig. 2.22, the viewing volume for the parallel projection is like a box. The result of the parallel projection is a less realistic view but can be used for exact measurements. The viewing volume for the perspective projection is like a truncated pyramid, and the result looks more realistic in many cases, but does not preserve sizes in the display — objects further away are smaller.

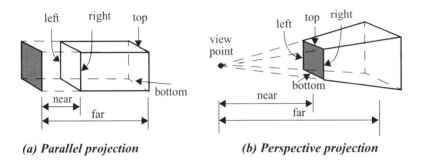

(a) Parallel projection   *(b) Perspective projection*

Fig. 2.22 View volumes and projection methods

In the following, we use the OpenGL system as an example to demonstrate how 3D viewing is achieved. The OpenGL viewing pipeline includes normalization, clipping, perspective division, and viewport transformation (Fig. 2.23). Except for clipping, all other transformation steps can be achieved by matrix multiplications. Therefore, viewing is mostly achieved by geometric transformation. In the OpenGL system, these transformations are achieved by matrix multiplications on the PROJECTION matrix stack.

Specifying a viewing volume. A parallel projection is called an *orthographic projection* if the projection lines are all perpendicular to the view plane. *glOrtho*(left, right, bottom, top, near, far) specifies an orthographic projection as shown in Fig. 2.22a. *glOrtho()* also defines six plane equations that cover the orthographic viewing volume: x=left, x=right, y=bottom, y=top, z=−near, and z=−far. We can see that (left, bottom, −near) and (right, top, −near) specify the (x, y, z) coordinates of the lower-left and upper-right corners of the near clipping plane. Similarly, (left, bottom, −far) and (right, top, −far) specify the (x, y, z) coordinates of the lower-left and upper-right corners of the far clipping plane.

glFrustum(left, right, bottom, top, near, far) specifies a perspective projection as shown in Fig. 2.22b. *glFrustum()* also defines six planes that cover the perspective viewing volume. We can see that (left, bottom, −near) and (right, top, −near) specify the (x, y, z) coordinates of the lower-left and upper-right corners of the near clipping plane. The far clipping plane is a cross section at z=−far with the projection lines converging to the viewpoint, which is fixed at the origin looking down the negative z axis.

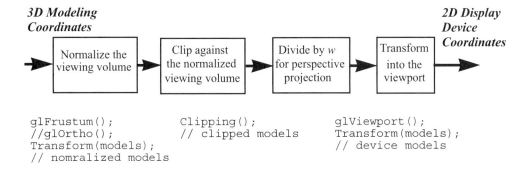

3D Modeling Coordinates

2D Display Device Coordinates

| Normalize the viewing volume | Clip against the normalized viewing volume | Divide by w for perspective projection | Transform into the viewport |

```
glFrustum();           Clipping();            glViewport();
//glOrtho();           // clipped models      Transform(models);
Transform(models);                            // device models
// nomralized models
```

Fig. 2.23 3D viewing pipeline

As we can see, both *glOrtho()* and *glFrustum()* specify viewing volumes oriented with left and right edges on the near clipping plane parallel to y axis. In general, we use a vector *up* to represent the orientation of the viewing volume, which when projected on to the near clipping plane is parallel to the left and right edges.

Normalization. Normalization transformation is achieved by matrix multiplication on the PROJECTION matrix stack. In the following code section, we first load the identity matrix onto the top of the matrix stack. Then, we multiply the identity matrix by a matrix specified by *glOrtho()*.

```
// hardware set to use projection matrix stack
gl.glMatrixMode (GL.GL_PROJECTION);
gl.glLoadIdentity ();
gl.glOrtho(-Width/2,Width/2,-Height/2,Height/2,-1.0, 1.0);
```

In OpenGL, *glOrtho()* actually specifies a matrix that transforms the specified viewing volume into a *normalized* viewing volume, which is a cube with six clipping planes as shown in Fig. 2.24 ($x=1$, $x=-1$, $y=1$, $y=-1$, $z=1$, and $z=-1$). Therefore, instead of calculating the clipping and projection directly, the normalization transformation is carried out first to simplify the clipping and the projection. Similarly, *glFrustum()* also specifies a matrix that transforms the perspective viewing volume into a normalized viewing volume as in Fig. 2.24. Here a division is needed to map the homogeneous coordinates into 3D coordinates. In OpenGL, a 3D vertex is represented by (x, y, z, w) and transformation matrices are 4×4 matrices. When $w=1$, (x, y, z) represents the 3D coordinates of the vertex. If $w=0$, (x, y, z) represents a direction. Otherwise, $(x/w, y/w, z/w)$ represents the 3D coordinates. A perspective division is needed simply because after the *glFrustum()* matrix transformation, $w \neq 1$. In OpenGL, the perspective division is carried out after clipping.

Clipping. Because *glOrtho()* and *glFrustum()* both transform their viewing volumes into a normalized viewing volume, we only need to develop one clipping algorithm. Clipping is carried out in homogeneous coordinates to accommodate certain curves. Therefore, all vertices of the models are first transformed into the normalized viewing coordinates, clipped against the planes of the normalized viewing volume ($x=-w, x=w, y=-w, y=w, z=-w, z=w$), and then transformed and projected into the 2D viewport.

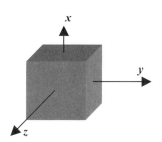

Fig. 2.24 Normalized viewing volume — a cube with (-1 to 1) along each axis

Perspective division. The perspective normalization transformation *glFrustum()* results in homogenous coordinates with $w \neq 1$. Clipping is carried out in homogeneous coordinates. However, a division for all the coordinates of the model $(x/w, y/w, z/w)$ is needed to transform homogeneous coordinates into 3D coordinates.

Viewport transformation. All vertices are kept in 3D. We need the z values to calculate hidden-surface removal. From the normalized viewing volume after dividing by w, the viewport transformation calculates each vertex's (x, y, z) corresponding to the pixels in the viewport and invokes scan-conversion algorithms to draw the model into the viewport. Projecting into 2D is nothing more than ignoring the z values when scan-converting the model's pixels into the frame buffer. It is not necessary but we may consider that the projection plane is at $z=0$. In Fig. 2.22, the shaded projection planes are arbitrarily specified.

Summary of the viewing pipeline. Before scan-conversion, an OpenGL model will go through the following transformation and viewing processing steps:

- *Modeling*: Each vertex of the model will be transformed by the current matrix on the top of the MODELVIEW matrix stack.

- *Normalization*: After the above MODELVIEW transformation, each vertex will be transformed by the current matrix on the top of the PROJECTION matrix stack.

- *Clipping*: Each primitive (point, line, polygon, etc.) is clipped against the clipping planes in homogeneous coordinates.

- *Perspective division*: All primitives are transformed from homogeneous coordinates into Cartesian coordinates.

- *Viewport transformation*: The model is scaled and translated into the viewport for scan-conversion.

2.4.3 The Logical Orders of Transformation Steps

Modeling and viewing transformations are carried out by the OpenGL system automatically. For programmers, it is more practical to understand how to specify a viewing volume through *glOrtho()* or *glFrustum()* on the PROJECTION matrix stack and to make sure that the model is in the viewing volume after being transformed by the current matrix on the MODELVIEW matrix stack. The PROJECTION matrix is multiplied with the MODELVIEW matrix, and the result is used to transform (normalize) the original model's vertices. The final matrix, if you view it from how it is constructed, represents an expression or queue of matrices from left-most where you specify normalization matrix to right-most where you specify a vertex in drawing.

When we analyze a model's transformation steps, logically speaking, the order of transformation steps is from right to left in the matrix expression. However, we can look at the matrix expression from left to right if our logical is transforming the projection (camera) instead of the model. We will discuss these two different logical reasoning orders here.

The following demonstrates how to specify the modelview and projection matrices on the two stacks in the example *J2_12_RobotSolar.java*, as shown in Fig. 2.25. Here the logical reasoning is from where we specify the model to where we specify the projection matrix.

1. In *display()*, a robot arm is calculated at the origin of the modeling coordinates.

2. As we discussed before, although the matrices are multiplied from the top-down transformation commands, when we analyze a model's transformations, logically speaking, the order of transformation steps are bottom-up

Fig. 2.25 Viewing in 3D [*See Color Plate 2*]

from the closest transformation above the drawing command on the MODELVIEW matrix stack to where we specify the viewing volume on the PROJECTION matrix stack.

3. OpenGL provides PROJECTION and MODELVIEW matrix stacks to facilitate viewing and transformation separately, which is a nice separation and logical structure. Theoretically, we do not have to require two pieces of hardware, because the matrix on top of the PROJECTION matrix stack and the matrix on top of the MODELVIEW matrix stack are multiplied together to transform the models into the canonical viewing volume. Therefore, we can view these two matrices as one matrix expression, and some of the transformations can be on either of the matrix stacks. The following transformation step is an example.

4. In *Reshape()*, the robot arm is translated along z axis $-(zNear + zFar)/2$ in order to be put in the middle of the viewing volume. This translation here can be the first matrix in the MODELVIEW matrix expression or the last matrix in the PROJECTION matrix expression.

5. *glOrtho()* or *glFrustum()* specify the viewing volume. The models in the viewing volume will appear in the viewport area on the display.

6. *glViewport()* in *Reshape()* specifies the rendering area within the display window. The viewing volume will be projected into the viewport area. When we reshape the drawing area, the viewport aspect ratio (w/h) changes accordingly. We may specify

a different viewport using *glViewport()* and draw into that area. In other words, we may have multiple viewports with different renderings in each display, which will be discussed later.

/* 3D transformation and viewing */

```
import net.java.games.jogl.*;


public class J2_12_RobotSolar extends
    J2_11_ConeSolarCollision {

  public void reshape(
      GLDrawable glDrawable,
      int x,
      int y,
      int w,
      int h) {

    WIDTH = w;
    HEIGHT = h;

    // enable zbuffer for hidden-surface removal
    gl.glEnable(GL.GL_DEPTH_TEST);

    // specify the drawing area within the frame window
    gl.glViewport(0, 0, w, h);

    // projection is carried on the projection matrix
    gl.glMatrixMode(GL.GL_PROJECTION);
    gl.glLoadIdentity();
    // specify perspective projection using glFrustum
    gl.glFrustum(-w/4, w/4, -h/4, h/4, w/2, 4*w);

    // put the models at the center of the viewing volume
    gl.glTranslatef(0, 0, -2*w);

    // transformations are on the modelview matrix
    gl.glMatrixMode(GL.GL_MODELVIEW);
    gl.glLoadIdentity();
  }


  public void display(GLDrawable glDrawable) {

    cnt++;
```

```
depth = (cnt/100)%6;

gl.glClear(GL.GL_COLOR_BUFFER_BIT|
           GL.GL_DEPTH_BUFFER_BIT);

if (cnt%60--0) {
  aalpha = -aalpha;
  abeta = -abeta;
  agama = -agama;
}
alpha += aalpha;
beta += abeta;
gama += agama;

drawRobot(O, A, B, C, alpha, beta, gama);

try {
  Thread.sleep(15);
} catch (Exception ignore) {}
}


void drawRobot (float O, float A, float B, float C,
    float alpha, float beta, float gama) {

gl.glLineWidth(8);
drawColorCoord(WIDTH/4, WIDTH/4, WIDTH/4);

gl.glPushMatrix();

gl.glRotatef(cnt, 0, 1, 0);
gl.glRotatef(alpha, 0, 0, 1);
// R_z(alpha) is on top of the matrix stack
drawArm(O, A);

gl.glTranslatef(A, 0, 0);
gl.glRotatef(beta, 0, 0, 1);
// R_z(alpha)T_x(A)R_z(beta) is on top of the stack
drawArm(A, B);

gl.glTranslatef(B-A, 0, 0);
gl.glRotatef(gama, 0, 0, 1);
// R_z(alpha)T_x(A)R_z(beta)T_x(B)R_z(gama) is on top
drawArm(B, C);

// put the solar system at the end of the robot arm
gl.glTranslatef(C-B, 0, 0);
drawSolar(WIDTH/4, 2.5f*cnt, WIDTH/6, 1.5f*cnt);
```

```
  gl.glPopMatrix();
}

public static void main(String[] args) {
  J2_12_RobotSolar f = new J2_12_RobotSolar();

  f.setTitle("JOGL J2_12_RobotSolar");
  f.setSize(WIDTH, HEIGHT);
  f.setVisible(true);
}
}
```

Another way of looking at the modeling and viewing transformation is that the matrix expression transforms the viewing method instead of the model. Translating a model along the negative z axis is like moving the viewing volume (camera) along the positive z axis. Similarly, rotating a model along an axis by a positive angle is like rotating the viewing volume along the axis by a negative angle. When we analyze a model's transformation by thinking about transforming its viewing, the order of transformation steps are top-down from where we specify the viewing volume to where we specify the drawing command. We should

Fig. 2.26 Transform the viewing [*See* **Color Plate 2**]

remember that the signs of the transformation are logically negated in this perspective. Example *J2_12_RobotSolar.java*, specifies transformation in *myCamera()* from the top-down point of view. The result is shown in Fig. 2.26.

/* going backwards to the moon in generalized solar system */

```
import net.java.games.jogl.*;

public class J2_13_TravelSolar extends J2_12_RobotSolar {

  public void display(GLDrawable glDrawable) {
```

```
   cnt++;
   depth = (cnt/50)%6;

gl.glClear(GL.GL_COLOR_BUFFER_BIT|GL.GL_DEPTH_BUFFER_BIT);

   if (cnt%60==0) {
     aalpha = -aalpha; abeta = -abeta; agama = -agama;
   }
   alpha += aalpha; beta += abeta; gama += agama;

   gl.glPushMatrix();
   if (cnt%1000<500) {
     // look at the solar system from the moon
     myCamera(A, B, C, alpha, beta, gama);
   }
   drawRobot(O, A, B, C, alpha, beta, gama);
   gl.glPopMatrix();

 void myCamera(float A, float B, float C,
     float alpha, float beta, float gama) {

   float E = WIDTH/4; float e = 2.5f*cnt;
   float M = WIDTH/6; float m = 1.5f*cnt;

   //1. camera faces the negative x axis
   gl.glRotatef(-90, 0, 1, 0);

   //2. camera on positive x axis
   gl.glTranslatef(-M*2, 0, 0);

   //3. camera rotates with the cylinder
   gl.glRotatef(-cylinderm, 0, 1, 0);

   // and so on reversing the solar transformation
   gl.glTranslatef(0, -E, 0);
   gl.glRotatef(-alpha, 0, 0, 1); // tilt angle
   // rotating around the "sun"; proceed angle
   gl.glRotatef(-e, 0, 1, 0);

   // and reversing the robot transformation
   gl.glTranslatef(-C+B, 0, 0);
   gl.glRotatef(-gama, 0, 0, 1);
   gl.glTranslatef(-B+A, 0, 0);
   gl.glRotatef(-beta, 0, 0, 1);
   gl.glTranslatef(-A, 0, 0);
   gl.glRotatef(-alpha, 0, 0, 1);
   gl.glRotatef(-cnt, 0, 1, 0);
 }
```

```
public static void main(String[] args) {
    J2_13_TravelSolar f = new J2_13_TravelSolar();

    f.setTitle("JOGL J2_13_TravelSolar");
    f.setSize(WIDTH, HEIGHT);
    f.setVisible(true);
  }
}
```

2.4.4 gluPerspective and gluLookAt

The OpenGL Utility (GLU) library, which is considered part of OpenGL, contains several groups of convenience functions that are built on top of OpenGL functions and complement the OpenGL library. The prefix for OpenGL Utility library functions is "glu" rather than "gl." We have only focused on the OpenGL library. For further understanding viewing, here we discuss two GLU library functions: *gluPerspective()* and *gluLookAt()*. More GLU library functions are discussed in Chapter 5.

gluPerspective() sets up a perspective projection matrix as follows:

```
void gluPerspective(
    double fovy,   // the field of view angle in y-direction
    double aspect,  // width/height of the near clipping plane
    double zNear,  // distance from the origin to the near
    double zFar    // distance from the origin to far
);
```

The parameters of *gluPerspective()* are explained in Fig. 2.27. Compared with *glFrustum()*, *gluPerspective()* is easier to use for some programmers, but it is less powerful. The *fovy* (field of view) angle is symmetric around z axis in y direction, and its near and far clipping planes are symmetric around z axis as well. Therefore, *gluPerspective()* can only specify a symmetric viewing frustum around z axis, whereas *glFrustum()* has no such restriction. The following example *J2_14_Perspective.java* shows an implementation of *myPerspective(double fovy, double aspect, double near, double far)*:

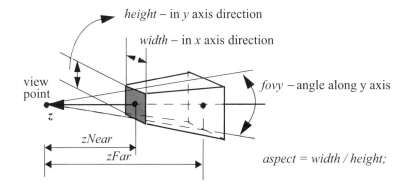

height – in *y* axis direction

width – in *x* axis direction

view
point

z

fovy – angle along y axis

zNear

zFar

aspect = *width* / *height;*

Fig. 2.27 *gluPerspective* **specifies a viewing frustum symmetric around** *z* **axis**

/* simulate gluPerspective */

```
import net.java.games.jogl.*;
import java.lang.Math;


public class J2_14_Perspective extends
    J2_13_TravelSolar {

  public void myPerspective(double fovy, double aspect,
                            double near, double far) {
    double left, right, bottom, top;

    fovy = fovy*Math.PI/180; // convert degree to arc

    top = near*Math.tan(fovy/2);
    bottom = -top;
    right = aspect*top;
    left = -right;

    gl.glMatrixMode(GL.GL_PROJECTION);
    gl.glLoadIdentity();
    gl.glFrustum(left, right, bottom, top, near, far);
  }

  public void reshape(GLDrawable glDrawable,
       int x, int y, int width, int height) {
```

```
WIDTH = width;
HEIGHT = height;

// enable zbuffer for hidden-surface removal
gl.glEnable(GL.GL_DEPTH_TEST);
gl.glViewport(0, 0, width, height);

myPerspective(45, 1, width/2, 4*width);

gl.glMatrixMode(GL.GL_MODELVIEW);
gl.glLoadIdentity();
gl.glTranslatef(0, 0, -2*width);
}


public static void main(String[] args) {
  J2_14_Perspective f = new J2_14_Perspective();

  f.setTitle("JOGL J2_14_Perspective");
  f.setSize(WIDTH, HEIGHT);
  f.setVisible(true);
}
}
```

glOrtho(), *glFrustum()*, and gluPerspective all specify a viewing volume oriented with left and right edges on the near clipping plane parallel to y axis. As we mentioned earlier, we use an *up* vector to represent the orientation of the viewing volume. In other words, by default the projection of *up* onto the near clipping plane is always parallel to the y axis. Because we can transform a viewing volume (camera) now as discussed in the past section, if we specify an orientation vector (*upX, upY, upZ*), we can orient the viewing volume accordingly. Here the angle between y axis and *up*'s projection on the *xy* plane is *atan(upX/upY)*, we just need to rotate the viewing volume −*atan(upX/upY)* to achieve this. This can go further. We do not necessarily have to look from the origin down to the negative z axis. Instead, we can specify the viewpoint as a point *eye* looking down to another point *center*, with *up* as the orientation of the viewing volume. This seems complex, but an equivalent transformation seems much simpler. Given a triangle in 3D (*eye, center, up*), can we build up a transformation matrix so that after the transformation *eye* will be at the origin, *center* will be in the negative z axis, and *up* in the *yz* plane? The answer is shown in the method *myLookAt()* in the example *J2_15_LookAt.java* in the next section. *myLookAt()* and *myGluLookAt()* in the example are equivalent simulations of *gluLookAt()*, which defines a viewing transformation from viewpoint *eye* to another point *center* with *up* as the viewing frustum's orientation vector:

```
void gluLookAt (double eyeX
             , double eyeY
             , double eyeZ
             , double centerX
             , double centerY
             , double centerZ
             , double upX
             , double upY
             , double upZ
             );
```

Here the *eye* and *center* are points, but *up* is a vector. This is slightly different from our triangle example, where up is a point as well. As we can see, the *up* vector cannot be parallel to the line (*eye*, *center*).

2.4.5 Multiple Viewports

glViewport(int x, int y, int width, int height) specifies the rendering area within the frame of the display window. By default *glViewport(0, 0, w, h)* is implicitly called in the *reshape(GLDrawable glDrawable, int x, int y, int w, int h)* with the same area as the display window. The viewing volume will be projected into the viewport area accordingly.

We may specify a different viewport using *glViewport()* with lower-left corner (*x, y*) goes from (*0, 0*) to (*w, h*) and the viewport region is an area of *width* to *height* in pixels confined in the display window. All drawing functions afterwards will draw into the current viewport region. That is, the projection goes to the viewport. Also, we may specify multiple viewports at different regions in a drawing area and draw different scenes into these viewports. For example, *glViewport(0, 0, width/2, height/2)* will be the lower-left quarter of the drawing area, and *glViewport(width/2, height/2, width/2, height/2)* will be the upper-right quarter of the drawing area. In our example *J2_15_LookAt.java* below, we also specified different projection methods to demonstrate *myLookAt(), mygluLookat(), and myPerspective()* functions. If we don't specify different projection methods in different viewports, the same projection matrix will be used for different viewports. Fig. 2.28 is a snapshot of the multiple viewports rendering.

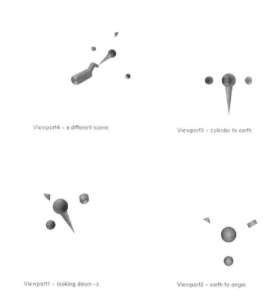

Viewport4 - a different scene

Viewport3 - cylinder to earth

Viewport1 - looking down -z

Viewport2 - earth to origin

Fig. 2.28 **Multiple viewports with different LookAt projections**

/* simulate gluLookAt and display in multiple viewports */

```
import net.java.games.jogl.*;
import java.lang.Math;
import net.java.games.jogl.util.GLUT;


public class J2_15_LookAt extends J2_14_Perspective {
  GLUT glut = new GLUT();

  public void display(GLDrawable glDrawable) {
    cnt++;
    depth = 4;
    gl.glClear(GL.GL_COLOR_BUFFER_BIT|
               GL.GL_DEPTH_BUFFER_BIT);

    viewPort1();
    drawSolar(WIDTH/4, cnt, WIDTH/12, cnt);
    // the objects' centers are retrieved from above call
```

```
    viewPort2();
    drawSolar(WIDTH/4, cnt, WIDTH/12, cnt);
    viewPort3();
    drawSolar(WIDTH/4, cnt, WIDTH/12, cnt);
    viewPort4();
    drawRobot(O, A, B, C, alpha, beta, gama);

    try {
      Thread.sleep(10);
    } catch (Exception ignore) {}
}

public void viewPort1() {
  int w = WIDTH, h = HEIGHT;

  gl.glViewport(0, 0, w/2, h/2);

  // use a different projection
  gl.glMatrixMode(GL.GL_PROJECTION);
  gl.glLoadIdentity();
  gl.glOrtho(-w/2, w/2, -h/2, h/2, -w, w);
  gl.glRasterPos3f(-w/3, -h/3, 0); // start position
  glut.glutBitmapString(gl, GLUT.BITMAP_HELVETICA_18,
                        "Viewport1 - looking down -z.");

  gl.glMatrixMode(GL.GL_MODELVIEW);
  gl.glLoadIdentity();
}


public void viewPort2() {
  int w = WIDTH, h = HEIGHT;
  gl.glViewport(w/2, 0, w/2, h/2);

  gl.glMatrixMode(GL.GL_PROJECTION);
  gl.glLoadIdentity();

  // make sure the cone is within the viewing volume
  gl.glFrustum(-w/8, w/8, -h/8, h/8, w/2, 4*w);
  gl.glTranslatef(0, 0, -2*w);
  gl.glRasterPos3f(-w/3, -h/3, 0); // start position
  glut.glutBitmapString(gl, GLUT.BITMAP_HELVETICA_18,
                        "Viewport2 - earth to origin.");

  // earthC retrieved in drawSolar() before viewPort2
  myLookAt(earthC[0], earthC[1], earthC[2],
           0, 0, 0, 0, 1, 0);
```

```
    gl.glMatrixMode(GL.GL_MODELVIEW);
    gl.glLoadIdentity();

}


public void viewPort3() {
    int w = WIDTH, h = HEIGHT;

    gl.glViewport(w/2, h/2, w/2, h/2);

    gl.glMatrixMode(GL.GL_PROJECTION);
    gl.glLoadIdentity();
    // make sure the cone is within the viewing volume
    gl.glFrustum(-w/8, w/8, -h/8, h/8, w/2, 4*w);
    gl.glTranslatef(0, 0, -2*w);

    gl.glRasterPos3f(-w/3, -h/3, 0); // start position
    glut.glutBitmapString(gl, GLUT.BITMAP_HELVETICA_18,
                    "Viewport3 - cylinder to earth.");

    // earthC retrieved in drawSolar() before viewPort3
    mygluLookAt(cylinderC[0], cylinderC[1], cylinderC[2],
                earthC[0], earthC[1], earthC[2],
                earthC[0], earthC[1], earthC[2]);

    gl.glMatrixMode(GL.GL_MODELVIEW);
    gl.glLoadIdentity();
}


public void viewPort4() {
    int w = WIDTH, h = HEIGHT;

    gl.glViewport(0, h/2, w/2, h/2);

    gl.glMatrixMode(GL.GL_PROJECTION);
    gl.glLoadIdentity();
    // implemented in superclass J2_14_Perspective
    myPerspective(45, w/h, w/2, 4*w);
    gl.glTranslatef(0, 0, -1.5f*w);

    gl.glMatrixMode(GL.GL_MODELVIEW);
    gl.glLoadIdentity();

    gl.glRasterPos3f(-w/2.5f, -h/2.1f, 0);
     glut.glutBitmapString(gl, GLUT.BITMAP_HELVETICA_18,
                    "Viewport4 - a different scene.");
}
```

```
public void myLookAt(
    double eX, double eY, double eZ,
    double cX, double cY, double cZ,
    double upX, double upY, double upZ) {
//eye and center are points, but up is a vector

  //1. change center into a vector:
  // glTranslated(-eX, -eY, -eZ);
  cX = cX-eX; cY = cY-eY; cZ = cZ-eZ;

  //2. The angle of center on xz plane and x axis
  // i.e. angle to rot so center in the neg. yz plane
  double a = Math.atan(cZ/cX);
  if (cX>=0) {
    a = a+Math.PI/2;
  } else {
    a = a-Math.PI/2;
  }

  //3. The angle between the center and y axis
  // i.e. angle to rot so center in the negative z axis
  double b = Math.acos(
      cY/Math.sqrt(cX*cX+cY*cY+cZ*cZ));
  b = b-Math.PI/2;

  //4. up rotate around y axis (a) radians
  double upx = upX*Math.cos(a)+upZ*Math.sin(a);
  double upz = -upX*Math.sin(a)+upZ*Math.cos(a);
  upX = upx; upZ = upz;

  //5. up rotate around x axis (b) radians
  double upy = upY*Math.cos(b)-upZ*Math.sin(b);
  upz = upY*Math.sin(b)+upZ*Math.cos(b);
  upY = upy; upZ = upz;

  double c = Math.atan(upX/upY);
  if (upY<0) {
    //6. the angle between up on xy plane and y axis
    c = c+Math.PI;
  }
  gl.glRotated(Math.toDegrees(c), 0, 0, 1);
  // up in yz plane
  gl.glRotated(Math.toDegrees(b), 1, 0, 0);
  // center in negative z axis
  gl.glRotated(Math.toDegrees(a), 0, 1, 0);
  //center in yz plane
  gl.glTranslated(-eX, -eY, -eZ);
  //eye at the origin
}
```

```
public void mygluLookAt(
     double eX, double eY, double eZ,
     double cX, double cY, double cZ,
     double upX, double upY, double upZ) {
  //eye and center are points, but up is a vector

  double[] F = new double[3];
  double[] UP = new double[3];
  double[] s = new double[3];
  double[] u = new double[3];
  F[0] = cX-eX; F[1] = cY-eY; F[2] = cZ-eZ;
  UP[0] = upX; UP[1] = upY; UP[2] = upZ;
  normalize(F); normalize(UP);
  crossProd(F, UP, s); crossProd(s, F, u);

  double[] M = new double[16];
  M[0] = s[0]; M[1] = u[0]; M[2] = -F[0];
  M[3] = 0; M[4] = s[1]; M[5] = u[1];
  M[6] = -F[1]; M[7] = 0; M[8] = s[2];
  M[9] = u[2]; M[10] = -F[2]; M[11] = 0;
  M[12] = 0; M[13] = 0; M[14] = 0; M[15] = 1;

  gl.glMultMatrixd(M);
  gl.glTranslated(-eX, -eY, -eZ);
}


public void normalize(double v[]) {
  double d = Math.sqrt(v[0]*v[0]+v[1]*v[1]+v[2]*v[2]);

  if (d==0) {
    System.out.println("0 length vector: normalize().");
    return;
  }
  v[0] /= d; v[1] /= d; v[2] /= d;
}


public void crossProd(double U[],
                      double V[], double W[]) {
  // W = U X V
  W[0] = U[1]*V[2]-U[2]*V[1];
  W[1] = U[2]*V[0]-U[0]*V[2];
  W[2] = U[0]*V[1]-U[1]*V[0];
}
```

```
public static void main(String[] args) {
    J2_15_LookAt f = new J2_15_LookAt();

    f.setTitle("JOGL J2_15_LookAt");
    f.setSize(WIDTH, HEIGHT);
    f.setVisible(true);
  }
}
```

2.5 *Review Questions*

1. An octahedron has v1=(1,0,0), v2=(0,1,0), v3=(0,0,1), v4=(−1,0,0), v5=(0,−1,0), v6=(0,0,−1). Please choose the triangles that face the outside of the octahedron.

    a. (v1v2v3, v1v3v5, v1v5v6,v1v2v6)   b. (v2v3v1, v2v1v6, v2v6v4, v2v4v3)
    c. (v3v2v1, v3v5v1, v3v4v2, v3v4v5)   d. (v4v2v1, v4v5v1, v3v4v2, v3v4v5)

2. If we subdivide the above octahedron 8 times (depth=8), how many triangles we will have in the final sphere.

    No. of triangles: _____

3. Choose the *matrix expression* that would transform square ABCD into square A'B'C'D' in 3D as shown in the figure below.

    a. $T(-1,-1, 0)R_y(-90)$
    b. $R_y(-90) T(-1,-1, 0)$
    c. $T(-2,-2, 0)R_z(-90)R_y(90)$
    d. $R_y(90)R_z(-90)T(-2,-2, 0)$

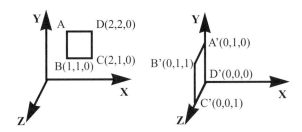

4. *myDrawTop()* will draw a top below on the left. Write a section of OpenGL code so that the top will appear as specified on the right with tip at A(x1, y1, z1), tilted α, and proceeded θ around an axis parallel to *y* axis.

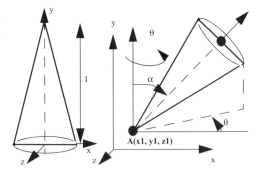

5. *myDrawTop()* will draw an objects in oblique pro-jection as in the question above with height equals 1 and radius equals 0.5. Please draw two displays in <u>orthographic</u> projection according to the program on the right (as they will appear on the screen where the *z* axis is perpendicular to the plane).

```
glLoadIdentity();
glRotatef (-90, 0.0, 1.0, 0.0);
myDrawTop(); // left
glRotatef(-90, 0.0, 0.0, 1.0);

glPushMatrix();
glTranslatef (0.0, 0.0, 1.0);
myDrawTop(); //right
glPopMatrix();
```

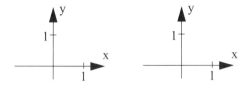

6. In the scan-line algorithm for filling polygons, if z-buffer is used, when should the program call the z-buffer algorithm function?

a. at the beginning of the program   b. at the beginning of each scan-line
c. at the beginning of each pixel   d. at the beginning of each polygon

7. *Collision detection* **avoids two models in an animation penetrating each other; which of the following is FALSE:**

a. bounding boxes are used for efficiency purposes in collision detection
b. both animated and stationary objects are covered by the bounding boxes
c. animated objects can move whatever distance between frames of calculations
d. collision detection can be calculated in many different ways

8. After following transformations, what is on top of the matrix stack at *drawObject2()***?**

glLoadIdentity(); glPushMatrix(); glMultMatrixf(S); glRotatef(a,1,0,0); glTranslatef(t,0,0);
drawObject1(); glGetFloatv(GL_MODELVIEW_MATRIX, &tmp); glPopMatrix();
glPushMatrix(); glMultMatrixf(S); glMultMatrixf(&tmp);*drawObject2();* glPopMatrix();

a. $SSR_x(a)T_x(t)$ b. $ST_x(t)R_x(a)S$ c. $T_x(t)R_x(a)SS$
d. $R_x(a)SST_x(t)$ e. $SR_x(a)T_x(t)$

9. Given glViewport (u, v, w, h) and gluOrtho2D(xmin, xmax, ymin, ymax), choose the 2D transformation <u>matrix expression</u> that maps a point in the modeling (modelview) coordinates to the device (viewport) coordinates.

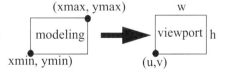

a. $S(1/(xmax - xmin),1/(ymax - ymin))$
$\quad\quad\quad T(-xmin,-ymin)T(u,v)S(w,h)$
b. $S(1/(xmax - xmin),1/(ymax - ymin))S(w,h)T(-xmin,-ymin)T(u,v)$
c. $T(u,v)S(w,h)S(1/(xmax - xmin),1/(ymax - ymin))T(-xmin,-ymin)$
d. $T(-xmin,-ymin)T(u,v)S(1/(xmax - xmin),1/(ymax - ymin))S(w,h)$

10. Given a 2D model and a modeling window, please draw the object in normalized coordinates after clipping and in the device as it appears on a display.

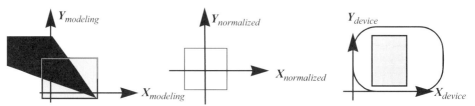

11. In the OpenGL graphics pipeline, please order the following according to their order of operations:

(____) clipping   (____) viewport transformation
(____) modelview transformation   (____) normalization
(____) perspective division   (____) scan conversion

12. Please implement the following viewing command: gmuPerspective(fx, fy, d, s), where the viewing direction is from the origin looking down the negative z axis. fx is the field of view angle in the x direction; fy is the field of view angle in the y direction; d is the distance from the viewpoint to the center of the viewing volume, which is a point on the negative z axis; s is the distance from d to the near or far clipping planes.

gmuPerspective(fx, fy, d, s) {

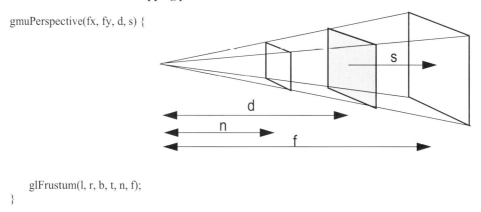

glFrustum(l, r, b, t, n, f);
}

2.6 *Programming Assignments*

1. Implement myLoadIdentity, myRotatef, myTranslatef, myScalef, myPushMatrix, and myPop-Matrix just like their corresponding OpenGL commands. Then, in the rest of the programming assignments, you can interchange them with OpenGL commands.

2. Check out online what is polarview transformation; implement your own polarview with a demonstration of the function.

3. As shown in the figure on the right, use 2D transformation to rotate the stroke font and the star.

4. The above problem can be extended into 3D: the outer
circle rotates along *y* axis, the inner circle rotates around *x*
axis, and the star rotates around *z* axis.

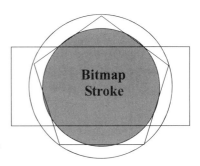

5. Draw a cone, a cylinder, and a sphere that bounce back
and forth along a circle, as shown in the figure. When the
objects meet, they change their directions of movement.
The program must be in double-buffer mode and have hidden surface removal.

6. Draw two circles with the same animation as above. At the same time,
one circle rotates around *x* axis, and the other rotates around *y* axis.

7. Implement a 3D robot arm animation as in the book, and put the
above animation system on the palm of the robot arm. The system on the
palm can change its size periodically, which is achieved through scaling.

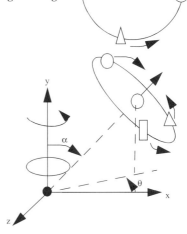

8. Draw a cone, a cylinder, and a sphere that move and
collide in the moon's trajectory in the generalized solar
system. When the objects meet, they change their directions of movement.

9. Put the above system on the palm of the robot arm.

10. Implement myPerspective and myLookAt just like
gluPerspective and gluLookAt. Then, use them to look
from the cone to the earth or cylinder in the system above.

11. Display different perspectives or direction of viewing
in multiple viewports.

3
Color and Lighting

Chapter Objectives:

- Introduce RGB color in the hardware, eye characteristics, and gamma correction
- Understand color interpolation and smooth shading in OpenGL
- Set up OpenGL lighting: ambient, diffuse, specular, and multiple light sources
- Understand back-face culling and surface shading models

3.1 Color

In a display, a pixel color is specified as a red, green, and blue (RGB) vector. The RGB colors are also called the *primaries*, because our eye sees a different color in a vector of different primary values. The RGB colors are additive primaries — we construct a color on the black background by adding the primaries together. For example, with equal amounts of R, G, and B: G+B $\Rightarrow$ cyan, R+B $\Rightarrow$ magenta, R+G $\Rightarrow$ yellow, and R+G+B $\Rightarrow$ white. RGB colors are used in the graphics hardware, which we will discuss in more detail.

Cyan, magenta, and yellow (CMY) colors are the complements of RGB colors, respectively. The CMY colors are subtractive primaries — we construct a color on a white background by removing the corresponding RGB primaries. Similarly, with equal amounts of R, G, and B: C = RGB - R, M = RGB - G, and Y = RGB - B.

The CMY colors are used in color printers. Adding certain amounts of CMY inks to a point on a white paper is like removing certain amounts of RGB from the white color at that point. The resulting color at the point on the paper depends on the portions of individual inks. Black ink is used to generate different levels of grays replacing use of equal amounts of CMY inks.

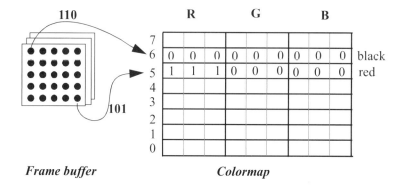

Fig. 3.1 Color-index mode and colormap

3.1.1 RGB Mode and Index Mode

If each pixel value in the frame buffer is an RGB vector, the display is in *RGB mode*. Each pixel value can also be an index into a color look-up table called a *colormap*, as shown in Fig. 3.3.1. Then, the display is in *index mode*. The pixel color is specified in the colormap instead of the frame buffer.

Let's assume that we have 3 bits per entry in the frame buffer. That is, the frame buffer has 3 *bitplanes*. In RGB mode, we have access to 8 different colors: black, red, green, blue, cyan, magenta, yellow, and white. In index mode, we still have access to only 8 different colors, but the colors can vary depending on how we load the colormap. If the graphics hardware has a limited number of bitplanes for the frame buffer, index mode allows more color choices, even though the number of colors is the same as that of RGB mode at the same time. For example, in the above example, if we have 12 bitplanes per entry in the colormap, we can choose 8 colors from $2^{12} = 4096$ different colors. The colormap does not take much space in memory, which had been a significant advantage when fast memory chips were very expensive. In GLUT, we use *glutInitDisplayMode(GLUT_INDEX)* to choose the index mode. RGB mode is the default. Index mode can also be useful for doing various animation tricks. However, in general, because memory is no longer a limitation and RGB mode is easier and more flexible, we use it in the examples. Also, in OpenGL programming, each color component (R, G, or B) value is in the range of 0 to 1. The system will scale the value to the corresponding hardware bits during compilation transparent to the users.

3.1.2 Eye Characteristics and Gamma Correction

A pixel color on a display is the emission of light that reaches our eye. An RGB vector is a representation of the *brightness* level that our eye perceives. The *intensity* is the amount of physical energy used to generate the brightness. Our eye sees a different color for a different RGB vector. We may not have noticed, but certain colors cannot be produced by RGB mixes and hence cannot be shown on an RGB display device.

The eye is more sensitive to yellow-green light. In general, the eye's sensitivities to different colors generated by a constant intensity level are different. Also, for the same color, the eye's perceived brightness levels are not linearly proportional to the intensity levels. To generate evenly spaced brightness levels, we need to use logarithmically-spaced intensity levels. For example, to generate n evenly-spaced brightness levels for a color component λ (which represents R, G, or B), we need corresponding intensity levels at

$$I_{i\lambda} = r^i I_{0\lambda} \text{ for } i = 0, 1, ..., n\text{-}1, \tag{EQ 54}$$

where $I_{0\lambda}$ is the lowest intensity available in the display hardware and $r=(1/I_{0\lambda})^{1/(n-1)}$.

For a CRT display monitor, $I_{i\lambda}$ depends on the energy in voltage that is applied to generate the electrons lighting the corresponding screen pixels (phosphor dots):

$$I_{i\lambda} = KV^{\gamma}. \tag{EQ 55}$$

The value of γ is about 2.2 to 2.5 for most CRTs. Therefore, given an intensity $I_{i\lambda}$, we can find the corresponding voltage needed in the hardware:

$$V = (I_{i\lambda}/K)^{1/\gamma}. \tag{EQ 56}$$

This is called *gamma correction*, because γ is used in the equation to find the voltage to generate the correct intensity. Without gamma correction, the brightness levels are not even, and high brightness pixels appear to be darker. Different CRTs have different K's and γ's. Instead of calculating the voltages, CRT manufacturers can build up a look-up table for a CRT (in the CRT monitor or in the corresponding graphics card that refreshes the CRT) by measuring the corresponding brightness levels and voltages. In the look-up table, the indices are the brightness levels and the values are the corresponding voltages.

Usually, the hardware gamma correction allows software modifications. That is, we can change the contents of the look-up table. Today, most color monitors have hardware gamma corrections. Due to different material properties (phosphor composites) and gamma corrections, the same RGB vector appears in different colors and brightness on individual monitors. Effort is needed to make two CRT monitors appear exactly the same.

To simplify the matter, because the difference between the intensity and the brightness is solved in the hardware, we use the intensity to mean the brightness or the RGB value directly. Also, we use I_λ to represent the brightness level i of an RGB component directly. That is, I_λ represents a perceived brightness level instead of an energy level.

3.2 Color Interpolation

In OpenGL, we use *glShadeModel(GL_FLAT)* or *glShadeModel(GL_SMOOTH)* to choose between two different models (flat shading and smooth shading) of using colors for a primitive. With *GL_FLAT*, we use one color that is specified by *glColor3f()* for all the pixels in the primitive. For example, in *J3_1_Shading.java*, if we call *glShadeModel(GL_FLAT)*, only one color will be used in *drawtriangle()*, even though we have specified different colors for different vertices. Depending on the OpenGL systems, the color may be the color specified for the last vertex in a primitive.

For a line, with *GL_SMOOTH*, the vertex colors are linearly interpolated along the pixels between the two end vertices. For example, if a line has 5 pixels, and the end point colors are (0, 0, 0) and (0, 0, 1), then, after the interpolation, the 5 pixel colors will be (0, 0, 0), (0, 0, 1/4), (0, 0, 2/4), (0, 0, 3/4), and (0, 0, 1), respectively. The intensity of each RGB component is interpolated separately. In general, given the end point intensities ($I_{\lambda 1}$ and $I_{\lambda 2}$) and the number of pixels along the line (N), the intensity increment of the linear interpolation is

$$\Delta I_\lambda = \frac{I_{\lambda 2} - I_{\lambda 1}}{N - 1}.$$
(EQ 57)

That is, for each pixel from the starting pixel to the end pixel, the color component changes ΔI_λ.

For a polygon, OpenGL first interpolates along the edges, and then along the horizontal scan-lines during scan-conversion. All we need to do to carry out interpolation in OpenGL is to call *glShadeModel(GL_SMOOTH)* and set up different vertex colors, as shown in the following example (Fig. 3.3.2).

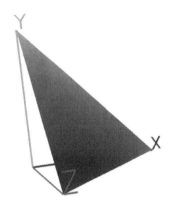

Fig. 3.2 Smooth shading [*See Color Plate 3*]

/* OpenGL flat or smooth shading */

```java
import net.java.games.jogl.*;

public class J3_1_Shading extends
J2_13_TravelSolar {

   // static float vdata[3][3]
   static float vdata[][] = { {1.0f, 0, 0}
                            , {0, 1.0f, 0}
                            , {0, 0, 1.0f}
   };

   public void display(GLDrawable glDrawable) {

     cnt++;

     gl.glClear(GL.GL_COLOR_BUFFER_BIT|
               GL.GL_DEPTH_BUFFER_BIT);

     // alternate between flat and smooth
     if (cnt%50==0) {
       gl.glShadeModel(GL.GL_SMOOTH);
     }
     if (cnt%100==0) {
       gl.glShadeModel(GL.GL_FLAT);
     }
```

```
gl.glPushMatrix();
gl.glRotatef(cnt, 1, 1, 1);
gl.glScalef(WIDTH/2, WIDTH/2, WIDTH/2);
drawColorCoord(1.0f, 1.0f, 1.0f);
drawColorTriangle(vdata[0], vdata[1], vdata[2]);
gl.glPopMatrix();

try {
  Thread.sleep(20);
} catch (Exception ignore) {}
}


private void drawColorTriangle(float[] v1,
                               float[] v2,
                               float[] v3) {

gl.glBegin(GL.GL_TRIANGLES);
gl.glColor3f(1, 0, 0);
gl.glVertex3fv(v1);
gl.glColor3f(0, 1, 0);
gl.glVertex3fv(v2);
gl.glColor3f(0, 0, 1);
gl.glVertex3fv(v3);
gl.glEnd();
}


public static void main(String[] args) {
  J3_1_Shading f = new J3_1_Shading();

  f.setTitle("JOGL J3_1_Shading");
  f.setSize(WIDTH, HEIGHT);
  f.setVisible(true);
}
}
```

3.3 Lighting

A pixel color is a reflection or emission of light from a point on a model to our eye. Therefore, instead of specifying a color for a point directly, we can specify light sources and material properties for the graphics system to calculate the color of the point according to a lighting model. The real-world lighting is very complex. In graphics, we adopt simplified methods (i.e., lighting or illumination models) that work relatively fast and well.

We use the OpenGL lighting system as an example to explain lighting. The OpenGL lighting model includes four major components: ambient, diffuse, specular, and emission. The final color is the summation of these components. The lighting model is developed to calculate the color of each individual pixel that corresponds to a point on a primitive. The method of calculating the lighting for all pixels in a primitive is called the *shading model*. As introduced in Section 3.2, OpenGL calculates vertex pixel colors and uses interpolation to find the colors of all pixels in a primitive when we call *glShadeModel(GL_SMOOTH)*. If we use *glShadeModel(GL_FLAT)*, only one vertex color is used for the primitive. However, the vertex colors are calculated by the lighting model instead of being specified by *glColor()*.

3.3.1 Lighting Components

Emissive component. The emission intensity of a vertex pixel with an emissive material is calculated as follows:

$$I_{\lambda e} = M_{\lambda emission},$$

(EQ 58)

where λ is an RGB component or A (alpha), and $M_{\lambda emission}$ is the material's emission property. Each color component is calculated independently. Because the *alpha* value will be discussed in the next chapter, we can ignore it in our current examples. In OpenGL, *emission* is a material property that is neither dependent on any light source nor considered a light source. Emissive material does not emit light, it displays its own color. The vertex's corresponding surface has two sides, the front and the back, which can be specified with different material properties.

In Example *J3_2_Emission.java*, the material is emitting a white color and all objects will be white until we change the emission material component to something else. Here according to Equation 58, the calculated RGB color is (*1., 1., 1.*). If we only specify the emission component, the effect is the same as specifying *glColor3f(1., 1., 1.)*.

/* emissive material component */

```
import net.java.games.jogl.*;

public class J3_2_Emission extends J2_13_TravelSolar {
float white[] = {1, 1, 1, 1};

  public void init(GLDrawable glDrawable) {

    super.init(glDrawable);

    gl.glEnable(GL.GL_LIGHTING);
    gl.glMaterialfv(GL.GL_FRONT, GL.GL_EMISSION, white);
  }

  public static void main(String[] args) {
    J3_2_Emission f = new J3_2_Emission();

    f.setTitle("JOGL J3_2_Emission");
    f.setSize(WIDTH, HEIGHT);
    f.setVisible(true);
  }
}
```

When lighting is enabled, *glColor3f()* is turned off. In other words, even though we may have *glColor3f()s* in the program, they are not used. Instead, the OpenGL system uses the current lighting model to calculate the vertex color automatically. We may use *glColorMaterial()* with *glEnable(GL_COLOR_MATERIAL)* to tie the color specified by *glColor3f()* to a material property.

Ambient component. The ambient intensity of a vertex pixel is calculated as follows:

$$I_{\lambda a} = L_{\lambda a} M_{\lambda a}, \qquad \text{(EQ 59)}$$

where $L_{\lambda a}$ represents the light source's ambient intensity and $M_{\lambda a}$ is the material's ambient property. Ambient color is the overall intensity of multiple reflections generated from a light source in an environment. We do not even care where the light source is as long as it exists. In Example *J3_3_Ambient.java*, according to Equation 59, the calculated RGB color is *(1., 1., 0)*.

/* ambient component */

```
import net.java.games.jogl.GL;
import net.java.games.jogl.GLDrawable;


public class J3_3_Ambient extends J3_2_Emission {

    float white[] = {1, 1, 1, 1};
    float black[] = {0, 0, 0, 1};
    float red[] = {1, 0, 0, 1};
    float green[] = {0, 1, 0, 1};
    float blue[] = {0, 0, 1, 1};
    float cyan[] = {0, 1, 1, 1};
    float magenta[] = {1, 0, 1, 1};
    float yellow[] = {1, 1, 0, 1};

    public void init(GLDrawable glDrawable) {

        super.init(glDrawable);

        gl.glEnable(GL.GL_LIGHTING);

        gl.glEnable(GL.GL_LIGHT0);
        gl.glLightfv(GL.GL_LIGHT0, GL.GL_AMBIENT, white);

        gl.glMaterialfv(GL.GL_FRONT, GL.GL_AMBIENT, yellow);
        gl.glMaterialfv(GL.GL_FRONT, GL.GL_EMISSION, black);
    }


    public static void main(String[] args) {

        J3_3_Ambient f = new J3_3_Ambient();

        f.setTitle("JOGL J3_3_Ambient");
        f.setSize(WIDTH, HEIGHT);

        f.setVisible(true);
    }
}
```

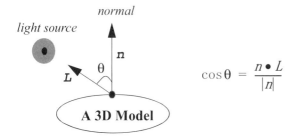

Fig. 3.3 The angle between L and n at the vertex

Diffuse component. The diffuse intensity of a vertex pixel is calculated as follows:

$$I_{\lambda d} = L_{\lambda d} M_{\lambda d} (n \bullet L), \qquad \text{(EQ 60)}$$

where $L_{\lambda d}$ is the light source's diffuse intensity, $M_{\lambda d}$ is the material's diffuse property, **L** is the light source direction, and **n** is the surface normal direction from the pixel, which is a vector perpendicular to the surface. Here the light source is a point generating equal intensity in all directions. Diffuse color is the reflection from a dull surface material that appears equally bright from all viewing directions.

In OpenGL, **L** is a unit vector (or normalized vector) pointing from the current vertex to the light source position. The normal is specified by *glNormal*() right before we specify the vertex. As shown in Fig. 3.3.3, $\cos\theta = \dfrac{n \bullet L}{|n|}$, which is between *0* and *1* when θ is between *0°* and *90°*. When θ is greater than *90°*, the diffuse intensity is set to zero.

The length of the normal is a factor in Equation 60. We can initially specify the normal to be a unit vector. However, normals are transformed similar to vertices so that the lengths of the normals may be scaled. (Actually, normals are transformed by the inverse transpose of the current matrix on the matrix stack.) If we are not sure about the length of the normals, we can call *glEnable(GL_NORMALIZE)*, which enables the OpenGL system to normalize each normal before calculating the lighting. This, however, incurs the extra normalization calculations. Also, the light source position has four parameters: (*x, y, z, w*) as in homogeneous coordinates. If *w* is *1*, (*x, y, z*) is the light source position. If *w* is *0*, (*x, y, z*) represents the light source direction at infinity, in which case the light source is in the same direction for all pixels at different locations. If a point light source is far away from the object, it has essentially the same angle with all surfaces that have the same surface normal direction. Example *J3_4_Diffuse.java* shows how to specify the diffuse parameters in OpenGL.

/* diffuse light & material components */

```
import net.java.games.jogl.*;

public class J3_4_Diffuse extends J3_3_Ambient {
   float whitish[] = {0.7f, 0.7f, 0.7f, 1};
   float position[] = {0, 0, 1, 0};

   public void init(GLDrawable glDrawable) {

     super.init(glDrawable);

     gl.glEnable(GL.GL_LIGHTING);
     gl.glEnable(GL.GL_NORMALIZE);

     gl.glEnable(GL.GL_LIGHT0);
     gl.glLightfv(GL.GL_LIGHT0, GL.GL_POSITION, position);
     gl.glLightfv(GL.GL_LIGHT0, GL.GL_DIFFUSE, white);

     gl.glMaterialfv(GL.GL_FRONT, GL.GL_DIFFUSE, whitish);
     gl.glMaterialfv(GL.GL_FRONT, GL.GL_AMBIENT, black);
     gl.glMaterialfv(GL.GL_FRONT, GL.GL_EMISSION, black);
   }


   private void drawSphereTriangle(float v1[],
                                   float v2[], float v3[]) {

     gl.glBegin(GL.GL_TRIANGLES);
     gl.glNormal3fv(v1);
     gl.glVertex3fv(v1);
     gl.glNormal3fv(v2);
     gl.glVertex3fv(v2);
     gl.glNormal3fv(v3);
     gl.glVertex3fv(v3);
     gl.glEnd();
   }
```

```
private void drawConeSide(float v1[], float v2[],
                          float v3[]) {

   float v11[] = new float[3];
   float v22[] = new float[3];
   float v33[] = new float[3];

   for (int i = 0; i<3; i++) {
     v11[i] = v1[i]+v3[i]; // normal for cone vertex 1
     v22[i] = v2[i]+v3[i]; // normal for vertex 2
     v33[i] = v11[i]+v22[i]; // normal for vertex 3
   }

   gl.glBegin(GL.GL_TRIANGLES);
   gl.glNormal3fv(v11);
   gl.glVertex3fv(v1);
   gl.glNormal3fv(v22);
   gl.glVertex3fv(v2);
   gl.glNormal3fv(v33);
   gl.glVertex3fv(v3);
   gl.glEnd();
}

private void drawBottom(float v1[], float v2[], float v3[])
{
   float vb[] = {0, 0, 1};
   // normal to the cylinder bottom

   if (v3[2]<0.1) { //  bottom on the xy plane
     vb[2] = -1;
   }

   gl.glBegin(GL.GL_TRIANGLES);
   gl.glNormal3fv(vb);
   gl.glVertex3fv(v3);
   gl.glVertex3fv(v2);
   gl.glVertex3fv(v1);
   gl.glEnd();
}

private void subdivideSphere( float v1[],
     float v2[], float v3[], long depth) {

   float v12[] = new float[3];
   float v23[] = new float[3];
```

```
    float v31[] = new float[3];

    if (depth==0) {
      gl.glColor3f(v1[0]*v1[0], v2[1]*v2[1], v3[2]*v3[2]);
      drawSphereTriangle(v1, v2, v3);
      return;
    }
    for (int i = 0; i<3; i++) {
      v12[i]  = v1[i]+v2[i];
      v23[i]  = v2[i]+v3[i];
      v31[i]  = v3[i]+v1[i];
    }
    normalize(v12);
    normalize(v23);
    normalize(v31);

    subdivideSphere(v1, v12, v31, depth-1);
    subdivideSphere(v2, v23, v12, depth-1);
    subdivideSphere(v3, v31, v23, depth-1);
    subdivideSphere(v12, v23, v31, depth-1);
}


public void drawSphere() {
    subdivideSphere(sVdata[0], sVdata[1], sVdata[2], depth);
    subdivideSphere(sVdata[0], sVdata[2], sVdata[4], depth);
    subdivideSphere(sVdata[0], sVdata[4], sVdata[5], depth);
    subdivideSphere(sVdata[0], sVdata[5], sVdata[1], depth);

    subdivideSphere(sVdata[3], sVdata[1], sVdata[5], depth);
    subdivideSphere(sVdata[3], sVdata[5], sVdata[4], depth);
    subdivideSphere(sVdata[3], sVdata[4], sVdata[2], depth);
    subdivideSphere(sVdata[3], sVdata[2], sVdata[1], depth);
}


void subdivideCone(float v1[], float v2[], int depth) {

    float v11[]  = {0, 0, 0};
    float v22[]  = {0, 0, 0};
    float v00[]  = {0, 0, 0};
    float v12[]  = {0, 0, 0};

    if (depth==0) {

      gl.glColor3f(v1[0]*v1[0], v1[1]*v1[1], v1[2]*v1[2]);

      for (int i = 0; i<3; i++) {
        v11[i]  = v1[i];
```

```
      v22[i] = v2[i];
    }
    drawBottom(v11, v22, v00);
    // bottom cover of the cone

    v00[2] = 1; // height of cone, the tip on z axis
    drawConeSide(v11, v22, v00);
    // side cover of the cone

    return;
  }

  for (int i = 0; i<3; i++) {
    v12[i] = v1[i]+v2[i];
  }
  normalize(v12);

  subdivideCone(v1, v12, depth-1);
  subdivideCone(v12, v2, depth-1);
}


public void drawCone() {

  subdivideCone(cVdata[0], cVdata[1], depth);
  subdivideCone(cVdata[1], cVdata[2], depth);
  subdivideCone(cVdata[2], cVdata[3], depth);
  subdivideCone(cVdata[3], cVdata[0], depth);
}


void subdivideCylinder(float v1[],
                       float v2[], int depth) {
  float v11[] = {0, 0, 0};
  float v22[] = {0, 0, 0};
  float v00[] = {0, 0, 0};
  float v12[] = {0, 0, 0};
  float v01[] = {0, 0, 0};
  float v02[] = {0, 0, 0};

  if (depth==0) {
    gl.glColor3f(v1[0]*v1[0], v1[1]*v1[1], v1[2]*v1[2]);

    for (int i = 0; i<3; i++) {
      v01[i] = v11[i] = v1[i];
      v02[i] = v22[i] = v2[i];
    }
    drawBottom(v11, v22, v00);
    // draw sphere at the cylinder's bottom
```

```
      // the height of the cone along z axis
      v01[2] = v02[2] = v00[2] = 1;

      gl.glBegin(GL.GL_POLYGON);
      // draw the side rectangles of the cylinder
      gl.glNormal3fv(v11);
      gl.glVertex3fv(v11);
      gl.glNormal3fv(v22);
      gl.glVertex3fv(v22);
      gl.glNormal3fv(v22);
      gl.glVertex3fv(v02);
      gl.glNormal3fv(v11);
      gl.glVertex3fv(v01);
      gl.glEnd();

      drawBottom(v02, v01, v00);
      // draw sphere at the cylinder's bottom

      return;
    }
    v12[0] = v1[0]+v2[0];
    v12[1] = v1[1]+v2[1];
    v12[2] = v1[2]+v2[2];
    normalize(v12);

    subdivideCylinder(v1, v12, depth-1);
    subdivideCylinder(v12, v2, depth-1);
  }


  public void drawCylinder() {

    subdivideCylinder(cVdata[0], cVdata[1], depth);
    subdivideCylinder(cVdata[1], cVdata[2], depth);
    subdivideCylinder(cVdata[2], cVdata[3], depth);
    subdivideCylinder(cVdata[3], cVdata[0], depth);
  }


  public static void main(String[] args) {
    J3_4_Diffuse f = new J3_4_Diffuse();

    f.setTitle("JOGL J3_4_Diffuse");
    f.setSize(WIDTH, HEIGHT);
    f.setVisible(true);
  }
}
```

Object shading depends on how we specify the normals as well. For example (Fig. 3.3.4), if we want to display a pyramid, the normals for the triangle vertices v1, v2, and v3 should be the same and perpendicular to the triangle. If we want to approximate a cone, the normals should be perpendicular to the cone's surface. If we assume that the radius of the cone's base and the height of the cone have the same length, then the normals are $n1$ = v1 + v3, $n2$ = v2 + v3, and $n3$ = $n1$ + $n2$. Here, the

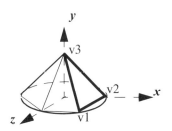

Fig. 3.4 The radius and the height of the cone are the same (unit length)

additions are vector additions, as in the function *drawConeSide()* in Example *J3_4_Diffuse.java* above. The OpenGL system interpolates the pixel colors in the triangle. We can set all the vertex normals to $n3$ to display a pyramid.

Specular component. The specular intensity of a vertex pixel is calculated as follows:

$$I_{\lambda s} = L_{\lambda s} M_{\lambda s} \left(\frac{n \bullet (L + V)}{|L + V|} \right)^{shininess} \tag{EQ 61}$$

where $L_{\lambda s}$ is the light source's specular intensity, $M_{\lambda s}$ is the material's specular property, V is the viewpoint direction from the pixel, and *shininess* is the material's shininess property. Specular color is the highlight reflection from a smooth-surface material that depends on the reflection direction R (which is L reflected along the normal) and the viewing direction V. As shown in Fig. 3.3.5, $\cos \alpha = \dfrac{n \bullet (L + V)}{|n||L + V|}$,

which is between 0 and 1 when α is between $0°$ and $90°$. When θ or α is greater than $90°$, the specular intensity is set to zero. The viewer can see specularly reflected light from a mirror only when the angle α is close to zero. When the *shininess* is a very large number, $(\cos \alpha)^{shininess}$ is attenuated toward zero unless $(\cos \alpha)$ equals one.

The viewpoint, as we discussed in the viewing transformation, is at the origin (facing the negative z axis). We use *glLightModeli(GL_LIGHT_MODEL_LOCAL_VIEWER, GL_TRUE)* to specify the viewpoint at (0, 0, 0). However, to simplify the lighting calculation, OpenGL allows us to specify the viewpoint at infinity in the (0, 0, 1)

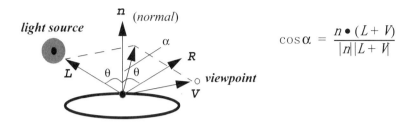

Fig. 3.5 The angle between _n_ and (_L+V_) at the vertex

direction. This is the default in the same direction for all vertex pixels. Because this assumption is only used to simplify lighting calculations, the viewpoint is not changed for other graphics calculations, such as projection. Example _J3_5_Specular.java_ shows how to specify the specular parameters in OpenGL.

/* specular light & material components */

```
import net.java.games.jogl.*;

public class J3_5_Specular extends J3_4_Diffuse {
  public void init(GLDrawable glDrawable) {
    super.init(glDrawable);

    gl.glEnable(GL.GL_LIGHTING);

    gl.glEnable(GL.GL_NORMALIZE);

    gl.glEnable(GL.GL_LIGHT0);

    gl.glLightfv(GL.GL_LIGHT0, GL.GL_POSITION, position);
    gl.glLightfv(GL.GL_LIGHT0, GL.GL_SPECULAR, white);

    gl.glMaterialfv(GL.GL_FRONT, GL.GL_SPECULAR, white);
    gl.glMaterialf(GL.GL_FRONT, GL.GL_SHININESS, 50.0f);

    gl.glMaterialfv(GL.GL_FRONT, GL.GL_DIFFUSE, black);
    gl.glMaterialfv(GL.GL_FRONT, GL.GL_AMBIENT, black);
```

```
    gl.glMaterialfv(GL.GL_FRONT, GL.GL_EMISSION, black);
  }

  public static void main(String[] args) {
    J3_5_Specular f = new J3_5_Specular();
    f.setTitle("JOGL J3_5_Specular");

    f.setSize(WIDTH, HEIGHT);
    f.setVisible(true);
  }
}
```

3.3.2 OpenGL Lighting Model

Both the light source and the material have multiple components: ambient, diffuse, and specular. The final vertex color is an integration of all these components:

$$I_\lambda = I_{\lambda e} + I_{\lambda a} + I_{\lambda d} + I_{\lambda s}. \qquad \text{(EQ 62)}$$

We can simplify Equation 62 as:

$$I_\lambda = I_{\lambda e} + I_{\lambda L}, \qquad \text{(EQ 63)}$$

where $I_{\lambda L} = I_{\lambda a} + I_{\lambda d} + I_{\lambda s}$. Whereas ambient, diffuse, and specular intensities depend on the light source, emissive intensity does not. OpenGL scales and normalizes the final intensity to a value between 0 and 1.

In previous examples, even though we didn't specify all the components, OpenGL used the default values that are predefined. If necessary, we can specify all different lighting components (Example *J3_6_Materials.java*). Fig. 3.3.6 is a comparison among the different lighting component effects from the examples we have discussed.

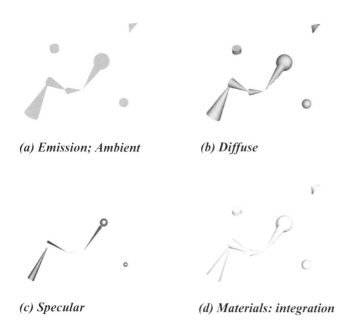

(a) Emission; Ambient   *(b) Diffuse*

(c) Specular   *(d) Materials: integration*

Fig. 3.6 The OpenGL lighting components and their integration

/* multiple light and material components */

```
import net.java.games.jogl.*;
import net.java.games.jogl.util.GLUT;

public class J3_6_Materials extends J3_5_Specular {
  float blackish[] = {0.3f, 0.3f, 0.3f, 0.3f};

  public void init(GLDrawable glDrawable) {

    super.init(glDrawable);

    gl.glEnable(GL.GL_LIGHTING);
    gl.glEnable(GL.GL_NORMALIZE);

    gl.glEnable(GL.GL_LIGHT0);
    gl.glLightfv(GL.GL_LIGHT0, GL.GL_POSITION, position);
```

```
    gl.glLightfv(GL.GL_LIGHT0, GL.GL_AMBIENT, whitish);
    gl.glLightfv(GL.GL_LIGHT0, GL.GL_DIFFUSE, white);
    gl.glLightfv(GL.GL_LIGHT0, GL.GL_SPECULAR, white);

    gl.glMaterialfv(GL.GL_FRONT, GL.GL_AMBIENT, blackish);
    gl.glMaterialfv(GL.GL_FRONT, GL.GL_DIFFUSE, whitish);
    gl.glMaterialfv(GL.GL_FRONT, GL.GL_SPECULAR, white);
    gl.glMaterialf(GL.GL_FRONT, GL.GL_SHININESS, 100.0f);
    gl.glMaterialfv(GL.GL_FRONT, GL.GL_EMISSION, black);
}


public void drawColorCoord(float xlen,
                           float ylen, float zlen) {

    GLUT glut = new GLUT();

    gl.glBegin(GL.GL_LINES);
    gl.glMaterialfv(GL.GL_FRONT, GL.GL_EMISSION, red);
    gl.glColor3f(1, 0, 0);
    gl.glVertex3f(0, 0, 0); gl.glVertex3f(0, 0, zlen);
    gl.glMaterialfv(GL.GL_FRONT, GL.GL_EMISSION, green);
    gl.glColor3f(0, 1, 0);
    gl.glVertex3f(0, 0, 0); gl.glVertex3f(0, ylen, 0);
    gl.glMaterialfv(GL.GL_FRONT, GL.GL_EMISSION, blue);
    gl.glColor3f(0, 0, 1);
    gl.glVertex3f(0, 0, 0); gl.glVertex3f(xlen, 0, 0);
    gl.glEnd();

    // coordinate labels: X, Y, Z
    gl.glPushMatrix();
    gl.glTranslatef(xlen, 0, 0);
    gl.glScalef(xlen/WIDTH, xlen/WIDTH, 1);
    glut.glutStrokeCharacter(gl, GLUT.STROKE_ROMAN, 'X');
    gl.glPopMatrix();

    gl.glPushMatrix();
    gl.glMaterialfv(GL.GL_FRONT, GL.GL_EMISSION, green);
    gl.glColor3f(0, 1, 0);
    gl.glTranslatef(0, ylen, 0);
    gl.glScalef(ylen/WIDTH, ylen/WIDTH, 1);
    glut.glutStrokeCharacter(gl, GLUT.STROKE_ROMAN, 'Y');
    gl.glPopMatrix();

    gl.glPushMatrix();
    gl.glMaterialfv(GL.GL_FRONT, GL.GL_EMISSION, red);
    gl.glColor3f(1, 0, 0);
    gl.glTranslatef(0, 0, zlen);
    gl.glScalef(zlen/WIDTH, zlen/WIDTH, 1);
```

```
    glut.glutStrokeCharacter(gl, GLUT.STROKE_ROMAN, 'Z');
    gl.glPopMatrix();

    gl.glMaterialfv(GL.GL_FRONT, GL.GL_EMISSION, black);
  }


  public static void main(String[] args) {
    J3_6_Materials f = new J3_6_Materials();

    f.setTitle("JOGL J3_6_Materials");
    f.setSize(WIDTH, HEIGHT);
    f.setVisible(true);
  }

}
```

Movable light source. In OpenGL, a light source is invisible. The light source position is transformed as a geometric object by the current matrix when it is specified. In other words, if the matrix is modified at runtime, the light source can be moved around like an object. Lighting is calculated according to the transformed position. To simulate a visible light source, we can specify the light source and draw an object at the same position. As in Example *J3_7_MoveLight.java*, the light source and the sphere are transformed by the same matrix. We may specify the sphere's emission property to correspond to the light source's parameters, so that the sphere looks like the light source (Fig. 3.3.7).

Fig. 3.7 **A moving light source**

/* movable light source */

```java
import net.java.games.jogl.*;

public class J3_7_MoveLight extends J3_6_Materials {
  float origin[] = {0, 0, 0, 1};

  public void drawSolar(float E, float e, float M, float m) {

    // Global coordinates
    gl.glLineWidth(2);
    drawColorCoord(width/6, width/6, width/6);

    gl.glPushMatrix();

    gl.glRotatef(e, 0, 1, 0);
    // rotating around the "sun"; proceed angle
    gl.glRotatef(alpha, 0, 0, 1); // tilt angle
    gl.glTranslatef(0, E, 0);

    gl.glPushMatrix();
    gl.glTranslatef(0, E, 0);
    gl.glScalef(E, E, E);
    drawSphere(); // the "earth"
    gl.glPopMatrix();

    gl.glPushMatrix();
    gl.glScalef(E/4, E, E/4);
    gl.glRotatef(90, 1, 0, 0); // orient the cone
    drawCone();
    gl.glPopMatrix();

    gl.glTranslatef(0, E/2, 0);
    gl.glRotatef(4*m, 0, 1, 0); // rot around the "earth"

    gl.glPushMatrix();
    gl.glTranslatef(2*M, 0, 0);
    gl.glLineWidth(1);
    drawColorCoord(width/8, width/8, width/8);
    gl.glScalef(E/8, E/8, E/8);
    gl.glMaterialfv(GL.GL_FRONT, GL.GL_EMISSION, whitish);
    gl.glLightfv(GL.GL_LIGHT0, GL.GL_POSITION, origin);
    drawSphere();
    gl.glMaterialfv(GL.GL_FRONT, GL.GL_EMISSION, black);
    gl.glPopMatrix();

    gl.glPopMatrix();
  }
```

Color Plate 1

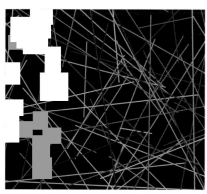

Fig. 1.5
(page 28)

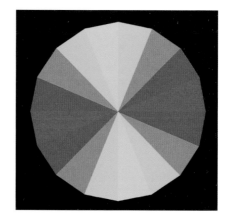

Fig. 1.7
(page 30)

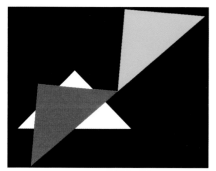

Fig. 2.4
(page 47)

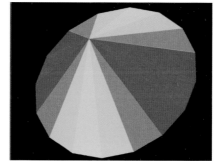

Fig. 2.12
(page 71)

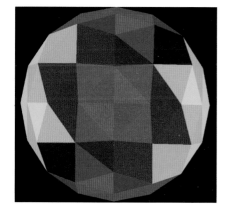

Fig. 2.14c
(page 76)

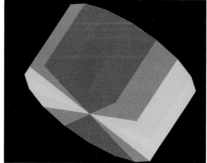

Fig. 2.13
(page 73)

Color Plate 2

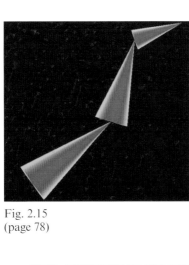

Fig. 2.15
(page 78)

Fig. 2.20
(page 88)

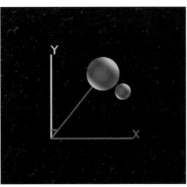

Fig. 2.18
(page 85)

Fig. 2.25
(page 98)

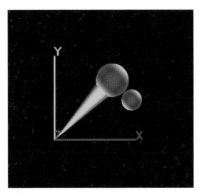

Fig. 2.19c
(page 87)

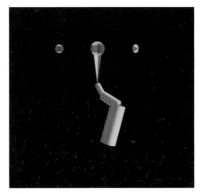

Fig. 2.26
(page 101)

Color Plate 3

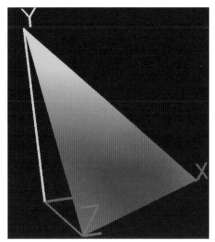

Fig. 3.2
(page 121)

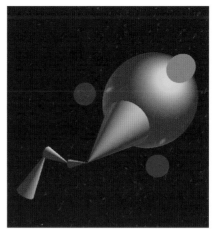

Fig. 3.12b
(page 147)

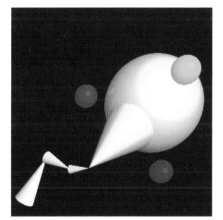

Fig. 3.12a
(page 147)

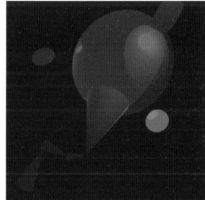

Fig. 3.12c
(page 147)

Color Plate 4

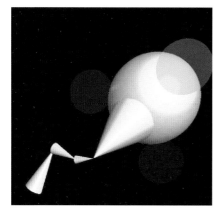

Fig. 4.1
(page 160)

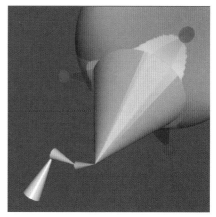

Fig. 4.3
(page 172)

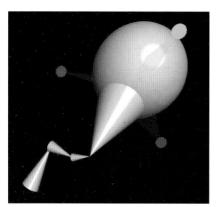

Fig. 4.2
(page 163)

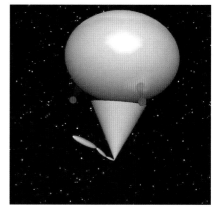

Fig. 4.4
(page 174)

Color Plate 5

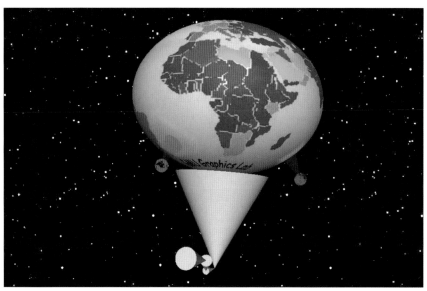

Fig. 4.6
(page 181)

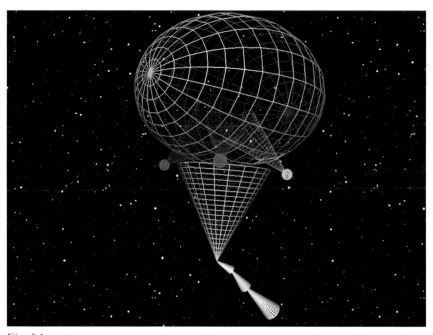

Fig. 5.1
(page 195)

Color Plate 6

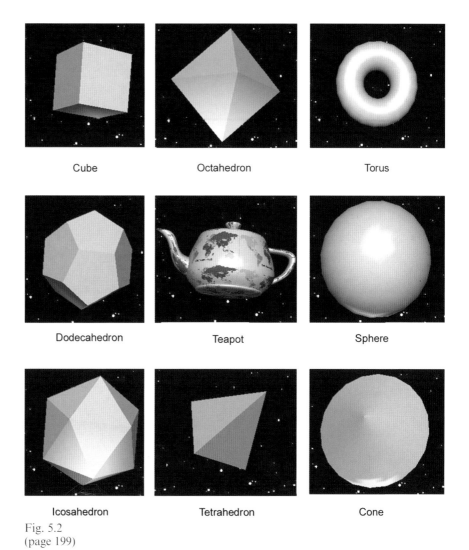

Cube   Octahedron   Torus

Dodecahedron   Teapot   Sphere

Icosahedron   Tetrahedron   Cone

Fig. 5.2
(page 199)

Color Plate 7

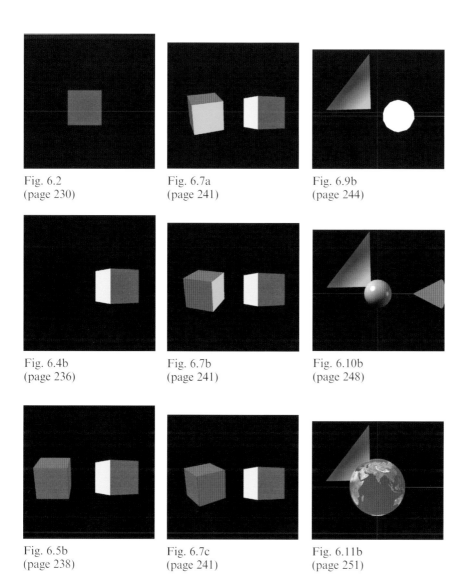

Fig. 6.2
(page 230)

Fig. 6.7a
(page 241)

Fig. 6.9b
(page 244)

Fig. 6.4b
(page 236)

Fig. 6.7b
(page 241)

Fig. 6.10b
(page 248)

Fig. 6.5b
(page 238)

Fig. 6.7c
(page 241)

Fig. 6.11b
(page 251)

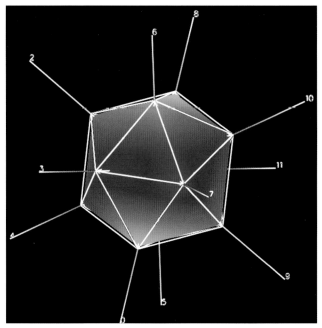

Fig. 7.3
(page 269)

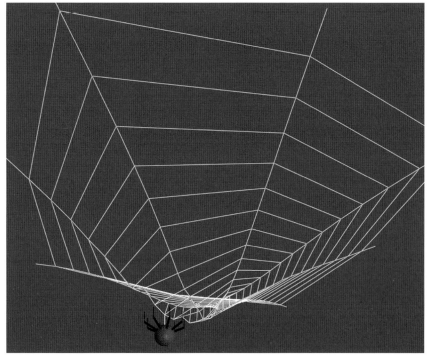

Fig. 7.5
(page 273)

```
public static void main(String[] args) {
    J3_7_MoveLight f = new J3_7_MoveLight();

    f.setTitle("JOGL J3_7_MoveLight");
    f.setSize(WIDTH, HEIGHT);
    f.setVisible(true);
  }
}
```

Spotlight effect. A real light source may not generate equa intensity in all directions:

$$I_\lambda = I_{\lambda e} + f_{spot} I_{\lambda L} \qquad\qquad \textbf{(EQ 64)}$$

where f_{spot} is called the *spotlight effect factor*. In OpenGL, it is calculated as follows:

$$f_{spot} = (-L \bullet D_{spot})^{spotExp} \qquad\qquad \textbf{(EQ 65)}$$

where $(-L)$ is a unit vector pointing from the light source to the vertex pixel, D_{spot} is the direction of the light source, and *spotExp* is a specified constant. As shown in Fig. 3.3.8, $\cos\gamma = \dfrac{(-L) \bullet D_{spot}}{|D_{spot}|}$. When the *spotExp* is a large number, $(\cos\gamma)^{spotExp}$ is attenuated toward zero and the light is concentrated along the D_{spot} direction.

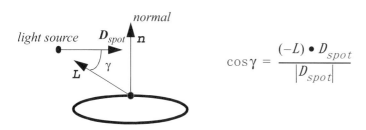

Fig. 3.8 The angle between (-L) and D_{spot}

The light source may have a *cutoff angle* as shown in Fig. 3.3.9, so that only the vertex pixels inside the cone area are lit. There is no light outside the cone area. To be exact, the cone area is infinite in the D_{spot} direction without a bottom.

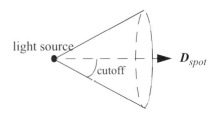

Example *J3_8_SpotLight.java* shows how to specify spotlight parameters. The effect is shown in Fig. 3.3.10. The D_{spot} direction

Fig. 3.9 The light source cutoff angle

vector is also transformed by the current modelview matrix, as the vertex normals.

/* spotlight effect */

```
import net.java.games.jogl.*;


public class J3_8_SpotLight extends J3_7_MoveLight {
    float spot_direction[] = {-1, 0, 0, 1};

    public void drawSolar(float E, float e, float M, float m) {

        // Global coordinates
        gl.glLineWidth(2);
        drawColorCoord(WIDTH/6, WIDTH/6, WIDTH/6);

        gl.glPushMatrix();

        gl.glRotatef(e, 0, 1, 0);
        // rotating around the "sun"; proceed angle
        gl.glRotatef(alpha, 0, 0, 1); // tilt angle
        gl.glTranslatef(0, E, 0);

        gl.glPushMatrix();
        gl.glTranslatef(0, E, 0);
        gl.glScalef(E, E, E);
        drawSphere();
        gl.glPopMatrix();

        gl.glPushMatrix();
        gl.glScalef(E/4, E, E/4);
        gl.glRotatef(90, 1, 0, 0); // orient the cone
        drawCone();
        gl.glPopMatrix();
```

```
        gl.glTranslatef(0, E/2, 0);
        gl.glRotatef(m, 0, 1, 0);
        // 1st moon rotating around the "earth"

        gl.glPushMatrix();
        gl.glTranslatef(2.5f*M, 0, 0);
        gl.glLineWidth(1);
        drawColorCoord(WIDTH/8, WIDTH/8, WIDTH/8);
        gl.glScalef(E/8, E/8, E/8);
        gl.glLightf(GL.GL_LIGHT0, GL.GL_SPOT_CUTOFF, 15f);
        gl.glLightfv(GL.GL_LIGHT0, GL.GL_SPOT_DIRECTION,
                    spot_direction); // facing x axis initially
        gl.glLightf(GL.GL_LIGHT0, GL.GL_SPOT_EXPONENT, 2f);
        gl.glLightfv(GL.GL_LIGHT0, GL.GL_POSITION, origin);
        gl.glMaterialfv(GL.GL_FRONT, GL.GL_EMISSION, whitish);
        drawSphere();
        gl.glMaterialfv(GL.GL_FRONT, GL.GL_EMISSION, black);
        gl.glPopMatrix();

        gl.glPopMatrix();
    }


    public static void main(String[] args) {
        J3_8_SpotLight f = new J3_8_SpotLight();

        f.setTitle("JOGL J3_8_SpotLight");
        f.setSize(WIDTH, HEIGHT);
        f.setVisible(true);
    }
}
```

Fig. 3.10 Spotlight effect

Fig. 3.11 Light source attenuation effect

Light source attenuation. The intensity from a point light source to a vertex pixel can be attenuated by the distance the light travels:

$$I_\lambda = I_{\lambda e} + f_{att} f_{spot} I_{\lambda L},$$ **(EQ 66)**

where f_{att} is called the *light source attenuation factor*. In OpenGL, f_{att} is calculated as follows:

$$f_{att} = \frac{1}{A_c + A_1 d_L + A_q d_L^2},$$ **(EQ 67)**

where d_L is the distance from the point light source to the lit vertex pixel, and A_c, A_1, and A_q are constant, linear, and quadratic attenuation factors. Example *J3_9_AttLight.java* shows how to specify these factors. The effect is shown in Fig. 3.3.11.

/* light source attenuation effect */

```
import net.java.games.jogl.*;
```

```
public class J3_9_AttLight extends J3_8_SpotLight {
  float dist = 0;

  public void drawSolar(float E, float e, float M, float m) {

    drawColorCoord(WIDTH/6, WIDTH/6, WIDTH/6);

    gl.glPushMatrix();

    gl.glRotatef(e, 0.0f, 1.0f, 0.0f);
    // rotating around the "sun"; proceed angle
    gl.glRotatef(alpha, 0.0f, 0.0f, 1.0f); // tilt angle
    gl.glTranslatef(0.0f, E, 0.0f);

    gl.glPushMatrix();
    gl.glTranslatef(0, E, 0);
    gl.glScalef(E, E, E);
    drawSphere();
    gl.glPopMatrix();

    gl.glPushMatrix();
    gl.glScalef(E/4, E, E/4);
    gl.glRotatef(90f, 1.0f, 0.0f, 0.0f); // orient the cone
    drawCone();
    gl.glPopMatrix();

    gl.glTranslatef(0, E/2, 0);
    gl.glRotatef(m, 0.0f, 1.0f, 0.0f);
    // 1st moon rotating around the "earth"

    gl.glPushMatrix();
    if (dist>5*M) {
      flip = -1;
    } else if (dist<M) {
      flip = 1;
    }
    if (dist==0) {
      dist = 1.5f*M;
    }
    dist = dist+flip;

    gl.glTranslatef(-dist, 0, 0);
    gl.glScalef(E/8, E/8, E/8);

    gl.glLightf(GL.GL_LIGHT0, GL.GL_CONSTANT_ATTENUATION, 1);
    gl.glLightf(GL.GL_LIGHT0, GL.GL_LINEAR_ATTENUATION,
                0.001f);
    gl.glLightf(GL.GL_LIGHT0, GL.GL_QUADRATIC_ATTENUATION,
```

```
                    0.0001f);
  gl.glLightfv(GL.GL_LIGHT0, GL.GL_POSITION, origin);
  gl.glMaterialfv(GL.GL_FRONT, GL.GL_EMISSION, whitish);
  drawSphere();
  gl.glPopMatrix();

  gl.glPopMatrix();
}


public static void main(String[] args) {

  J3_9_AttLight f = new J3_9_AttLight();

  f.setTitle("JOGL J3_9_AttLight");
  f.setSize(WIDTH, HEIGHT);
  f.setVisible(true);
}
}
```

Multiple light sources. We can also specify multiple light sources:

$$I_\lambda = I_{\lambda e} + \sum_{i=0}^{k-1} f_{atti} f_{spoti} I_{\lambda Li}, \qquad \text{(EQ 68)}$$

where k is the number of different light sources. Each light source's parameters and position can be specified differently. There may be fixed as well as moving light sources with different properties. The emission component, which is a material property, does not depend on any light source. We can also use *glLightModel()* to specify a global ambient light that does not depend on any light source. Fig. 3.3.12 is a comparison among the different lighting component effects: fixed global light, local movable lights, and light sources with cutoff angles.

/* fixed and multiple moving light sources */

```
import net.java.games.jogl.*;


public class J3_10_Lights extends J3_9_AttLight {
```

```
float redish[] = {.3f, 0, 0, 1};
float greenish[] = {0, .3f, 0, 1};
float blueish[] = {0, 0, .3f, 1};
float yellish[] = {.7f, .7f, 0.0f, 1};

public void init(GLDrawable glDrawable) {

  super.init(glDrawable);

  gl.glEnable(GL.GL_LIGHTING);
  gl.glEnable(GL.GL_NORMALIZE);
  gl.glEnable(GL.GL_CULL_FACE);
  gl.glCullFace(GL.GL_BACK);

  gl.glEnable(GL.GL_LIGHT1);
  gl.glEnable(GL.GL_LIGHT2);
  gl.glEnable(GL.GL_LIGHT3);

  gl.glLightfv(GL.GL_LIGHT0, GL.GL_POSITION, position);
  gl.glLightfv(GL.GL_LIGHT0, GL.GL_AMBIENT, blackish);
  gl.glLightfv(GL.GL_LIGHT0, GL.GL_DIFFUSE, whitish);
  gl.glLightfv(GL.GL_LIGHT0, GL.GL_SPECULAR, white);

  gl.glLightfv(GL.GL_LIGHT1, GL.GL_AMBIENT, redish);
  gl.glLightfv(GL.GL_LIGHT1, GL.GL_DIFFUSE, red);
  gl.glLightfv(GL.GL_LIGHT1, GL.GL_SPECULAR, red);

  gl.glLightfv(GL.GL_LIGHT2, GL.GL_AMBIENT, greenish);
  gl.glLightfv(GL.GL_LIGHT2, GL.GL_DIFFUSE, green);
  gl.glLightfv(GL.GL_LIGHT2, GL.GL_SPECULAR, green);

  gl.glLightfv(GL.GL_LIGHT3, GL.GL_AMBIENT, blueish);
  gl.glLightfv(GL.GL_LIGHT3, GL.GL_DIFFUSE, blue);
  gl.glLightfv(GL.GL_LIGHT3, GL.GL_SPECULAR, blue);

  myMaterialColor(blackish, whitish, white, black);
}


public void myMaterialColor(
    float myA[],
    float myD[],
    float myS[],
    float myE[]) {

  gl.glMaterialfv(GL.GL_FRONT, GL.GL_AMBIENT, myA);
  gl.glMaterialfv(GL.GL_FRONT, GL.GL_DIFFUSE, myD);
  gl.glMaterialfv(GL.GL_FRONT, GL.GL_SPECULAR, myS);
  gl.glMaterialfv(GL.GL_FRONT, GL.GL_EMISSION, myE);
```

```
}

public void drawSolar(float E, float e,
                      float M, float m) {

  // Global coordinates
  gl.glLineWidth(2);
  drawColorCoord(WIDTH/6, WIDTH/6, WIDTH/6);

  myMaterialColor(blackish, whitish, white, black);

  gl.glPushMatrix();

  gl.glRotatef(e, 0, 1, 0);
  // rotating around the "sun"; proceed angle
  gl.glRotatef(alpha, 0, 0, 1); // tilt angle
  gl.glTranslatef(0, 1.5f*E, 0);

  gl.glPushMatrix();
  gl.glTranslatef(0, E, 0);
  gl.glScalef(E, E, E);
  drawSphere();
  gl.glPopMatrix();

  gl.glPushMatrix();
  gl.glScalef(E/2, 1.5f*E, E/2);
  gl.glRotatef(90, 1, 0, 0); // orient the cone
  drawCone();
  gl.glPopMatrix();

  gl.glTranslatef(0, E/2, 0);
  gl.glRotatef(m, 0, 1, 0); // 1st moon

  gl.glPushMatrix();
  gl.glTranslatef(2*M, 0, 0);
  gl.glLineWidth(1);
  drawColorCoord(WIDTH/4, WIDTH/4, WIDTH/4);
  gl.glScalef(E/4, E/4, E/4);
  myMaterialColor(redish, redish, red, redish);
  gl.glLightfv(GL.GL_LIGHT1, GL.GL_POSITION, origin);
  drawSphere();
  gl.glPopMatrix();

  gl.glRotatef(120, 0, 1, 0); // 2nd moon

  gl.glPushMatrix();
  gl.glTranslatef(2*M, 0, 0);
  drawColorCoord(WIDTH/4, WIDTH/4, WIDTH/4);
```

```
    gl.glLightfv(GL.GL_LIGHT2, GL.GL_POSITION, origin);
    gl.glScalef(E/4, E/4, E/4);
    myMaterialColor(greenish, greenish, green, greenish);
    drawSphere();
    gl.glPopMatrix();

    gl.glRotatef(120, 0f, 1f, 0f); // 3rd moon
    gl.glTranslatef(2*M, 0, 0);
    gl.glLightfv(GL.GL_LIGHT3, GL.GL_POSITION, origin);
    drawColorCoord(WIDTH/4, WIDTH/4, WIDTH/4);
    gl.glScalef(E/4, E/4, E/4);
    myMaterialColor(blueish, blueish, blue, blueish);
    drawSphere();

    gl.glPopMatrix();

    myMaterialColor(blackish, whitish, white, black);
  }

  public static void main(String[] args) {
    J3_10_Lights f = new J3_10_Lights();

    f.setTitle("JOGL J3_10_Lights");
    f.setSize(WIDTH, HEIGHT);
    f.setVisible(true);
  }
}
```

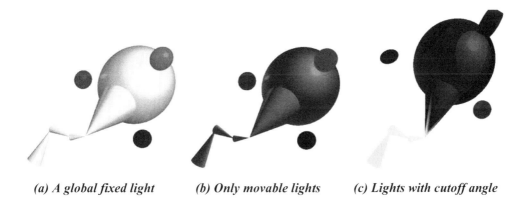

(a) A global fixed light   *(b) Only movable lights*   *(c) Lights with cutoff angle*

Fig. 3.12 Light sources: fixed, movable, and directional [*See* Color Plate 3]

3.4 Visible-Surface Shading

Shading models are methods for calculating the lighting of a surface instead of just one vertex or point pixel. As we discussed, OpenGL provides flat shading and smooth shading for polygonal surfaces. A polygon on a surface is also called a *face*. We will discuss some issues related to improving the efficiency and quality of face shading.

3.4.1 Back-Face Culling

We can speed up drawing by eliminating some of the hidden surfaces before rendering. Given a solid object such as a polygonal sphere, we can see only half of the faces. The visible faces are called *front-facing* polygons or *front faces*, and the invisible faces are called *back-facing* polygons or *back faces*. The invisible back faces should be eliminated from processing as early as possible, even before the z-buffer algorithm is called. The z-buffer algorithm, as discussed in Section 2.3.3 on page 69, needs significant hardware calculations. Eliminating back-facing polygons before rendering is called *back-face culling*.

In OpenGL, if the order of the polygon vertices is counter-clockwise from the viewpoint, the polygon is front-facing (Fig. 3.3.13). Otherwise, it is back-facing. We use *glEnable(GL_CULL_FACE)* to turn on culling and call *glCullFace(GL_BACK)* to achieve back-face culling. Therefore, if we use back-face culling, we should make sure that the order of the vertices are correct when we specify a face by a list of vertices. Otherwise, we will see some holes (missing faces) on the surface displayed. Also, as in

$$n = (v2 - v1) \times (v3 - v2)$$

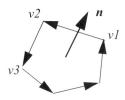

Fig. 3.13 A front face and its norm

the following function (Example *J3_10_Lights.java*), we often use the cross-product of two edge vectors of a face to find its normal *n*. An edge vector is calculated by the difference of two neighbor vertices. The correctness of the surface normal depends on the correct order and direction of the edge vectors in the cross-product, which in turn depend on the correct order of the vertices as well. The faces that have normals facing the wrong direction will not be shaded correctly.

```
void drawBottom(float *v1, float *v2, float *v3){
    // normal to the cone or cylinder bottom
    float v12[3], v23[3], vb[3];
    int i;

    for (i=0; i<3; i++) { // two edge vectors
        v12[i] = v2[i] - v1[i];
        v23[i] = v3[i] - v2[i];
    }

    // vb = normalized cross prod. of v12 X v23
    ncrossprod(v12, v23, vb);
    gl.glBegin(GL.GL_TRIANGLES);
        gl.glNormal3fv(vb);
        gl.glVertex3fv(v1);
        gl.glVertex3fv(v2);
        gl.glVertex3fv(v3);
    gl.glEnd();
}
```

Given a hollow box or cylinder without a cover, we will see both front and back faces. In this case, we cannot use back-face culling. We may turn on lighting for both front and back faces: *glLightModeli(GL_LIGHT_MODEL_TWO_SIDE, TRUE)*. If we turn on two-side lighting, each polygon has two sides with opposite normals and OpenGL will decide to shade the side that the normal is facing the viewpoint. We may also supply different material properties for both the front-facing polygons and the back-facing polygons: *glMaterialfv(GL_FRONT, GL_AMBIENT, red); glMaterialfv(GL_BACK, GL_AMBIENT, green)*.

3.4.2 Polygon Shading Models

The appearances of a surface under different shading models differ greatly. Flat shading, which is the simplest and fastest, is used to display a flat-face object instead of a curved-face object. In approximating a curved surface, using flat shading with a finer polygon mesh turns out to be ineffective and slow. Smooth shading (also called Gouraud shading), which calculates the colors of the vertex pixels and interpolates the colors of every other pixel in a polygon, is often used to approximate the shading of a curved face. In OpenGL, we can use *glShadeModel(GL_FLAT)* or *glShadeModel(GL_SMOOTH)* to choose between the two different shading models (flat shading and smooth shading), and the shadings are calculated by the OpenGL system. In OpenGL, the vertex normals are specified at the programmer's discernment. To eliminate intensity discontinuities, the normal of a vertex is often calculated by averaging the normals of the faces sharing the vertex on the surface. In general, we try to specify a vertex normal that is perpendicular to the curved surface instead of the polygon. Also, we may specify normals in the directions we prefer in order to achieve special effects.

Here we present an example to demonstrate how Gouraud shading is achieved. As shown in Fig. 3.3.14, the light source and the viewpoint are both at P, the normal N_A is parallel to CP that is perpendicular to AE, N_E is pointing toward P, ABCDEP is in a plane, and AP=EP=2CP. We can calculate the colors at A and E using a given lighting model, such as Equation 63 on page 134. Then, as discussed in Section 3.2 on page 120, we can

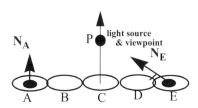

Fig. 3.14 Shading calculations

interplate and find the colors for all pixels on the line. For example, let's calculate an intensity according to the following lighting model (which includes only diffuse and specular components):

$$I = \frac{n \bullet L + \left(\dfrac{n \bullet (L+V)}{|L+V|} \right)^2}{2}.$$ (EQ 69)

Then,

$$I_A = \frac{N_A \bullet \overrightarrow{AP} + \left(\dfrac{N_A \bullet (\overrightarrow{AP} + \overrightarrow{AP})}{|\overrightarrow{AP} + \overrightarrow{AP}|} \right)^2}{2} = \frac{\cos 60^o + (\cos 60^o)^2}{2} = \frac{3}{8},$$ (EQ 70)

$$I_E = \frac{N_E \bullet \overrightarrow{AP} + \left(\dfrac{N_E \bullet (\overrightarrow{EP} + \overrightarrow{EP})}{|\overrightarrow{EP} + \overrightarrow{EP}|} \right)^2}{2} = \frac{\cos 0^o + (\cos 0^o)^2}{2} = 1,$$ (EQ 71)

and

$$\Delta I = \frac{I_E - I_A}{N - 1} = \frac{1 - \frac{3}{8}}{5 - 1} = \frac{5}{32}. \tag{EQ 72}$$

According to the Gouraud shading method discussed in Section 3.2 on page 120, with the intensities at A and B, the intensities at B, C, and D can be calculated, respectively:

$$I_B = I_A + \Delta I = \frac{3}{8} + \frac{5}{32} = \frac{17}{32}, \tag{EQ 73}$$

$$I_C = I_B + \Delta I = \frac{17}{32} + \frac{5}{32} = \frac{11}{16}, \tag{EQ 74}$$

$$I_D = I_C + \Delta I = \frac{11}{16} + \frac{5}{32} = \frac{27}{32}. \tag{EQ 75}$$

Another popular shading model, the normal-vector interpolation shading (called Phong shading), calculates the normals of the vertex pixels and interpolates the normals of all other pixels in a polygon. Then, the color of every pixel is calculated using a lighting model and the interpolated normals. Phong shading is much slower than Gouraud shading and therefore is not implemented in the OpenGL system.

For example, we use the same example and lighting model as shown in Fig. 3.3.14 to demonstrate Phong shading. First we calculate the normals through interpolations:

$$\Delta N = \frac{N_E - N_A}{N - 1} = \frac{0 - 60^o}{5 - 1} = 15^o \tag{EQ 76}$$

Therefore,

$$N_B = N_A + \Delta N = 60^o - 15^o = 45^o, \tag{EQ 77}$$

$$N_C = N_B + \Delta N = 45^o - 15^o = 30^o, \qquad \text{(EQ 78)}$$

$$N_D = N_C + \Lambda N = 30^o - 15^o = 15^o. \qquad \text{(EQ 79)}$$

Then, all the pixel intensities are calculated by the lighting model:

$$I_B = \frac{N_B \bullet \overrightarrow{BP} + \left(\dfrac{N_B \bullet (\overrightarrow{BP} + \overrightarrow{BP})}{|\overrightarrow{BP} + \overrightarrow{BP}|}\right)^2}{2} = \frac{\cos 45^o + (\cos 45^o)^2}{2} = 0.604 \qquad \text{(EQ 80)}$$

$$I_C = \frac{N_C \bullet \overrightarrow{CP} + \left(\dfrac{N_B \bullet (\overrightarrow{CP} + \overrightarrow{CP})}{|\overrightarrow{CP} + \overrightarrow{CP}|}\right)^2}{2} = \frac{\cos 30^o + (\cos 30^o)^2}{2} = 0.808 \qquad \text{(EQ 81)}$$

$$I_D = \frac{N_D \bullet \overrightarrow{DP} + \left(\dfrac{N_B \bullet (\overrightarrow{DP} + \overrightarrow{DP})}{|\overrightarrow{DP} + \overrightarrow{DP}|}\right)^2}{2} = \frac{\cos 15^o + (\cos 15^o)^2}{2} = 0.949 \qquad \text{(EQ 82)}$$

Phong shading allows specular highlights to be located in a polygon, whereas Gouraud shading does not. In contrast, if a highlight is within a polygon, smooth shading will fail to show it, because the intensity interpolation makes it such that the highest intensity is only possible at a vertex. Also, if we have a spotlight source and the vertices fall outside the cutoff angle, smooth shading will not calculate the vertex colors and thus the polygon will not be shaded. You may have noticed that when the sphere subdivisions are not enough, lighting toward the sphere with a small cutoff angle may not show up.

All of the above shading models are approximations. Using polygons to approximate curved faces is much faster than handling curved surfaces directly. The efficiency of polygon rendering is still the benchmark of graphics systems. In order to achieve better realism, we may calculate each surface pixel's color directly without using interpolations. However, calculating the lighting of every pixel on a surface is in general very time consuming.

3.4.3 Ray Tracing and Radiosity

Ray tracing and *radiosity* are advanced global lighting and rendering models that achieve better realism, which are not provided in OpenGL. They are time-consuming methods so that no practical real-time animation is possible with the current graphics hardware. Here we only introduce the general concepts.

Ray tracing is an extension to the lighting model we learned. The light rays travel from the light sources to the viewpoint. The simplest ray tracing method is to follow the rays in reverse from the viewpoint to the light sources. A ray is sent from the viewpoint through a pixel on the projection plane to the scene to calculate the lighting of that pixel. If we simply use the lighting model (Equation 68) once, we would produce a similar image as if we use the OpenGL lighting directly without ray tracing. Instead, ray tracing accounts for the global specular reflections among objects and calculates the ray's recursive intersections that include reflective bounces and refractive transmissions. Lighting is calculated at each point of intersection. The final pixel color is an accumulation of all fractions of intensity values from the bottom up. At any point of intersection, three lighting components are calculated and added together: current intensity, reflection, and transmission.

The current intensity of a point is calculated using the lighting method we learned already, except that we may take shadows into consideration. Rays (named feeler rays or shadow rays) are fired from the point under consideration to the light sources to decide the point's current intensity using Equation 68. If an object is between the point and a light source, the point under consideration will not be affected by the blocked light source directly, so the corresponding shadows will be generated.

The reflection and transmission components at the point are calculated by recursive calls following the reflected ray and transmitted ray (Fig. 3.3.15). For example, we can modify Equation 68:

$$I_\lambda = I_{\lambda e} + \sum_{i=0}^{k-1} f_{atti} f_{spoti} I_{\lambda Li} + I_{\lambda r} + I_{\lambda t}, \qquad \text{(EQ 83)}$$

where $I_{\lambda r}$ accounts for the reflected light component, and $I_{\lambda t}$ accounts for the transmitted light component, as shown in Fig. 3.3.15.

The reflection component $I_{\lambda r}$ is a specular component, which is calculated recursively by applying Equation 83. Here, we assume that the "viewpoint" is the starting point of the reflected ray R and the point under consideration is the end point of R:

$$I_{\lambda r} = M_{\lambda s} I_{\lambda},$$ (EQ 84)

where $M_{\lambda s}$ is the "viewpoint" material's specular property. The transmission component $I_{\lambda t}$ is calculated similarly:

$$I_{\lambda t} = M_{\lambda t} I_{\lambda},$$ (EQ 85)

where $M_{\lambda t}$ is the "viewpoint" material's transmission coefficient.

The recursion terminates when a user-defined depth is achieved where further reflections and transmissions are omitted, or when the reflected and transmitted rays don't hit objects. Computing the intersections of the ray with the objects and the normals at the intersections is the major part of a ray tracing program, which may take hidden-surface removal, refractive transparency, and shadows into its implementation considerations.

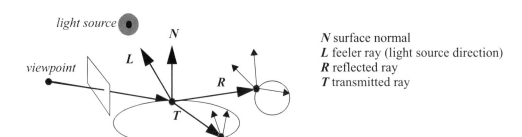

N surface normal
L feeler ray (light source direction)
R reflected ray
T transmitted ray

Fig. 3.15 Recursive ray tracing

Radiosity assumes that each small area or patch is an emissive as well as reflective light source. The method is based on thermal energy radiosity. We need to break up the environment into small discrete patches that emit and reflect light uniformly in the entire area. Also, we need to calculate the fraction of the energy that leaves from a patch and arrives at another, taking into account the shape and orientation of both patches. The shading of a patch is a summation of its own emission and all the emissions from other patches that reach the patch. The finer the patches, the better the results are at the expense of longer calculations.

Although both ray tracing and radiosity can be designed to account for all lighting components, ray tracing is viewpoint dependent, which is better for specular appearance, and radiosity is viewpoint independent, which is better for diffuse appearance.

3.5 Review Questions

1. Which of the following statements is correct:

  a. RGB are subtractive primaries.   b. CMY are additive primaries.
  c. CMY are the complements of RGB.   d. RGB are color inks in printers.

2. An RGB mode 512*512 frame buffer has 24 bits per pixel.

  What is the total memory size needed in bits?   (   )
  How many distinct color choices are available?   (   )
  How many different colors can be displayed in a frame? (   )

3. An index mode 1280*1024 frame buffer has 8 bits per entry. The color look-up table (CLT) has 24 bits per entry.

  What is the total memory size (frame buffer+CLT) in bits? (   )
  How many distinct color choices are available?   (   )
  How many different colors can be displayed in a frame? (   )

4. An index display has 2 bits per pixel and a look-up table with 6 bits per entry (2 bits for R, G, and B, respectively). We scan-converted an object as shown in the frame buffer: a 5-pixel blue horizontal line, a 3-pixel green vertical line, and two red pixels. The rest are black. Please provide the pixel values in the frame buffer.

Frame buffer

	R		G		B	
0	0	0	0	0	0	0
1	0	0	0	0	1	1
2	0	0	1	1	0	0
3	1	1	0	0	0	0

Color look-up table

5. An index raster display has 3 bits per pixel and a color look-up table (color map) with 9 bits per entry (3 bits each for R, G, and B, respectively). We want to load the color map for scan-converting a grayscale object. Assuming the index in the frame buffer corresponds to the intensity, please load the complete color map.

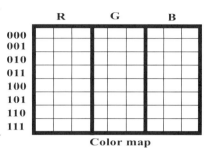

Color map

6. **Which of the following statements is WRONG?**

    a. Our eyes are sensitive to ratios of intensity.
    b. Our eyes average fine detail of the overall intensity.
    c. Our eyes have constant sensitivity to all colors.
    d. Some colors cannot be generated on an RGB display device.

7. **Given the vertex (pixel) colors of the triangle as specified, please use interpolation to find the pixel color in the middle (specified as bold).**

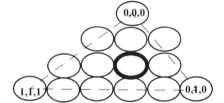

Color = (_____ , _____ , _____)

8. **About a movable light source, which of the following is correct about its location?**

    a. It should be specified at its physical location.
    b. It should be visible once it is specified.
    c. It should be specified at infinity in the direction of its physical location.
    d. It is used for lighting calculation at its specified location.

9. **The vertex normals ($N = N_A = N_B = N_C$) are perpendicular to the triangle. The light source L is making 30^0 angle with N_A, N_B, and N_C. The viewpoint V is at infinite in the direction of N, the normal of the triangle. Please use Gouraud shading and Phong shading to find the pixel color in the middle (specified as bold).**
Reminder: $I_\lambda = [1 + (N \cdot L) + (R \cdot V)^3]/3$, where λ is R, G, or B; N, L, R, and V are all normalized.

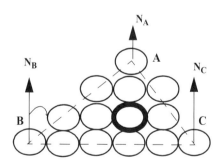

Gouraud shading = (_____ , _____ , _____)

Phong shading = (_____ , _____ , _____)

10. **The light source (P) & the viewpoint (V) are at the same position as in the figure, which is right in the normal of vertex C. The vertex normals of triangle ABC are in the same direction perpendicular to the triangle. Angle VAC = 30 degree. Angle VBC = 45 degree. Please use the following equation to calculate the intensities of the vertices, and use interpolation to find the pixel intensity in the middle (specified as bold).**

Reminder: $I = [1 + (N \cdot L) + (R \cdot V)^2]/3$, where N is the normal direction, L is the light source direction, R is the reflection direction, and V is the viewpoint direction from the vertex in consideration. All vectors are normalized vectors.

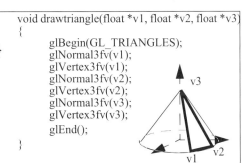

a. $N_A \cdot L_A =$ _____ ; $R_A \cdot V_A =$ _____ ;

b. Intensity A = _____ ; B = _____ ; C = _____

c. Intensity at the bold pixel = _____

11. **In an OpenGL program, we have a local light source with a small cutoff angle facing the center of a triangle. However, we cannot see any light on the triangle. Which of the following is least likely the problem?**

    a. The light source is too close to the triangle.   b. The cutoff angle is too small.
    c. The triangle is too small.   d. The normals of the vertices are facing the wrong direction.

12. **Light source attenuation is calculated according to the distance?**

    a. from the viewpoint to the pixel   b. from the pixel to the light source
    c. from the light to the origin   d. from the origin to the viewpoint
    e. from the pixel to the origin   f. from the origin to the pixel

13. **drawtriangle() on the right draws a piece on the side of the cone. The normals are specified wrong. If the radius equals the height of the cone, which of the following is correct for the normal of v1?**

    a. glNormal3fv(normalize(v1+v2));
    b. glNormal3fv(normalize(v1+v3));
    c. glNormal3fv(normalize(v2+v3));
    d. glNormal3fv(normalize(v1));
    (here "+" is a vector operator)

```
void drawtriangle(float *v1, float *v2, float *v3)
{
    glBegin(GL_TRIANGLES);
        glNormal3fv(v1);
        glVertex3fv(v1);
        glNormal3fv(v2);
        glVertex3fv(v2);
        glNormal3fv(v3);
        glVertex3fv(v3);
    glEnd();
}
```

14. **In OpenGL, normals are transformed with the associated vertices. Prove that normals are transformed by the inverse transpose of the matrix that transforms the corresponding vertices.**

3.6 Programming Assignments

**1. Make the cone, cylinder, and sphere three different
movable light sources pointing toward the center of the
earth in the previous problem in the past chapter. The
light sources are bouncing back and forth with collision
detection. Design your own light source and material
properties.**

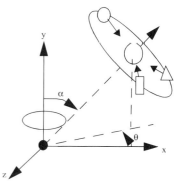

**2. Modify the above program with multiple viewports.
Each viewport demonstrates one lighting property of your
choice. For example, we can demonstrate light source
attenuation interactively as follows: turn on just one light
source and gradually move it away from the earth. When
the lighting is dim, move it toward the earth.**

**3. Implement a OpenGL smooth-shading environment
that has a sphere, box, and cone on a plane. You can specify the light source and materials of your
own.**

**4. Implement a Phong-shading and a corresponding ray-tracing environment that has a sphere,
box, and cone on a plane. You can specify the light source and materials of your own.**

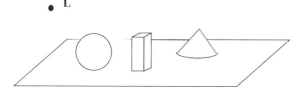

4

Blending and Texture Mapping

Chapter Objectives:

- Understand OpenGL blending to achieve transparency, antialiasing, and fog
- Use images for rendering directly or for texture mapping
- Understand OpenGL texture mapping programs

4.1 Blending

Given two color components $I_{\lambda 1}$ and $I_{\lambda 2}$, the blending of the two values is a linear interpolation between the two:

$$I_{\lambda} = \alpha I_{\lambda 1} + (1 - \alpha) I_{\lambda 2} \qquad \text{(EQ 86)}$$

where α is called the alpha blending factor, and λ is R, G, B, or A. Transparency is achieved by blending. Given two transparent polygons, every pixel color is a blending of the corresponding points on the two polygons along the projection line.

In OpenGL, without blending, each pixel will overwrite the corresponding value in the frame buffer during scan-conversion. In contrast, when blending is enabled, the current pixel color component (namely the source $I_{\lambda 1}$) is blended with the corresponding pixel color component already in the frame buffer (namely the destination $I_{\lambda 2}$). The blending function is an extension of Equation 86:

$$I_{\lambda} = B_1 I_{\lambda 1} + B_2 I_{\lambda 2} \qquad \text{(EQ 87)}$$

where B_1 and B_2 are the source and destination blending factors, respectively.

The blending factors are decided by the function *glBlendFunc(B1, B2)*, where *B1* and *B2* are predefined constants to indicate how to compute B_1 and B_2, respectively. As shown in Example *J4_1_Blending.java* (Fig. 4.1), *B1* = *GL_SRC_ALPHA* indicates that the source blending factor is the source color's alpha value, which is the A in the source pixel's RGBA, where A stands for *alpha*. That is, B_1 = A, and *B2* = *GL_ONE_MINUS_SRC_ALPHA* indicates that B_2 = 1-A. When we specify a color directly, or specify a material property in lighting, we now specify and use the alpha value as well. In Example *J4_1_Blending.java*, when we specify

Fig. 4.1 **Transparent spheres** [*See* **Color Plate 4**]

the material properties, we choose A=0.3 to represent the material's transparency property. Here, if we choose A=0.0, the material is completely transparent. If A=1.0, the material is opaque.

/* transparent spheres */

```
import net.java.games.jogl.*;


public class J4_1_Blending extends J3_10_Lights {

    // alpha 4 transparency
    float tred[] = {1, 0, 0, 0.3f};
    float tgreen[] = {0, 1, 0, 0.3f};
    float tblue[] = {0, 0, 1, 0.3f};


    public void drawSolar(float E, float e,
                          float M, float m) {

gl.glLineWidth(2);
    drawColorCoord(WIDTH/6, WIDTH/6, WIDTH/6);

    myMaterialColor(blackish, whitish, white, black);

    gl.glPushMatrix();
```

```
gl.glRotatef(e, 0, 1, 0);
// rotating around the "sun"; proceed angle
gl.glRotatef(alpha, 0, 0, 1); // tilt angle
gl.glTranslatef(0, 1.5f*E, 0);

gl.glPushMatrix();
gl.glTranslatef(0, E, 0);
gl.glScalef(E, E, E);
drawSphere();
gl.glPopMatrix();

gl.glPushMatrix();
gl.glScalef(E/2, 1.5f*E, E/2);
gl.glRotatef(90, 1, 0, 0); // orient the cone
drawCone();
gl.glPopMatrix();

// enable blending for moons
gl.glEnable(GL.GL_BLEND);
gl.glBlendFunc(GL.GL_SRC_ALPHA,
               GL.GL_ONE_MINUS_SRC_ALPHA);

gl.glTranslatef(0, E/2, 0);
gl.glRotatef(m, 0, 1, 0); // 1st moon
gl.glPushMatrix();
gl.glTranslatef(2*M, 0, 0);
gl.glLineWidth(1);
drawColorCoord(WIDTH/4, WIDTH/4, WIDTH/4);
gl.glScalef(E/2, E/2, E/2);
myMaterialColor(tred, tred, tred, tred); // transparent
gl.glLightfv(GL.GL_LIGHT1, GL.GL_POSITION, origin);
drawSphere();
gl.glPopMatrix();

gl.glRotatef(120, 0, 1, 0); // 2nd moon
gl.glPushMatrix();
gl.glTranslatef(2*M, 0, 0);
drawColorCoord(WIDTH/4, WIDTH/4, WIDTH/4);
gl.glLightfv(GL.GL_LIGHT2, GL.GL_POSITION, origin);
gl.glScalef(E/2, E/2, E/2);
myMaterialColor(tgreen, tgreen, tgreen, tgreen); // trans.
drawSphere();
gl.glPopMatrix();

gl.glRotatef(120, 0f, 1f, 0f); // 3rd moon
gl.glTranslatef(2*M, 0, 0);
gl.glLightfv(GL.GL_LIGHT3, GL.GL_POSITION, origin);
drawColorCoord(WIDTH/4, WIDTH/4, WIDTH/4);
gl.glScalef(E/2, E/2, E/2);
```

```
    myMaterialColor(tblue, tblue, tblue, tblue);
    drawSphere();

    gl.glPopMatrix();
    myMaterialColor(blackish, whitish, white, black);
  }


  public static void main(String[] args) {
    J4_1_Blending f = new J4_1_Blending();

    f.setTitle("JOGL J4_1_Blending");
    f.setSize(WIDTH, HEIGHT);
    f.setVisible(true);
  }
}
```

4.1.1 OpenGL Blending Factors

Example *J4_1_Blending.java* chooses the alpha blending factor as in Equation 86, which is a special case. OpenGL provides more constants to indicate how to compute the source or destination blending factors through *glBlendFunc()*.

If the source and destination colors are (R_s, G_s, B_s, A_s) and (R_d, G_d, B_d, A_d) and the source (src) and destination (dst) blending factors are (S_r, S_g, S_b, S_a) and (D_r, D_g, D_b, D_a), then the final RGBA value in the frame buffer is $(R_sS_r + R_dD_r, G_sS_g + G_dD_g, B_sS_b + B_dD_b, A_sS_a + A_dD_a)$. Each component is eventually clamped to $[0, 1]$. The predefined constants to indicate how to compute (S_r, S_g, S_b, S_a) and (D_r, D_g, D_b, D_a) are as follows:

Constant	Relevant Factor	Computed Blend Factor
GL_ZERO	src or dst	$(0, 0, 0, 0)$
GL_ONE	src or dst	$(1, 1, 1, 1)$
GL_DST_COLOR	src	(R_d, G_d, B_d, A_d)
GL_SRC_COLOR	dst	(R_s, G_s, B_s, A_s)
GL_ONE_MINUS_DST_COLOR	src	$(1,1,1,1) - (R_d, G_d, B_d, A_d)$
GL_ONE_MINUS_SRC_COLOR	dst	$(1,1,1,1) - (R_s, G_s, B_s, A_s)$
GL_SRC_ALPHA	src or dst	(A_s, A_s, A_s, A_s)
GL_ONE_MINUS_SRC_ALPHA	src or dst	$(1,1,1,1) - (A_s, A_s, A_s, A_s)$
GL_DST_ALPHA	src or dst	(A_d, A_d, A_d, A_d)
GL_ONE_MINUS_DST_ALPHA	src or dst	$(1,1,1,1) - (A_d, A_d, A_d, A_d)$
GL_SRC_ALPHA_SATURATE	src	$(f, f, f, 1);\ f=\min(A_s, 1-A_d)$

Depending on how we choose the blending factors and other parameters, we can achieve different effects of transparency, antialiasing, and fog, which will be discussed later.

OpenGL blending achieves nonrefractive transparency. The blended points are along the projection line. In other words, the light ray passing through the transparent surfaces is not bent. Refractive transparency, which needs to take the geometrical and optical properties into consideration, is significantly more time consuming. Refractive transparency is often integrated with ray tracing.

4.1.2 Transparency and Hidden-Surface Removal

It is fairly complex to achieve the correct transparency through blending if we have multiple transparent layers, because the order of blending of these layers matters. As in Equation 87, the source and the destination parameters are changed if we switch the order of drawing two polygons. We would like to blend the corresponding transparent points on the surfaces in the order of their distances to the viewpoint. However, this requires keeping track of the distances for all points on the different surfaces, which we avoid doing because of time and memory requirements.

If we enabled the depth-buffer (z-buffer) in OpenGL, obscured polygons may not be used for blending. To avoid this problem, while drawing transparent polygons, we may make the depth buffer read-only. Also, we should draw opaque objects first, and then enable blending to draw transparent objects. This causes the transparent polygons' depth values to be compared with the values established by the opaque polygons, and blending factors to be specified by the transparent polygons. As in *J4_2.Opaque.java, glDepthMask(GL_FALSE)* makes the depth-buffer become read-only, whereas *glDepthMask(GL_TRUE)* restores the normal depth-buffer operation (Fig. 4.2).

Fig. 4.2 Depth-buffer read only [*See* **Color Plate 4**]

/* transparency / hidden-surface removal */

```java
import net.java.games.jogl.*;

public class J4_2_Opaque extends J4_1_Blending {
  float PI = (float)Math.PI;

  public void drawSolar(float E, float e,
                        float M, float m) {

    // Global coordinates
    gl.glLineWidth(2);
    drawColorCoord(WIDTH/6, WIDTH/6, WIDTH/6);

    gl.glPushMatrix();
    {
      gl.glRotatef(e, 0, 1, 0);
      // rotating around the "sun"; proceed angle
      gl.glRotatef(tiltAngle, 0, 0, 1); // tilt angle
      gl.glTranslatef(0, 1.5f*E, 0);

      gl.glPushMatrix();
      gl.glTranslatef(0, E, 0);
      gl.glScalef(E, E, E);
      drawSphere(); // the earth
      gl.glPopMatrix();

      gl.glPushMatrix();
      gl.glScalef(E/2, 1.5f*E, E/2);
      gl.glRotatef(90, 1, 0, 0); // orient the top
      drawCone(); // the top
      gl.glPopMatrix();

      // moons moved up a little
      gl.glTranslatef(0, E/2, 0);
      gl.glRotatef(m, 0, 1, 0); // initial rotation

      // blend for transparency
      gl.glEnable(GL.GL_BLEND);
      gl.glBlendFunc(GL.GL_SRC_ALPHA,
                     GL.GL_ONE_MINUS_SRC_ALPHA);
      gl.glDepthMask(false); // no writting into zbuffer

      gl.glPushMatrix();
      {
        gl.glTranslatef(2.5f*M, 0, 0);
        gl.glLineWidth(1);
```

```
    drawColorCoord(WIDTH/4, WIDTH/4, WIDTH/4);
    gl.glLightfv(GL.GL_LIGHT1,
                 GL.GL_SPOT_DIRECTION, spot_direction);
    gl.glLightf(GL.GL_LIGHT1, GL.GL_SPOT_CUTOFF, 5);
    gl.glLightfv(GL.GL_LIGHT1, GL.GL_POSITION, origin);

    gl.glPushMatrix();
    myMaterialColor(red, red, red, red); // red lit source
    gl.glScalef(E/8, E/8, E/8);
    drawSphere();
    gl.glPopMatrix();

    gl.glScaled(2.5*M, 2.5*M*Math.tan(PI*5/180),
                2.5*M*Math.tan(PI*5/180)); // cutoff angle
    gl.glTranslatef(-1, 0, 0);
    gl.glRotatef(90, 0, 1, 0); // orient the cone
    myMaterialColor(tred, tred, tred, tred);
    drawCone(); // corresponds to the light source
}
gl.glPopMatrix();

gl.glRotatef(120, 0, 1, 0); // 2nd moon
gl.glPushMatrix();
{
    gl.glTranslatef(2.5f*M, 0, 0);

    drawColorCoord(WIDTH/4, WIDTH/4, WIDTH/4);
    gl.glLightfv(GL.GL_LIGHT2, GL.GL_POSITION, origin);
    gl.glLightfv(GL.GL_LIGHT2,
                 GL.GL_SPOT_DIRECTION, spot_direction);
    gl.glLightf(GL.GL_LIGHT2, GL.GL_SPOT_CUTOFF, 10f);
    myMaterialColor(green, green, green, green);
    gl.glPushMatrix();
    gl.glScalef(E/8, E/8, E/8);
    drawSphere(); // green light source
    gl.glPopMatrix();

    gl.glScaled(2.5*M, 2.5f*M*Math.tan(PI*1/18),
                2.5f*M*Math.tan(PI*1/18));
    gl.glTranslatef(-1, 0, 0);
    gl.glRotatef(90, 0, 1, 0); // orient the cone
    myMaterialColor(tgreen, tgreen, tgreen, tgreen);
    drawCone();
}
gl.glPopMatrix();

gl.glRotatef(120, 0f, 1f, 0f); // 3rd moon

gl.glTranslatef(2.5f*M, 0, 0);
```

```
    gl.glLightfv(GL.GL_LIGHT3, GL.GL_POSITION, origin);
    gl.glLightfv(GL.GL_LIGHT3,
                GL.GL_SPOT_DIRECTION, spot_direction);
    gl.glLightf(GL.GL_LIGHT3, GL.GL_SPOT_CUTOFF, 15f);
    drawColorCoord(WIDTH/4, WIDTH/4, WIDTH/4);
    myMaterialColor(blue, blue, blue, blue);
    gl.glPushMatrix();
    gl.glScalef(E/8, E/8, E/8);
    drawSphere();
    gl.glPopMatrix();

    gl.glScaled(2.5*M, 2.5*M*Math.tan(PI*15/180),
                2.5*M*Math.tan(PI*15/180));
    gl.glTranslatef(-1, 0, 0);
    gl.glRotatef(90, 0, 1, 0); // orient the cone
    myMaterialColor(tblue, tblue, tblue, tblue);
    drawCone();
    gl.glMaterialfv(GL.GL_FRONT, GL.GL_EMISSION, black);

  }

  gl.glPopMatrix();

  gl.glDepthMask(true); // allow writing into zbuffer
  gl.glDisable(GL.GL_BLEND); // no blending afterwards
  myMaterialColor(blackish, whitish, white, black);
}


public static void main(String[] args) {

  J4_2_Opaque f = new J4_2_Opaque();

  f.setTitle("JOGL J4_2_Opaque");
  f.setSize(WIDTH, HEIGHT);
  f.setVisible(true);

  }
}
```

Example *J4_3_TransLight.java* uses transparent cones to simulate the lighting volumes of the moving and rotating spotlight sources. Here the transparent cones are scaled corresponding to the lighting areas with defined cutoff angles. The light sources and cones are synchronized in their rotations.

/* cones to simulate moving spotlights */

```java
import net.java.games.jogl.*;

public class J4_3_TransLight extends J4_2_Opaque {
  float lightAngle = 0;

  public void drawSolar(float E, float e, float M, float m) {
    gl.glLineWidth(2);
    drawColorCoord(WIDTH/6, WIDTH/6, WIDTH/6);

    gl.glPushMatrix();
    {
      gl.glRotatef(e, 0, 1, 0);
      // rotating around the "sun"; proceed angle
      gl.glRotatef(tiltAngle, 0, 0, 1); // tilt angle
      gl.glTranslated(0, 2*E, 0);

      gl.glPushMatrix();
      gl.glTranslatef(0, 1.5f*E, 0);
      gl.glScalef(E*2, E*1.5f, E*2);
      drawSphere();
      gl.glPopMatrix();

      gl.glPushMatrix();
      gl.glScalef(E, 2*E, E);
      gl.glRotatef(90, 1, 0, 0); // orient the cone
      drawCone();
      gl.glPopMatrix();

      gl.glEnable(GL.GL_BLEND);
      gl.glBlendFunc(GL.GL_SRC_ALPHA,
                     GL.GL_ONE_MINUS_SRC_ALPHA);

      if (lightAngle==10) {
        flip = -1;
      }
      if (lightAngle==-85) {
        flip = 1;
      }
      lightAngle += flip;

      gl.glRotatef(m, 0, 1, 0); // 1st moon
      gl.glDepthMask(false);
      gl.glPushMatrix();
```

```
{
  gl.glTranslated(2.5*M, 0, 0);
  gl.glLineWidth(1);
  drawColorCoord(WIDTH/4, WIDTH/4, WIDTH/4);

  // light source rot up and down on earth center line
  gl.glRotatef(lightAngle, 0, 0, 1);

  gl.glLightfv(GL.GL_LIGHT1, GL.GL_POSITION, origin);
  gl.glLightfv(GL.GL_LIGHT1,
             GL.GL_SPOT_DIRECTION, spot_direction);
  gl.glLightf(GL.GL_LIGHT1, GL.GL_SPOT_CUTOFF, 15);
  gl.glPushMatrix();
  myMaterialColor(red, red, red, red);
  gl.glScalef(E/8, E/8, E/8);
  drawSphere(); // light source with cutoff=15
  gl.glPopMatrix();

  // lighting cone corresponds to the light source
  gl.glScaled(2.5*M, 2.5*M*Math.tan(PI*15/180),
             2.5*M*Math.tan(PI*15/180));
  gl.glTranslatef(-1, 0, 0);
  gl.glRotatef(90, 0, 1, 0); // orient the cone
  myMaterialColor(tred, tred, tred, tred); // trans.
  drawCone();
}
gl.glPopMatrix();

gl.glRotatef(120, 0, 1, 0); // 2nd moon
gl.glPushMatrix();
{
  gl.glTranslated(2.5*M, 0, 0);
  drawColorCoord(WIDTH/4, WIDTH/4, WIDTH/4);
  gl.glRotatef(lightAngle, 0, 0, 1);
  gl.glLightfv(GL.GL_LIGHT2, GL.GL_POSITION, origin);
  gl.glLightfv(GL.GL_LIGHT2,
             GL.GL_SPOT_DIRECTION, spot_direction);
  gl.glLightf(GL.GL_LIGHT2, GL.GL_SPOT_CUTOFF, 15f);
  myMaterialColor(green, green, green, green);
  gl.glPushMatrix();
  gl.glScalef(E/8, E/8, E/8);
  drawSphere();
  gl.glPopMatrix();

  gl.glScaled(2.5*M, 2.5*M*Math.tan(PI*15/180),
             2.5*M*Math.tan(PI*15/180));
  gl.glTranslatef(-1, 0, 0);
  gl.glRotatef(90, 0, 1, 0); // orient the cone
  myMaterialColor(tgreen, tgreen, tgreen, tgreen);
```

```
      drawCone();
   }

   gl.glPopMatrix();

   gl.glRotatef(120, 0, 1, 0); // 3rd moon
   gl.glTranslated(2.5*M, 0, 0);
   gl.glRotatef(lightAngle, 0, 0, 1);
   gl.glLightfv(GL.GL_LIGHT3, GL.GL_POSITION, origin);
   gl.glLightfv(GL.GL_LIGHT3,
               GL.GL_SPOT_DIRECTION, spot_direction);
   gl.glLightf(GL.GL_LIGHT3, GL.GL_SPOT_CUTOFF, 20f);
   drawColorCoord(WIDTH/4, WIDTH/4, WIDTH/4);
   myMaterialColor(blue, blue, blue, blue);
   gl.glPushMatrix();
   gl.glScalef(E/8, E/8, E/8);
   drawSphere();
   gl.glPopMatrix();

   gl.glScaled(2.5*M, 2.5*M*Math.tan(PI*20/180),
               2.5*M*Math.tan(PI*20/180));
   gl.glTranslatef(-1f, 0f, 0f);
   gl.glRotatef(90, 0f, 1f, 0f); // orient the cone
   myMaterialColor(tblue, tblue, tblue, tblue);
   drawCone();
   gl.glMaterialfv(GL.GL_FRONT, GL.GL_EMISSION, black);
   }
   gl.glPopMatrix();

   gl.glDepthMask(true); // allow hidden-surface removal
   gl.glDisable(GL.GL_BLEND); // turn off emission
   myMaterialColor(blackish, whitish, white, black);

}


public static void main(String[] args) {

   J4_3_TransLight f = new J4_3_TransLight();

   f.setTitle("JOGL J4_3_TransLight");
   f.setSize(WIDTH, HEIGHT);
   f.setVisible(true);
   }
}
```

4.1.3 Antialiasing

In OpenGL, antialiasing can be achieved by blending. If you call *glEnable()* with *GL_POINT_SMOOTH*, *GL_LINE_SMOOTH*, or *GL_POLYGON_SMOOTH*, OpenGL will calculate a coverage value based on the fraction of the pixel square that covers the point, line, or polygon edge with specified point size or line width and multiply the pixel's alpha value by the calculated coverage value. You can achieve antialiasing by using the resulting alpha value to blend the pixel color with the corresponding pixel color already in the frame buffer. The method is the same as the unweighted area sampling method discussed in Section 1.4.1 on page 22. You can even use *glHint()* to choose a faster or slower but better resulting quality sampling algorithm in the system. Example *J4_3_Antialiasing.java* achieves line antialiasing for all coordinates lines.

/* antialiasing through blending */

```
import net.java.games.jogl.GL;


public class J4_3_Antialiasing extends J4_3_TransLight {

  public void drawColorCoord(float xlen, float ylen,
                             float zlen) {
    boolean enabled = false;

    gl.glBlendFunc(GL.GL_SRC_ALPHA,
                   GL.GL_ONE_MINUS_SRC_ALPHA);
    gl.glHint(GL.GL_LINE_SMOOTH, GL.GL_NICEST);

    if (gl.glIsEnabled(GL.GL_BLEND)) {

      enabled = true;
    } else {

      gl.glEnable(GL.GL_BLEND);
    }

    gl.glEnable(GL.GL_LINE_SMOOTH);
    super.drawColorCoord(xlen, ylen, zlen);
    gl.glDisable(GL.GL_LINE_SMOOTH);

    // blending is only enabled for coordinates
    if (!enabled) {

      gl.glDisable(GL.GL_BLEND);
```

```
      }
   }

   public static void main(String[] args) {

      J4_3_Antialiasing f = new J4_3_Antialiasing();

      f.setTitle("JOGL J4_3_Antialiasing");
      f.setSize(WIDTH, HEIGHT);
      f.setVisible(true);
   }

}
```

4.1.4 Fog

Fog is the effect of the atmosphere between the rendered pixel and the eye, which is called the depth cuing or atmosphere attenuation effect. Fog is also achieved by blending:

$$I_\lambda = f I_{\lambda I} + (1 - f) I_{\lambda f} \qquad \text{(EQ 88)}$$

where f is the fog factor, $I_{\lambda I}$ is the incoming pixel component, and $I_{\lambda f}$ is the fog color. In OpenGL, as in Example *J4_4_Fog.java* (Fig. 4.3), the fog factor and the fog color are specified by *glFog*()*. The fog color can be the same as, or different from, the background color. The fog factor f depends on the distance (z) from the viewpoint to the pixel on the object. We can choose different equations if we specify the fog mode to *GL_EXP* (Equation 89), *GL_EXP2* (Equation 90), or *GL_LINEAR* (Equation 91):

$$f = e^{-(density \cdot z)} \qquad \text{(EQ 89)}$$

$$f = e^{-(density \cdot z)^2} \qquad \text{(EQ 90)}$$

$$f = \frac{end - z}{end - start} \qquad \text{(EQ 91)}$$

In Equation 91, when *z* changes from *start* to *end*, *f* changes from 1 to 0. According to Equation 88, the final pixel color will change from the incoming object pixel color to the fog color. Also, the distance *z* is from the viewpoint to the pixel under consideration. The viewpoint is at the origin, and the pixel's location is its initial location transformed by the MODELVIEW matrix at the drawing. It has nothing to do with PROJECTION transformation.

We may supply *GL_FOG_HINT* with *glHint()* to specify whether fog calculations are per pixel (*GL_NICEST*) or per vertex (*GL_FASTEST*) or whatever the system has (*GL_DONT_CARE*).

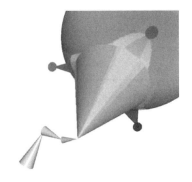

Fig. 4.3 Fog in OpenGL [*See Color Plate 4*]

/* fog and background colors */

```
import net.java.games.jogl.*;

public class J4_4_Fog extends J4_3_TransLight {

  public void init(GLDrawable glDrawable) {

    float fogColor[] = {0.3f, 0.3f, 0.0f, 1f};

    super.init(glDrawable);

    gl.glClearColor(0.3f, 0.3f, 0.1f, 1.0f);

    // lighting is calculated with viewpoint at origin
    // and models are transformed by MODELVIEW matrix
    // in our example, models are moved into -z by PROJECTION

    gl.glEnable(GL.GL_BLEND);
    gl.glEnable(GL.GL_FOG);

    // gl.glFogi (GL.GL_FOG_MODE, GL.GL_EXP);
    // gl.glFogi (GL.GL_FOG_MODE, GL.GL_EXP2);
    gl.glFogi(GL.GL_FOG_MODE, GL.GL_LINEAR);
    gl.glFogfv(GL.GL_FOG_COLOR, fogColor);
```

```
    // gl.glFogf (GL.GL_FOG_DENSITY, (float)(0.5/width));
    gl.glHint(GL.GL_FOG_HINT, GL.GL_NICEST);
    gl.glFogf(GL.GL_FOG_START, 0.1f*WIDTH);
    gl.glFogf(GL.GL_FOG_END, 0.5f*WIDTH);
  }

  public static void main(String[] args) {

    J4_4_Fog f = new J4_4_Fog();

    f.setTitle("JOGL J4_4_Fog");
    f.setSize(WIDTH, HEIGHT);
    f.setVisible(true);
  }
}
```

4.2 *Images*

We have discussed rendering and scan-converting 3D models. The result is an image, or an array of RGBAs stored in the frame buffer. Instead of going through transformation, viewing, hidden-surface removal, lighting, and other graphics manipulations, OpenGL provides some basic functions that manipulate image data in the frame buffer directly: *glReadPixels()* reads a rectangular array of pixels from the frame buffer into the (computer main) memory, *glDrawPixels()* writes a rectangular array of pixels into the frame buffer from the memory, *glBitmap()* writes a single bitmap (a binary image) into the frame buffer from the main memory, etc. The function *glRasterPos3f(x, y, z)* specifies the current raster position (*x, y, z*) where the system starts reading or writing. The position (*x, y, z*), however, goes through the transformation pipeline as a vertex in a 3D model. For example, if you want an image to be attached to a vertex (*x, y, z*) of a model, *glRasterPos3f(x, y, z)* will help decide where to display the image.

As an example, in Section 1.3.3 on page 20 we discussed bitmap fonts and outline (stroke) fonts. Bitmap fonts are images, which go into the frame buffer directly. Outline (stroke) fonts are 3D models, which go through transformation and viewing pipeline before scan-converted into the frame buffer.

The image data stored in the memory might consist of just the overall intensity of each pixel (R+G+B), or the RGBA components, respectively. As image data is transferred from memory into the frame buffer, or from the frame buffer into memory, OpenGL can perform several operations on it, such as magnifying or reducing the data if necessary. Also, there are certain formats for storing data in the memory that are required or are more efficient on certain kinds of hardware. We use *glPixelStore*()* to set the pixel-storage mode of how data is unpacked from the memory into the frame buffer or from the frame buffer into the memory. For example,

Fig. 4.4 **Image background** [*See Color Plate 4*]

gl.glPixelStorei(GL.GL_UNPACK_ALIGNMENT, 1) specifies that the pixels are aligned in memory one byte after another to be unpacked into the frame buffer accordingly. Example *J4_5_Image.java* (Fig. 4.4) uses Java's BufferedImage Class to instantiate and read a jpeg image from a file into an array in the memory, and then uses OpenGL imaging functions to draw the image array into the frame buffer directly as the background of the 3D rendering.

/* write an image into the frame buffer */

```
import java.awt.image.*;
import net.java.games.jogl.*;
import java.io.*;
import javax.imageio.*;


public class J4_5_Image extends J4_3_TransLight {
   static byte[] img;
   static int imgW, imgH, imgType;

   public void init(GLDrawable glDrawable) {

      super.init(glDrawable);

      readImage("STARS.JPG"); // read the image to img[]
      gl.glPixelStorei(GL.GL_UNPACK_ALIGNMENT, 1);
   }
```

```
public void display(GLDrawable drawable) {

  gl.glClear(GL.GL_COLOR_BUFFER_BIT
            |GL.GL_DEPTH_BUFFER_BIT);

  drawImage(-1.95f*WIDTH, -1.95f*HEIGHT, -1.99f*WIDTH);
  // remember : gl.glFrustum(-w/4,w/4,-h/4,h/4,w/2,4*w);
  //gl.glTranslatef(0, 0, -2*w);

  displayView();
}


public void readImage(String fileName) {
  File f = new File(fileName);
  BufferedImage bufimg;

  try {
    // read the image into BufferredImage structure
    bufimg = ImageIO.read(f);
    imgW = bufimg.getWidth();
    imgH = bufimg.getHeight();
    imgType = bufimg.getType();
    System.out.println("BufferedImage type: "+imgType);
    //TYPE_BYTE_GRAY  10
    //TYPE_3BYTE_BGR 5

    // retrieve the pixel array in raster's databuffer
    Raster raster = bufimg.getData();

    DataBufferByte dataBufByte = (DataBufferByte)raster.
                                 getDataBuffer();
    img = dataBufByte.getData();
    System.out.println("Image data's type: "+
                       dataBufByte.getDataType());
    // TYPE_BYTE 0

  } catch (IOException ex) {
    System.exit(1);
  }
}


protected void drawImage(float x, float y, float z) {

  gl.glRasterPos3f(x, y, z);
  gl.glDrawPixels(imgW, imgH, GL.GL_LUMINANCE,
                  GL.GL_UNSIGNED_BYTE, img);
}
```

```
public void displayView() {
  cnt++;
  depth = (cnt/100)%5;

  if (cnt%60==0) {
    dalpha = -dalpha;
    dbeta = -dbeta;
    dgama = -dgama;
  }
  alpha += dalpha;
  beta += dbeta;
  gama += dgama;

  gl.glPushMatrix();
  if (cnt%500>300) {
    // look at the solar system from the moon
    myCamera(A, B, C, alpha, beta, gama);
  }

  drawRobot(O, A, B, C, alpha, beta, gama);
  gl.glPopMatrix();

  try {
    Thread.sleep(15);
  } catch (Exception ignore) {}
}


public static void main(String[] args) {
  J4_5_Image f = new J4_5_Image();

  f.setTitle("JOGL J4_5_Image");
  f.setSize(WIDTH, HEIGHT);
  f.setVisible(true);
}
}
```

4.3 Texture Mapping

In graphics rendering, an image can be mapped onto the surface of a model. That is, when writing the color of a pixel into the frame buffer, the graphics system can use a color retrieved from an image. To do this we need to provide a piece of image called *texture. Texture mapping* is a process of using the texture pixels (namely *texels*) to modify or replace the model's corresponding pixels during scan-conversion. Texture mapping allows many choices. Here we introduce some basics with a couple of examples in texture mapping.

4.3.1 Pixel and Texel Relations

Let's consider mapping a square texture onto a rectangular polygon (Example *J4_6_Texture.java*).

First, we need to specify the corresponding vertices of the texture and the polygon. In OpenGL, this is done by associating each vertex in the texture with a vertex in the polygon, which is similar to the way of specifying each vertex normal. Given a point (s, t) in the 2D texture, the s and t are in the range of [0, 1]. *glTexCoord2f(s, t)* corresponds to a point in the texture. In our example, the points are the vertices of the texture, and the OpenGL system stretches or shrinks the texture to map exactly onto the polygon.

Second, in OpenGL, when the texture is smaller than the polygon, the system stretches the texture to match the polygon (magnification). Otherwise, the system shrinks the texture (minification). Either way the pixels corresponding to the texels after stretching or shrinking need to be calculated. The algorithms to calculate the mapping are called the magnification filter or minification filter (*GL_TEXTURE_MAG_FILTER* or *GL_TEXTURE_MIN_FILTER*), which are discussed below.

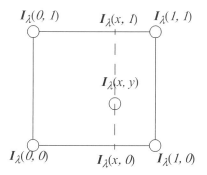

Fig. 4.5 Interpolation (GL_LINEAR)

Given a pixel location in the polygon, we can find its corresponding point in the texture. This point may be on a texel, on the line between two texels, or in the square with four texels at the corners as shown in Fig. 4.5. The resulting color of the point needs to be calculated. The simplest method OpenGL uses is to choose the texel that is nearest to the point as the mapping of the pixel (*GL_NEAREST*, as in *gl.glTexParameteri(GL.GL_TEXTURE_2D, GL.GL_TEXTURE_MIN_FILTER,*

GL.GL_NEAREST)), which in this case is $I_\lambda(x,y) = I_\lambda(1,0)$. We can also bi-linearly interpolate the four texels according to their distances to the point to find the mapping of the pixel (*GL_LINEAR*), which is smoother but slower than *GL_NEAREST* method. That is, first-pass linear interpolations are along x axis direction for two intermediate values:

$$I_\lambda(x, 0) = x I_\lambda(1, 0) + (1 - x) I_\lambda(0, 0) \qquad \textbf{(EQ 92)}$$

$$I_\lambda(x, 1) = x I_\lambda(1, 1) + (1 - x) I_\lambda(0, 1) \qquad \textbf{(EQ 93)}$$

and second-pass linear interpolation is along y axis direction for the final result:

$$I_\lambda(x, y) = y I_\lambda(x, 1) + (1 - y) I_\lambda(x, 0) \qquad \textbf{(EQ 94)}$$

Third, at each pixel, the calculated texel color components (texel RGBA represented by C_t and A_t) can be used to either replace or change (modulate, decal, or blend) incoming pixel color components (which is also called a fragment and is represented by C_f and A_f). A texture environment color (C_c), which is specified by *gl.glTexEnvf(GL.GL_TEXTURE_ENV, GL.GL_TEXTURE_ENV_COLOR, parameter)*, can also be used to modify the final color components (represented as C_v and A_v).

A texel can have up to four components. L_t indicates a one-component texture. A two-component texture has L_t and A_t. A three-component texture has C_t. A four-component texture has both C_t and A_t.

If the texels replace the pixels, lighting will not affect the appearance of the polygon (*gl.glTexEnvf(GL.GL_TEXTURE_ENV, GL.GL_TEXTURE_ENV_MODE, GL.GL_REPLACE)*). If the texel components are used to modulate the pixel components, each texture color component is multiplied by the corresponding pixel color component, and the original color and shading of the polygon are partially preserved. The following table lists all the corresponding functions for different mode:

glTexEnvf(GL_TEXTURE_ENV, GL_TEXTURE_VNV_MODE, *Parameter*).

Internal Formats	GL_ MODULATE	GL_DECAL	GL_BLEND	GL_ REPLACE	GL_ADD
1 or GL_ LUMINANCE	$C_v=L_tC_f$ $A_v=A_f$	*Undefined*	$C_v=(1-L_t)C_f$ $+L_tC_c; A_v=A_f$	$C_v=L_t$ $A_v=A_f$	$C_v=C_f+L_t$ $A_v=A_f$
2 or GL_ LUMINANCE _ALPHA	$C_v=L_tC_f$ $A_v=A_tA_f$	*Undefined*	$C_v=(1-L_t)C_f$ $+L_tC_c; A_v=A_tA_f$	$C_v=L_t$ $A_v=A_t$	$C_v=C_f+L_t$ $A_v=A_fA_t$
3 or GL_ RGB	$C_v=C_tC_f$ $A_v=A_f$	$C_v=C_t$ $A_v=A_f$	$C_v=(1-C_t)C_f$ $+C_tC_c; A_v=A_f$	$C_v=C_t$ $A_v=A_f$	$C_v=C_f$ $+Ct A_v=A_f$
4 or GL_ RGBA	$C_v=C_tC_f$ $A_v=A_tA_f$	$C_v=(1-A_t)C_f$ $+A_tC_t; A_v=A_f$	$C_v=(1-C_t)C_f$ $+C_tC_c; A_v=A_tA_f$	$C_v=C_t$ $A_v=A_t$	$C_v=C_f+C_t$ $A_v=A_fA_t$

Example *J4_6_Texture.java* maps an image to a polygon. Although Example *J4_5_Image.java* and Example *J4_6_Texture.java* executions look the same, the approaches are totally different.

/* simple texture mapping */

```
import net.java.games.jogl.*;


public class J4_6_Texture extends J4_5_Image {

  public void init(GLDrawable glDrawable) {
    super.init(glDrawable); // stars_image[] available
    initTexture(); // texture parameters initiated
  }


  public void display(GLDrawable drawable) {
    gl.glClear(GL.GL_COLOR_BUFFER_BIT
             |GL.GL_DEPTH_BUFFER_BIT);

    // texture on a quad covering most of the drawing area
    drawTexture(-2.5f*WIDTH, -2.5f*HEIGHT, -2.0f*WIDTH);
```

```
      displayView();
    }


    void initTexture() {
      gl.glTexParameteri(GL.GL_TEXTURE_2D,
            GL.GL_TEXTURE_MIN_FILTER, GL.GL_NEAREST);
      gl.glTexParameteri(GL.GL_TEXTURE_2D,
            GL.GL_TEXTURE_MAG_FILTER, GL.GL_NEAREST);
      gl.glTexImage2D(GL.GL_TEXTURE_2D, 0, GL.GL_LUMINANCE,
                    imgW, imgH, 0, GL.GL_LUMINANCE,
                    GL.GL_UNSIGNED_BYTE, img);
    }


    public void drawTexture(float x, float y, float z) {

      gl.glTexEnvf(GL.GL_TEXTURE_ENV, GL.GL_TEXTURE_ENV_MODE,
                  GL.GL_REPLACE);

      gl.glEnable(GL.GL_TEXTURE_2D);
      {
        gl.glBegin(GL.GL_QUADS);
        gl.glTexCoord2f(0.0f, 1.0f);
        gl.glVertex3f(x, y, z);
        gl.glTexCoord2f(1.0f, 1.0f);
        gl.glVertex3f(-x, y, z);
        gl.glTexCoord2f(1.0f, 0.0f);
        gl.glVertex3f(-x, -y, z);
        gl.glTexCoord2f(0.0f, 0.0f);
        gl.glVertex3f(x, -y, z);
        gl.glEnd();
      }
      gl.glDisable(GL.GL_TEXTURE_2D);
    }


    public static void main(String[] args) {
      J4_6_Texture f = new J4_6_Texture();

      f.setTitle("JOGL J4_6_Texture");
      f.setSize(WIDTH, HEIGHT);
      f.setVisible(true);
    }
  }
```

4.3.2 Texture Objects

If we use several textures in the same program (Fig. 4.6), we may load them into texture memory and associate individual texture parameters with their texture names before rendering. This way we do not need to load textures and their parameters from the disk files during rendering, which would otherwise be very slow. In OpenGL, this is done by calling *glGenTextures()* and *glBindTexture()*. When we call *glGenTextures()*, we can generate the texture names or texture objects. When we call *glBindTexture()* with a texture name, all subsequent *glTex*()* commands that specify the texture and its associated parameters are saved in the memory

Fig. 4.6 Multiple texture objects [*See* **Color Plate 5**]

corresponding to the named texture. After that, in the program, whenever we call *glBindTexture()* with a specific texture name, all drawing will employ the current bound texture. The example is shown in the next section.

4.3.3 Texture Coordinates

In OpenGL, *glTexCoord2f(s, t)* corresponds to a point in the texture, and *s* and *t* are in the range of [0, 1]. If the points are on the boundaries of the texture, then we stretch or shrink the entire texture to fit exactly onto the polygon. Otherwise, only a portion of the texture is used to map onto the polygon. For example, if we have a polygonal cylinder with four polygons and we want to wrap the texture around the cylinder (Example *J4_7_TexObjects.java*), we can divide the texture into four pieces with *s* in the range of [0, 0.25], [0.25, 0.5], [0.5, 0.75], and [0.75, 1.0]. When mapping a rectangular texture onto a sphere around the axis, texture geodesic distortion happens, especially toward the poles.

If we specify *glTexCoord2f(2, t)*, we mean to repeat the texture twice in the *s* direction. That is, we will squeeze two pieces of the texture in *s* direction into the polygon. If we specify *glTexCoord2f(1.5, t)*, we mean to repeat the texture 1.5 times in the *s* direction. In order to achieve texture repeating in *s* direction, we need to specify the following: *glTexParameteri(GL_TEXTURE_2D, GL_TEXTURE_WRAP_S, GL_REPEAT)*. In

OpenGL, the texture should have width and height in the form of 2^m number of pixels, where the width and height can be different.

/* Example 4.7.texobjects.c: texture objects and coordinates */

```java
import net.java.games.jogl.*;


public class J4_7_TexObjects extends J4_6_Texture {
  // name for texture objects
  static final int[] IRIS_TEX = new int[1];
  static final int[] EARTH_TEX = new int[1];
  static final int[] STARS_TEX = new int[1];

  void initTexture() {

// initialize IRIS1 texture obj
    gl.glGenTextures(1, IRIS_TEX);
    gl.glBindTexture(GL.GL_TEXTURE_2D, IRIS_TEX[0]);
    gl.glTexParameteri(GL.GL_TEXTURE_2D,
                       GL.GL_TEXTURE_MIN_FILTER,
                       GL.GL_LINEAR);
    gl.glTexParameteri(GL.GL_TEXTURE_2D,
                       GL.GL_TEXTURE_MAG_FILTER,
                       GL.GL_LINEAR);
    readImage("IRIS1.JPG");
    gl.glTexImage2D(GL.GL_TEXTURE_2D, 0, GL.GL_RGB8,
                    imgW, imgH, 0, GL.GL_BGR,
                    GL.GL_UNSIGNED_BYTE, img);

// initialize EARTH texture obj
    gl.glGenTextures(1, EARTH_TEX);
    gl.glBindTexture(GL.GL_TEXTURE_2D, EARTH_TEX[0]);
    gl.glTexParameteri(GL.GL_TEXTURE_2D,
      GL.GL_TEXTURE_MIN_FILTER, GL.GL_LINEAR);
    gl.glTexParameteri(GL.GL_TEXTURE_2D,
      GL.GL_TEXTURE_MAG_FILTER, GL.GL_LINEAR);
    readImage("EARTH2.JPG");
    gl.glTexImage2D(GL.GL_TEXTURE_2D, 0, GL.GL_RGB8,
                    imgW, imgH, 0, GL.GL_BGR,
                    GL.GL_UNSIGNED_BYTE, img);

// initialize STARS texture obj
    gl.glGenTextures(1, STARS_TEX);
    gl.glBindTexture(GL.GL_TEXTURE_2D, STARS_TEX[0]);
    gl.glTexParameteri(GL.GL_TEXTURE_2D,
                       GL.GL_TEXTURE_WRAP_S, GL.GL_REPEAT);
```

```
  gl.glTexParameteri(GL.GL_TEXTURE_2D,
                     GL.GL_TEXTURE_WRAP_T, GL.GL_REPEAT);
  gl.glTexParameteri(GL.GL_TEXTURE_2D,
                     GL.GL_TEXTURE_MIN_FILTER,
                     GL.GL_NEAREST);
  gl.glTexParameteri(GL.GL_TEXTURE_2D,
                     GL.GL_TEXTURE_MAG_FILTER,
                     GL.GL_NEAREST);
  readImage("STARS.JPG");
  gl.glTexImage2D(GL.GL_TEXTURE_2D, 0, GL.GL_LUMINANCE,
                  imgW, imgH, 0, GL.GL_LUMINANCE,
                  GL.GL_UNSIGNED_BYTE, img);
}


public void drawSphere() {

  if ((cnt%1000)<500) {
    gl.glBindTexture(GL.GL_TEXTURE_2D, EARTH_TEX[0]);
  } else {
    gl.glBindTexture(GL.GL_TEXTURE_2D, IRIS_TEX[0]);
  }
  gl.glTexEnvf(GL.GL_TEXTURE_ENV, GL.GL_TEXTURE_ENV_MODE,
               GL.GL_MODULATE);

  if (cnt%1111<900) { // could turn texture off
    gl.glEnable(GL.GL_TEXTURE_2D);
  }

  subdivideSphere(sVdata[0], sVdata[1], sVdata[2], depth);
  subdivideSphere(sVdata[0], sVdata[2], sVdata[4], depth);
  subdivideSphere(sVdata[0], sVdata[4], sVdata[5], depth);
  subdivideSphere(sVdata[0], sVdata[5], sVdata[1], depth);

  subdivideSphere(sVdata[3], sVdata[1], sVdata[5], depth);
  subdivideSphere(sVdata[3], sVdata[5], sVdata[4], depth);
  subdivideSphere(sVdata[3], sVdata[4], sVdata[2], depth);
  subdivideSphere(sVdata[3], sVdata[2], sVdata[1], depth);

  gl.glDisable(GL.GL_TEXTURE_2D);

  if (cnt%800<400) { // for the background texture
    gl.glBindTexture(GL.GL_TEXTURE_2D, STARS_TEX[0]);
  } else {
    gl.glBindTexture(GL.GL_TEXTURE_2D, IRIS_TEX[0]);
  }
}
```

```java
public void drawSphereTriangle(float v1[],
                               float v2[], float v3[]) {
  float[] s1 = new float[1], t1 = new float[1];
  float[] s2 = new float[1], t2 = new float[1];
  float[] s3 = new float[1], t3 = new float[1];

  texCoord(v1, s1, t1);
  texCoord(v2, s2, t2);
  texCoord(v3, s3, t3);

  // for coord at z=0
  if (s1[0]==-1.0f) {
    s1[0] = (s2[0]+s3[0])/2;
  } else if (s2[0]==-1.0f) {
    s2[0] = (s1[0]+s3[0])/2;
  } else if (s3[0]==-1.0f) {
    s3[0] = (s2[0]+s1[0])/2;
  }

  gl.glBegin(GL.GL_TRIANGLES);

  gl.glTexCoord2f(s1[0], t1[0]);
  gl.glNormal3fv(v1);
  gl.glVertex3fv(v1);
  gl.glTexCoord2f(s2[0], t2[0]);
  gl.glNormal3fv(v2);
  gl.glVertex3fv(v2);
  gl.glTexCoord2f(s3[0], t3[0]);
  gl.glNormal3fv(v3);
  gl.glVertex3fv(v3);

  gl.glEnd();
}


public void texCoord(float v[], float s[], float t[]) {
  // given the vertex on a sphere, find its texture (s,t)
  float x, y, z, PI = 3.14159f, PI2 = 6.283f;

  x = v[0];
  y = v[1];
  z = v[2];

  if (x>0) {
    if (z>0) {
      s[0] = (float)Math.atan(z/x)/PI2;
    } else {
      s[0] = 1f+(float)Math.atan(z/x)/PI2;
    }
```

```
  } else if (x<0) {
    s[0] = 0.5f+(float)Math.atan(z/x)/PI2;
  } else {
    if (z>0) {
      s[0] = 0.25f;
    }
    if (z<0) {
      s[0] = 0.75f;
    }
    if (z==0) {
      s[0] = -1.0f;
    }
  }
  t[0] = (float)Math.acos(y)/PI;
}


public void subdivideCyl(float v1[], float v2[],
                         int depth, float t1, float t2) {
  float v11[] = {0, 0, 0};
  float v22[] = {0, 0, 0};
  float v00[] = {0, 0, 0};
  float v12[] = {0, 0, 0};
  float v01[] = {0, 0, 0};
  float v02[] = {0, 0, 0};
  int i;

  if (depth==0) {
    drawBottom(v00, v1, v2);
    for (i = 0; i<3; i++) {
      v01[i] = v11[i] = v1[i];
      v02[i] = v22[i] = v2[i];
    }
    // the height of the cone along z axis
    v11[2] = v22[2] = 1;

    gl.glBegin(GL.GL_POLYGON);
    // draw the rectangles around the cylinder
    gl.glNormal3fv(v2);
    gl.glTexCoord2f(t1, 0.0f);
    gl.glVertex3fv(v1);
    gl.glTexCoord2f(t2, 0.0f);
    gl.glVertex3fv(v2);
    gl.glNormal3fv(v1);
    gl.glTexCoord2f(t2, 1.0f);
    gl.glVertex3fv(v22);
    gl.glTexCoord2f(t1, 1.0f);
    gl.glVertex3fv(v11);
    gl.glEnd();
```

```
      v00[2] = 1;
      drawBottom(v22, v11, v00); // draw the other bottom

      return;
    }
    v12[0] = v1[0]+v2[0];
    v12[1] = v1[1]+v2[1];
    v12[2] = v1[2]+v2[2];

    normalize(v12);

    subdivideCyl(v1, v12, depth-1, t1, (t2+t1)/2);
    subdivideCyl(v12, v2, depth-1, (t2+t1)/2, t2);
  }


  public void drawCylinder() {
    if ((cnt%1000)<500) {
      gl.glBindTexture(GL.GL_TEXTURE_2D, IRIS_TEX[0]);
    } else {
      gl.glBindTexture(GL.GL_TEXTURE_2D, EARTH_TEX[0]);
    }

    if (cnt%1100<980) { // turn off texture sometimes
      gl.glEnable(GL.GL_TEXTURE_2D);
    }

    subdivideCyl(cVdata[0], cVdata[1], depth, 0f, 0.25f);
    subdivideCyl(cVdata[1], cVdata[2], depth, 0.25f, 0.5f);
    subdivideCyl(cVdata[2], cVdata[3], depth, 0.5f, 0.75f);
    subdivideCyl(cVdata[3], cVdata[0], depth, 0.75f, 1.0f);
    gl.glDisable(GL.GL_TEXTURE_2D);
  }


  public static void main(String[] args) {
    J4_7_TexObjects f = new J4_7_TexObjects();

    f.setTitle("JOGL J4_7_TexObjects");
    f.setSize(WIDTH, HEIGHT);
    f.setVisible(true);
  }
}
```

4.3.4 Levels of Detail in Texture Mapping

In perspective projection, models further away from the viewpoint will appear smaller, and we cannot see that much detail. At the same time, for texture mapping, a large texture will need to be filtered by the minification filter to a much smaller size of the projected primitive (image). If the texture is significantly smaller than the original image, the filtering process takes time and the result may appear flashing or shimmering, as the texture on the cylinders in Example *J_4_7_TexObjects.java*.

OpenGL allows specifying multiple levels of detail (LOD) images at different resolutions for texture mapping. OpenGL will choose the appropriate texture image(s) according to the corresponding projected image size automatically. The different LOD images are called *mipmaps*, which must be at the dimension of power of 2. If you use LOD in OpenGL, you have to specify all mipmaps from the largest image down to the size of 1×1. For example, for a size 512×512 size image, you have to specify 512×512, 256×256, 128×128, 64×64, 32×32, 16×16, 8×8, 4×4, 2×2, and 1×1 texture images. The second parameter in *glTexImage2D()* when specifying a texture image is the *level* (of detail) of the current image, from 0 the largest image up to the 1×1 image. As shown in Example *J_4_8_Mipmap.java*, the levels are 0, 1, ..., 9 for the image sizes of 512×512, 256×256, ..., 1×1. Also, the minification filter has to be specified to choose the nearest mipmap image for texture mapping (*glTexParameteri(GL_TEXTURE_2D, GL_TEXTURE_MIN_FILTER, GL_NEAREST_MIPMAP_NEAREST)*) or linear for interpolation between the two closest textures in size to the projected primitive: (*glTexParameteri(GL_TEXTURE_2D, GL_TEXTURE_MIN_FILTER, GL_NEAREST_MIPMAP_LINEAR)*). The animation displayed in *J_4_8_Mipmap.java* does not have the shimmering effect.

/* Multiple LOD in OpenGL - mipmaps */

```
import net.java.games.jogl.*;

public class J4_8_Mipmap extends J4_7_TexObjects {
  public void init(GLDrawable glDrawable) {

    super.init(glDrawable); // texture objects available

    // Redifine LOD mipmap for IRIS
    gl.glBindTexture(GL.GL_TEXTURE_2D, IRIS_TEX[0]);
```

```
gl.glTexParameteri(GL.GL_TEXTURE_2D,
                   GL.GL_TEXTURE_MIN_FILTER,
                   GL.GL_LINEAR_MIPMAP_LINEAR);

readImage("IRIS1.JPG");
gl.glTexImage2D(GL.GL_TEXTURE_2D, 0, GL.GL_RGB8,
                imgW, imgH, 0, GL.GL_BGR,
                GL.GL_UNSIGNED_BYTE, img);

readImage("IRIS1_256_256.JPG");
gl.glTexImage2D(GL.GL_TEXTURE_2D, 1, GL.GL_RGB8,
                imgW, imgH, 0, GL.GL_BGR,
                GL.GL_UNSIGNED_BYTE, img);

readImage("IRIS1_128_128.JPG");
gl.glTexImage2D(GL.GL_TEXTURE_2D, 2, GL.GL_RGB8,
                imgW, imgH, 0, GL.GL_BGR,
                GL.GL_UNSIGNED_BYTE, img);

readImage("IRIS1_64_64.JPG");
gl.glTexImage2D(GL.GL_TEXTURE_2D, 3, GL.GL_RGB8,
                imgW, imgH, 0, GL.GL_BGR,
                GL.GL_UNSIGNED_BYTE, img);

readImage("IRIS1_32_32.JPG");
gl.glTexImage2D(GL.GL_TEXTURE_2D, 4, GL.GL_RGB8,
                imgW, imgH, 0, GL.GL_BGR,
                GL.GL_UNSIGNED_BYTE, img);

readImage("IRIS1_16_16.JPG");
gl.glTexImage2D(GL.GL_TEXTURE_2D, 5, GL.GL_RGB8,
                imgW, imgH, 0, GL.GL_BGR,
                GL.GL_UNSIGNED_BYTE, img);

readImage("IRIS1_8_8.JPG");
gl.glTexImage2D(GL.GL_TEXTURE_2D, 6, GL.GL_RGB8,
                imgW, imgH, 0, GL.GL_BGR,
                GL.GL_UNSIGNED_BYTE, img);

readImage("IRIS1_4_4.JPG");
gl.glTexImage2D(GL.GL_TEXTURE_2D, 7, GL.GL_RGB8,
                imgW, imgH, 0, GL.GL_BGR,
                GL.GL_UNSIGNED_BYTE, img);

readImage("IRIS1_2_2.JPG");
gl.glTexImage2D(GL.GL_TEXTURE_2D, 8, GL.GL_RGB8,
                imgW, imgH, 0, GL.GL_BGR,
                GL.GL_UNSIGNED_BYTE, img);
```

```
    readImage("IRIS1_1_1.JPG");
    gl.glTexImage2D(GL.GL_TEXTURE_2D, 9, GL.GL_RGB8,
                    imgW, imgH, 0, GL.GL_BGR,
                    GL.GL_UNSIGNED_BYTE, img);
}


  public static void main(String[] args) {
    J4_8_Mipmap f = new J4_8_Mipmap();

    f.setTitle("JOGL J4_8_Mipmap");
    f.setSize(WIDTH, HEIGHT);
    f.setVisible(true);
  }
}
```

4.4 Review Questions

1. Alpha blending is used for transparency, antialiasing, and so on. Please list all the applications we have learned in this chapter.

2. Please list the order of operation for the following:

(___). drawTransparentObject();   (___). glDepthMask(GL_FALSE)
(___). drawOpaqueObject();   (___). glDepthMask(GL_TRUE)

3. *Fog* is calculated according to which of the following distances?

a. from the light source to the viewpoint   b. from the viewpoint to the pixel
c. from the pixel to the light source   d. from the light source to the origin
e. from the origin to the viewpoint   f. from the pixel to the origin

4. glutBitmapString() will draw a string of bitmap characters at the current raster position. glutStrokeString() will draw a string of stroke characters at the current raster position. Please explain the differences between glutBitmapString() and glutStrokeString() in detail.

5. We have a rectangular image, and we'll wrap it around a cylinder, a sphere, and a cone as described earlier in the book. Please develop your methods of calculating your texture coordinates, and explain the distortions if any.

6. In OpenGL *texture mapping*, what is a <u>texture object</u>?

a. A 3D model on display   b. A name with associated data saved in the memory
c. A texture file   d. A blending of texture and material

| 7. Judging from the code on the right, which of the following is likely false about the complete program?

a. It has translucent objects
b. It has hidden surface removal
c. It has a moving light source
d. It has fogs in the environment
e. It has a sphere moving with a light source | ...
glEnable (GL_BLEND);
glDepthMask (GL_FALSE);
glBlendFunc (GL_SRC_ALPHA, GL_ONE);
glMaterialfv(GL_FRONT, GL_DIFFUSE, red);
glPushMatrix();
glRotatef(m, 0.0, 1.0, 0.);
glLightfv(GL_LIGHT1, GL_POSITION, pos);
drawSphere();
glPopMatrix();
glDisable (GL_BLEND); glDepthMask
    (GL_TRUE);
... |

8. Given a 3D cube with end points values A(0, 0 , 0) = a, B(0, 0, 1) = b, C(1, 0, 1) = c, D(1, 0, 0) = d, E(0, 1, 0) = e, F(0, 1, 1) = f, G(1, 1, 1) = g, and H(1, 1, 0) = h, please use tri-linear interpolation to calculate a point's value inside the cube at an arbitrary position P(x,y,z).

9. Calculate the intersection of an arbitrary line from the center of a cube and the cube's face.

4.5 Programming Assignments

1. Draw randomly generated lines with antialiasing at changeable width using OpenGL functions.

2. Please implement two functions myBitmapString() and myStrokeString() that simulate their glut counterparts. Here you cannot call any font drawing functions to achieve the goal.

3. Draw a generalized solar system on a robot arm with the earth transparent and the moons opaque. The center of the earth is a light source.

4. Extend J4_8_MipMap.java so that the cones are covered by an image of your choice. The image on the cone should be distorted.

5. Take 6 pictures in an environment so that you can form a cube with the 6 pictures. Then, consider our earth is a silver sphere in the center of the cube. Each sphere triangle's vertex is a ray penetrating the cube. In other words, each triangle has three intersections on the cube. Now, if we consider the 6 pictures as 6 texture objects, we can use the intersection to set up corresponding texture mapping. For a triangle penetrating more than one texture object, you can choose just one texture object and do something at your preference. Please implement such a texture mapping, and display a solid sphere in a transparent cube with texture mapping.

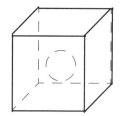

5
Curved Models

Chapter Objectives:

- Introduce existing 3D model functions in GLUT and GLU libraries

- Introduce theories and programming of basic cubic curves and bi-cubic curved surfaces

5.1 Introduction

Just as that there are numerous scan-conversion methods for a primitive, there exists different ways to create a 3D model as well. For example, we can create a sphere model through subdivision as discussed in Chapter 2. We can also use a sphere equation to find all the points on the sphere and render it accordingly. Further, we can find a set of points on a circle in the xy plane and rotate the points along x or y axis to find all the points on the corresponding sphere. Although generating 3D models is not exactly basic graphics drawing capabilities, it is part of the graphics theory. In this chapter, we introduce some existing 3D models and the corresponding function calls in GLUT and GLU libraries. Also, we provide the math foundations for some curved 3D models, including quadratic surfaces, cubic curves, and bi-cubic surfaces.

The degree of an equation with one variable in each term is the exponent of the highest power to which that variable is raised in the equation. For example, $(ax^2 + bx + c = 0)$ is a second-degree equation, as x is raised to the power of 2. When more than one variable appears in a term, as in $(axy^2 + bx + cy + d = 0)$, it is necessary to add the exponents of the variables within a term to get the degree of the equation, which is 3 in this example. Quadratic curves and surfaces are represented by second-degree equations. Cubic curves are third-degree equations.

5.2 Quadratic Surfaces

Quadratic surfaces, or simply quadrics, are defined by the following general form second-degree (quadratic) equation:

$$ax^2 + by^2 + cz^2 + dxy + exz + fyz + gx + hy + iz + j = 0. \qquad \text{(EQ 95)}$$

There are numerous models that can be generated by the above equation, including spheres, ellipsoids, cones, and cylinders.

5.2.1 Sphere

In Cartesian coordinates, a sphere at the origin with radius r is

$$x^2 + y^2 + z^2 = r^2. \qquad \text{(EQ 96)}$$

In parametric equation form, a sphere is

$$x = r\cos\phi\cos\theta, \quad 0 \le \phi \le \pi, \qquad \text{(EQ 97)}$$

$$y = r\cos\phi\sin\theta, \quad 0 \le \theta \le 2\pi, \qquad \text{(EQ 98)}$$

$$\text{and } z = r\sin\phi. \qquad \text{(EQ 99)}$$

So we can find all the points on a sphere through a double for-loop:

```
for (int i=0; i<nLongitudes; i++)
for (j=0; j<nLatitudes; i++)
   drawSherePoint (
      r*cos(i*PI/nLongitudes)*cos(j*2*PI/nLatitudes),
      r*cos(i*PI/nLongitudes)*sin(j*2*PI/nLatitudes),
      r*sin(i*PI/nLongitudes));
```

Both GLUT and GLU provide wireframe or solid sphere drawing functions, which are demonstrated in Example *J5_1_Quadrics.java*. In C binding:

```
// Using GLUT to draw a sphere
glutWireSphere(r, nLongitudes, nLatitudes);
glutSolidSphere(r, nLongitudes, nLatitudes);


// USING GLU to draw a sphere
GLUquadric *sphere = gluNewQuadric();
gluQuadricDrawStyle(shpere, GLU_LINE); //GLU_FILL
glusphere(sphere, r, nLongitudes, nLatitudes);
```

5.2.2 Ellipsoid

In Cartesian coordinates, an ellipsoid at the origin is

$$\left(\frac{x}{r_X}\right)^2 + \left(\frac{y}{r_y}\right)^2 + \left(\frac{z}{r_Z}\right)^2 = 1. \qquad \text{(EQ 100)}$$

In parametric equation form:

$$x = r_X \cos\phi\cos\theta, \qquad 0 \le \phi \le \pi, \qquad \text{(EQ 101)}$$

$$y = r_y \cos\phi\sin\theta, \qquad 0 \le \theta \le 2\pi, \qquad \text{(EQ 102)}$$

$$\text{and } z = r_Z \sin\phi. \qquad \text{(EQ 103)}$$

Similarly, we can find all points on an ellipsoid through a double for-loop. Because ellipsoids can be achieved by scaling a sphere in graphics programming, neither GLUT nor GLU provides drawing them.

5.2.3 Cone

A cone with its height h on the z axis, bottom radius r in xy plane, and tip at the origin is

$$z^2 = (x^2 + y^2)\left(\frac{h}{r}\right)^2.$$

(EQ 104)

In parametric equation form:

$$x = r\left(\frac{h-u}{h}\right)\cos\theta, \qquad 0 \le u \le h,$$

(EQ 105)

$$y = r\left(\frac{h-u}{h}\right)\sin\theta, \qquad 0 \le \theta \le 2\pi,$$

(EQ 106)

$$\text{and } z = u.$$

(EQ 107)

GLUT provides wireframe or solid cone **drawing functions**, which are demonstrated in Example *J5_1_Quadrics.java*. The **function call is as** follows:

```
// USING GLUT to draw a cone
glut.glutSolidCone(glu, r, h, nLongitudes, nLatitudes);
```

5.2.4 Cylinder

In parametric equation form, a cylinder is

$$x = r\cos\theta,$$

(EQ 108)

$$y = r\sin\theta, \qquad 0 \le \theta \le 2\pi,$$

(EQ 109)

$$\text{and } z = z.$$

(EQ 110)

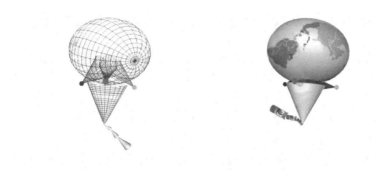

Fig. 5.1 GLUT and GLU models: wireframe or filled surfaces [*See* Color Plate 5]

Both GLUT and GLU provide wireframe or solid cylinder drawing functions, which are demonstrated in Example *J5_1_Quadrics.java*.

5.2.5 Texture Mapping on GLU Models

GLU provides automatic specifying texture coordinates in rendering its models, which is specified by *gluQuadricTexture()*. Therefore, texture mapping is made simple. We can just specify texture parameters and data as before, and we do not worry how the texture coordinates are specified on the primitives. GLUT only provides automatic texture coordinates specifications in rendering its teapot, which will be discussed later.

Figure 5.1 is a snapshot demonstrating GLUT and GLU library functions that are employed to draw spheres, cones, and cylinders in *J5_1_Quadrics.java*. The ellipsoid is achieved through scaling a sphere instead of direct rendering from ellipsoid parametric equations.

/* GLUT and GLU quadrics */

```
import net.java.games.jogl.GLU;
import net.java.games.jogl.*;


public class J5_1_Quadrics extends J4_8_Mipmap {
```

```
GLU glu = canvas.getGLU(); // glut int. is inherited
GLUquadric cylinder = glu.gluNewQuadric();
GLUquadric sphere = glu.gluNewQuadric();

public void drawSphere() {
  double r = 1;

  // number of points along longitudes and latitudes
  int nLongitudes = 20, nLatitudes = 20;

  // switch between two textures -- effect
  if ((cnt%1000)<500) {
    gl.glBindTexture(GL.GL_TEXTURE_2D, EARTH_TEX[0]);
  } else {
    gl.glBindTexture(GL.GL_TEXTURE_2D, IRIS_TEX[0]);
  }

  gl.glTexEnvf(GL.GL_TEXTURE_ENV,
               GL.GL_TEXTURE_ENV_MODE, GL.GL_MODULATE);

  if (cnt%950<400) { // draw solid sphere with GLU

    // automatic generate texture coords
    glu.gluQuadricTexture(sphere, true);
    gl.glEnable(GL.GL_TEXTURE_2D);

    // draw a filled sphere with GLU
    glu.gluQuadricDrawStyle(sphere, GLU.GLU_FILL);
    glu.gluSphere(sphere, r, nLongitudes, nLatitudes);
  } else {

    // draw wireframe sphere with GLUT.
    glut.glutWireSphere(glu, r, nLongitudes, nLatitudes);
  }

  gl.glDisable(GL.GL_TEXTURE_2D);

  if (cnt%800<400) { // for the background texture
    gl.glBindTexture(GL.GL_TEXTURE_2D, STARS_TEX[0]);
  } else {
    gl.glBindTexture(GL.GL_TEXTURE_2D, IRIS_TEX[0]);
  }
}


public void drawCone() {
  double r = 1, h = 1;
  int nLongitudes = 20, nLatitudes = 20;
```

```
    if (cnt%950>400) { // draw wireframe cone with GLUT
      glut.glutWireCone(glu, r, h, nLongitudes, nLatitudes);
    } else { //draw solid cone with GLUT
      glut.glutSolidCone(glu, r, h, nLongitudes, nLatitudes);
    }
  }


  public void drawCylinder() {
    double r = 1, h = 1;
    int nLongitudes = 20, nLatitudes = 20;

    // switching between two texture images
    if ((cnt%1000)<5000) {
      gl.glBindTexture(GL.GL_TEXTURE_2D, IRIS_TEX[0]);
    } else {
      gl.glBindTexture(GL.GL_TEXTURE_2D, EARTH_TEX[0]);
    }

    // automatic generate texture coords
    glu.gluQuadricTexture(cylinder, true);
    gl.glEnable(GL.GL_TEXTURE_2D);

    if (cnt%950<400) { // draw solid cylinder with GLU
      glu.gluQuadricDrawStyle(cylinder, GLU.GLU_FILL);
    } else { // draw point cylinder with GLU.
      glu.gluQuadricDrawStyle(cylinder, GLU.GLU_POINT);
    }

    // actually draw the cylinder
    glu.gluCylinder(cylinder, r, r, h, nLongitudes,
                    nLatitudes);

    gl.glDisable(GL.GL_TEXTURE_2D);
  }


  public static void main(String[] args) {

    J5_1_Quadrics f = new J5_1_Quadrics();

    f.setTitle("JOGL J5_1_Quadrics");
    f.setSize(WIDTH, HEIGHT);
    f.setVisible(true);
  }
}
```

5.3 Tori, Polyhedra, and Teapots in GLUT

In addition to drawing cone and sphere, GLUT provides a set of functions for rendering 3D models, including a torus, cube, tetrahedron, octahedron, dodecahedron, icosahedron, and teapot, in both solid shapes and wireframes. They are easy to use for applications, as demonstrated in *J5_2_Solids.java*, where we replace drawing sphere in our previous program (*J5_1_Quadrics.java*) with different 3D models in GLUT.

5.3.1 Tori

A torus looks the same as a doughnut, as shown in Fig. 5.2. It can be generated by rotating a circle around a line outside the circle. Therefore, a torus has two radii: r_{in} of the inner circle which is a cross section inside the doughnut, and r_{out} of the outer circle which is the doughnut as a circle. Then, the equation in Cartesian coordinates for a torus azimuthally symmetric about the z-axis is

$$\left(r_{in} - \sqrt{x^2 + y^2} \right)^2 + z^2 = r_{out}^2,$$

(EQ 111)

and the parametric equations are

$$x = (r_{in} + r_{out} \cos\phi) \cos\theta, \qquad 0 \le \phi \le 2\pi,$$

(EQ 112)

$$y = (r_{in} + r_{out} \cos\phi) \sin\theta, \qquad 0 \le \theta \le 2\pi,$$

(EQ 113)

$$z = r_{out} \sin\phi.$$

(EQ 114)

5.3.2 Polyhedra

A *polyhedron* is an arbitrary 3D shape whose surface is a collection of flat polygons. A *regular* polyhedron is one whose faces and vertices all look the same. There are only five regular polyhedra: the *tetrahedron* — 4 faces with three equilateral triangles at a vertex; the *cube* — 6 faces with three squares at a vertex; the *octahedron* — 8 faces with four equilateral triangles at a vertex; the *dodecahedron* — 12 faces with three pentagons at a vertex; and the *icosahedron* — 20 faces with five equilateral triangles at a vertex. The regular polyhedron models can be found in many books and graphics packages. However, the complex polyhedron model requires effort to be constructed.

GLUT provides functions to draw the regular polyhedra, as shown in Fig. 5.2. Polyhedra are flat-surface models, therefore they are not really curved surface models. Their counterpart is a sphere. The difference between the sphere and the polyhedra is really how the normals are specified.

5.3.3 Teapots

glutSolidTeapot() and *glutWireTeapot()* render a solid and wireframe teapot, respectively. Both surface normals and texture coordinates for the teapot are generated by the program, so texture mapping is available, as shown in Fig. 5.2 Actually, the teapot is the only model in GLUT that comes with texture coordinates. The teapot is generated with OpenGL evaluators, which will be discussed later.

The teapot's surface primitives are all back-facing. That is, the polygon vertices are all ordered clockwise. For the back-face culling purpose, we need to specify the front face as *glFrontFace(GL_CW)* before drawing the teapot to conform to the back-face culling employed in the programs, and return to normal situation using *glFrontFace(GL_CCW)* after drawing it. The teapot is very finely tessellated, so it is very slow to be rendered.

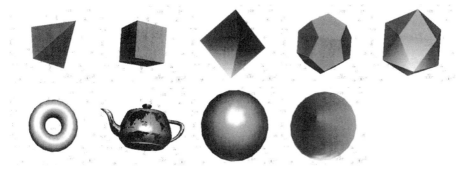

Fig. 5.2 3D models that GLUT renders [*See* Color Plate 6]

/* display GLUT solids: tori, polyhedra, and teapots */

```java
import net.java.games.jogl.GL;


public class J5_2_Solids extends J5_1_Quadrics {

  // replace the spheres with GLUT solids
  public void drawSphere() {

    gl.glPushMatrix();
    gl.glScaled(0.5, 0.5, 0.5);

    if (cnt%2000<100) {
      glut.glutSolidCone(glu, 1, 1, 20, 20);
    } else
    if (cnt%2000<200) {
      glut.glutWireCone(glu, 1, 1, 20, 20);
    } else
    if (cnt%2000<300) {
      glut.glutSolidCube(gl, 1);
    } else
    if (cnt%2000<400) {
      glut.glutWireCube(gl, 1);
    } else
    if (cnt%2000<500) {
      glut.glutSolidDodecahedron(gl);
    } else
    if (cnt%2000<600) {
      glut.glutWireDodecahedron(gl);
    } else
    if (cnt%2000<700) {
      glut.glutSolidIcosahedron(gl);
    } else
    if (cnt%2000<800) {
      glut.glutWireIcosahedron(gl);
    } else
    if (cnt%2000<900) {
      glut.glutSolidOctahedron(gl);
    } else
    if (cnt%2000<1000) {
      glut.glutWireOctahedron(gl);
    } else
    if (cnt%2000<1100) {
      glut.glutSolidSphere(glu, 1, 20, 20);
    } else
    if (cnt%2000<1200) {
      glut.glutWireSphere(glu, 1, 20, 20);
```

```java
    } else
    if (cnt%2000<1300) {
      gl.glBindTexture(GL.GL_TEXTURE_2D, EARTH_TEX[0]);
      gl.glTexEnvf(GL.GL_TEXTURE_ENV,
                   GL.GL_TEXTURE_ENV_MODE, GL.GL_MODULATE);
      gl.glEnable(GL.GL_TEXTURE_2D);

      gl.glFrontFace(GL.GL_CW);
      // the faces are clockwise
      glut.glutSolidTeapot(gl, 1);

      gl.glFrontFace(GL.GL_CCW);
      // return to normal

      gl.glDisable(GL.GL_TEXTURE_2D);
    } else
    if (cnt%2000<1400) {
      glut.glutWireTeapot(gl, 1);
    } else
    if (cnt%2000<1500) {
      glut.glutSolidTetrahedron(gl);
    } else
    if (cnt%2000<1600) {
      glut.glutWireTetrahedron(gl);
    } else
    if (cnt%2000<1700) {
      glut.glutSolidTorus(gl, 0.5, 1, 20, 20);
    } else if (cnt%2000<1800) {
      glut.glutWireTorus(gl, 0.5, 1, 20, 20);
    }
    gl.glPopMatrix();

    // for the background texture
    gl.glBindTexture(GL.GL_TEXTURE_2D, STARS_TEX[0]);
  }


  public static void main(String[] args) {

    J5_2_Solids f = new J5_2_Solids();

    f.setTitle("JOGL J5_2_Solids");
    f.setSize(WIDTH, HEIGHT);
    f.setVisible(true);
  }
}
```

5.4 Cubic Curves

Conic sections are quadratic curves, which includes circle, ellipse, parabola, and hyperbola. Their equations are in second-degree and they represent 2D curves that always fit into planes. Cubic curves, or simply cubics, are the lowest-degree curves that are non-planar in 3D. If we consider a curve like a worm wiggles in 2D changing direction along the curve, quadratic curves have at most one wiggle, and cubic curves have at most two wiggles. As you can see, higher degree curves will have more wiggles, but they are complex and time consuming. Instead, we can connect multiple cubic curves (segments) to form a curve with the number of wiggles and shape we want.

We study curves in parametric polynomial form. In general, a parametric polynomial is expressed as:

$$f(t) = a_0 + a_1 t + a_2 t^2 + \ldots + a_n t^n,$$

(EQ 115)

and a curve in 3D is

$$Q(t) = (x(t), y(t), z(t)),$$

(EQ 116)

where for a cubic curve segment,

$$0 \leq t \leq 1$$

(EQ 117)

and:

$$x(t) = a_{0x} + a_{1x} t + a_{2x} t^2 + a_{3x} t^3,$$

(EQ 118)

$$y(t) = a_{0y} + a_{1y} t + a_{2y} t^2 + a_{3y} t^3,$$

(EQ 119)

$$z(t) = a_{0z} + a_{1z} t + a_{2z} t^2 + a_{3z} t^3.$$

(EQ 120)

Because $x(t)$, $y(t)$, and $z(t)$ are in the same form but independent of each other except at drawing, where they are used together to specify a point, we discuss $p(t)$ in place of $x(t)$, $y(t)$, or $z(t)$. Therefore, we simplify the cubic parametric equations above into a representative equation as follows:

$$p(t) = a t^3 + b t^2 + c t + d, \text{ where } 0 \le t \le 1.$$ (EQ 121)

In matrix form, we have

$$p(t) = \begin{bmatrix} t^3 & t^2 & t & 1 \end{bmatrix} \begin{bmatrix} a \\ b \\ c \\ d \end{bmatrix}$$ (EQ 122)

5.4.1 Continuity Conditions

The first derivative at a point on a curve, $\dfrac{d(Q(t))}{dt} = Q(t) = (x'(t), y'(t), z'(t))$, is the tangent vector at a specific t. For easier understanding, we may assume that t is the time, then from time $t = 0$ to $t = 1$ a point moves from $Q(0)$ to $Q(1)$ and the tangent vector is the velocity (direction and speed) of the point tracing out the curve.

As we discussed, a cubic curve is a segment where $0 \le t \le 1$ (Equation 116, Equation 117 on page 202). We can connect multiple cubic curves to form a longer curve. The smoothness condition of the connection is determined by the continuity conditions as discussed below for two curves.

Parametric continuity. Zero-order parametric continuity, C^0, means that the ending-point of the first curve meets the starting-point of the second curve:

$$Q_1(1) = Q_2(0).$$ (EQ 123)

First-order parametric continuity, C^1, means that the first derivatives of the two successive curves are equal at their connection:

$$Q_1(1) = Q_2(0).$$
(EQ 124)

Second-order parametric continuity, C^2, means that both the first and second parametric derivatives of the two curves are the same at the intersection:

$$Q_1(1) = Q_2(0), \quad \text{and} \quad Q'_1(1) = Q'_2(0).$$
(EQ 125)

Higher-order continuity conditions are defined similarly, which are meaningful for higher degree curves.

Geometric continuity. Zero-order geometric continuity, G^0, means that the end point of the first curve meets the starting-point of the second curve:

$$Q_1(1) = Q_2(0).$$
(EQ 126)

First-order geometric continuity, G^1, means that the first derivatives of the two successive curves are proportional at their connection:

$$Q_1(1) = kQ_2(0).$$
(EQ 127)

where k is a constant. In other words, the two tangent vector's directions are still the same, but their lengths may not be the same.

Similarly, second-order geometric continuity, G^2, means that both the first and second parametric derivatives of the two curves are proportional at the intersection:

$$Q_1(1) = k_1 Q_2(0), \quad \text{and} \quad Q'_1(1) = k_2 Q'_2(0).$$
(EQ 128)

Compared to parametric continuity conditions, geometric continuity conditions are more flexible.

5.4.2 Hermite Curves

Hermite curves are specified by two end points $p(0)$ and $p(1)$ and two tangent vectors at the two ends $p'(0)$ and $p'(1)$. The end points and tangent vectors are called the *boundary constraints* of a Hermite curve. According to Equation 121 on page 203:

$$p(0) = d, \tag{EQ 129}$$

$$p(1) = a + b + c + d, \tag{EQ 130}$$

$$p'(0) = c, \text{ and} \tag{EQ 131}$$

$$p'(1) = 3a + 2b + c. \tag{EQ 132}$$

Therefore, from Equation 129 to Equation 132, we have:

$$a = 2p(0) - 2p(1) + p'(0) + p'(1), \tag{EQ 133}$$

$$b = -3p(0) + 3p(1) - 2p'(0) - p'(1), \tag{EQ 134}$$

$$c = p'(0), \tag{EQ 135}$$

$$\text{and } d = p(0). \tag{EQ 136}$$

Then, the equation for a Hermite curve is

$$p(t) = (2t^3 - 3t^2 + 1)p(0) + (-2t^3 + 3t^2)p(1) + \\ (at^3 - 2t^2)p'(0) + (t^3 - t^2)p'(1) \quad . \tag{EQ 137}$$

That is,

$$p(t) = H_0(t)p(0) + H_1(t)p(1) + H_2(t)p'(0) + H_3(t)p'(1), \tag{EQ 138}$$

where $H_0(t)$, $H_1(t)$, $H_2(t)$, and $H_3(t)$ are called the *blending functions* of a Hermite curve, because they blend the four boundary constraint values to obtain each position along the curve at a specific t.

As shown in Fig. 5.3, when $t = 0$, only $H_0(0)$ is nonzero, and therefore only $P(0)$ has an influence on the curve. When $t=1$, only $H_1(1)$ is nonzero, and therefore only $P(1)$ has an influence on the curve. For all $0 < t < 1$, all boundary constraints have influences on the curve. Because the tangent vectors at the end points are specified as constants, if we connect multiple Hermite curves, we can specify C^1 or

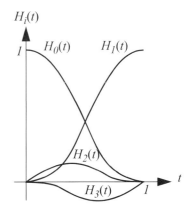

Fig. 5.3 Hermite blending functions

G^1 continuity conditions, but we cannot specify C^2 or G^2 because the second derivatives do not exist.

We often express Hermite equation in matrix form as follows:

$$p(t) = \begin{bmatrix} t^3 & t^2 & t & 1 \end{bmatrix} \begin{bmatrix} 2 & -2 & 1 & 1 \\ -3 & 3 & -2 & -1 \\ 0 & 0 & 1 & 0 \\ 1 & 0 & 0 & 0 \end{bmatrix} \begin{bmatrix} p(0) \\ P(1) \\ p'(0) \\ p'(1) \end{bmatrix}$$

(EQ 139)

That is,

$$p(t) = TM_h P$$

(EQ 140)

where M_h is called the Hermite matrix, and P includes, as we said earlier, the boundary constraints. The following program draws Hermite curves in place of spheres in the previous example:

/* draw a hermite curve */

```java
import net.java.games.jogl.GL;
import net.java.games.jogl.GLU;
import net.java.games.jogl.GLDrawable; /**

public class J5_3_Hermite extends J5_2_Solids {

  double ctrlp[][] = { {-0.5, -0.5, -0.5}, {-1.0, 1.0, 1.0},
                       {1.0, -1.0, 1.0}, {0.5, 0.5, 1.0}
  }; // control points: two end points, two tangent vectors

  public void myEvalCoordHermite(double t) {
    // evaluate the coordinates and specify the points
    double x, y, z, t_1, t2, t_2, t3, t_3;

    t_1 = 1-t;
    t2 = t*t;
    t_2 = t_1*t_1;
    t3 = t2*t;
    t_3 = t_2*t_1;

    x = t_3*ctrlp[0][0]+3*t*t_2*ctrlp[1][0]
        +3*t2*t_1*ctrlp[2][0]+t3*ctrlp[3][0];

    y = t_3*ctrlp[0][1]+3*t*t_2*ctrlp[1][1]
        +3*t2*t_1*ctrlp[2][1]+t3*ctrlp[3][1];

    z = t_3*ctrlp[0][2]+3*t*t_2*ctrlp[1][2]
        +3*t2*t_1*ctrlp[2][2]+t3*ctrlp[3][2];

    gl.glVertex3d(x, y, z);
  }


  public void drawSphere() {
    int i;

    myCameraView = true;

    gl.glLineWidth(4);
    gl.glBegin(GL.GL_LINE_STRIP);
    for (i = 0; i<=30; i++) {
      myEvalCoordHermite(i/30.0);
    }
    gl.glEnd();
```

```
/* The following code displays the control points
 as dots. */
gl.glPointSize(6.0f);
gl.glBegin(GL.GL_POINTS);
gl.glVertex3dv(ctrlp[0]);
gl.glVertex3dv(ctrlp[3]);
gl.glEnd();

// for the background texture
gl.glBindTexture(GL.GL_TEXTURE_2D, STARS_TEX[0]);
}


public void drawCone() {
}


public static void main(String[] args) {
  J5_3_Hermite f = new J5_3_Hermite();

  f.setTitle("JOGL J5_3_Hermite");
  f.setSize(WIDTH, HEIGHT);
  f.setVisible(true);
}
}
```

5.4.3 Bezier Curves

Bezier curves are specified by two end points: $p(0)$ and $p(1)$ and two control points C_1 and C_2 such that the tangent vectors at the two ends are $p'(0) = 3(C_1 - p(0))$ and $p'(1) = 3(p(1) - C_2)$. Similar to Hermite curve equation, according to Equation 121 on page 203 we have:

$$p(0) = d, \qquad \text{(EQ 141)}$$

$$p(1) = a + b + c + d, \qquad \text{(EQ 142)}$$

$$p'(0) = 3(C_1 - p(0)) = c, \text{ and} \qquad \text{(EQ 143)}$$

$$p'(1) = 3(p(1) - C_2) = 3a + 2b + c. \qquad \text{(EQ 144)}$$

Therefore, from Equation 141 to Equation 144, we have:

$$a = -p(0) + 3C_1 - 3C_2 + p(1),$$ (EQ 145)

$$b = 3p(0) - 6C_1 + 3C_2,$$ (EQ 146)

$$c = -3p(0) + 3C_1,$$ (EQ 147)

$$\text{and } d = p(0).$$ (EQ 148)

Then, the equation for Hermite curves is

$$p(t) = (1-t)^3 p(0) + 3t(1-t)^2 C_1 + 3t^2(1-t)C_2 + t^3 p(1).$$ (EQ 149)

That is,

$$p(t) = B_0(t)p(0) + B_1(t)C_1 + B_2(t)C_2 + B_3(t)p(1),$$ (EQ 150)

where $B_0(t)$, $B_1(t)$, $B_2(t)$, and $B_3(t)$ are Bezier curves' *blending functions*, because they blend the four boundary constraint points to obtain each position along the curve.

As shown in Fig. 5.4, when $t=0$, only $B_0(0)$ is nonzero, and therefore only $P(0)$ has an influence on the curve. When $t=1$, only $B_3(1)$ is nonzero, and therefore only $P(1)$ has an influence on the curve. For all $0<t<1$, all boundary constraints have influences on the curve. Because the tangent vectors at the end points are specified by the 4 constraints as constants, if we connect multiple Bezier curves, we can specify C^1 or G^1 continuity

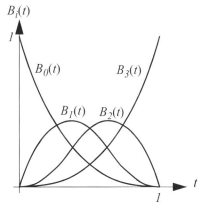

Fig. 5.4 Bezier blending functions

conditions, but we cannot specify C^2 or G^2 because the second derivatives do not exist.

Bezier curve has some important properties. If we use the four constraint points to form a convex hull in 3D (or convex polygon in 2D), the curve is cotangent to the two opposite edges defined by the $p(0)C_1$ and $C_2p(1)$ pairs. A convex hull, simply put, is a polyhedron with all of its vertices on only one side of each surface of the polyhedron. A cubic Bezier curve is just a weighted average of the four constraint points, and it is completely contained in the convex hull of the 4 control points. The sum of the four blending functions is equal to 1 for any t, and each polynomial is everywhere positive except at the two ends. As you can see, if we specify the constraint points on a line, according to the convex-hull property, the cubic Bezier curve is reduced to a line.

We often express Bezier curve equation in matrix form:

$$p(t) = \begin{bmatrix} t^3 & t^2 & t & 1 \end{bmatrix} \begin{bmatrix} -1 & 3 & -3 & 1 \\ 3 & -6 & 3 & 0 \\ -3 & 3 & 0 & 0 \\ 1 & 0 & 0 & 0 \end{bmatrix} \begin{bmatrix} p(0) \\ C_1 \\ C_2 \\ p(1) \end{bmatrix} \qquad \text{(EQ 151)}$$

That is,

$$p(t) = TM_bC, \qquad \text{(EQ 152)}$$

where M_b is called the Bezier matrix, and C includes the boundary constraints such that $C_0 = p(0)$ and $C_3 = p(1)$.

Bezier curves of general degree. Bezier curves can be easily extended into higher degrees. Given $n+1$ control point positions, we can blend them to produce the following:

$$p(t) = \sum_{k=0}^{n} C_k B_{k,n}(t), \qquad \text{(EQ 153)}$$

where the blending functions are called the Bernstein polynomials:

$$B_{k,n}(t) = C(n, k) t^k (1 - t)^{n-k}, \qquad \text{(EQ 154)}$$

$$\text{and } C(n, k) = \frac{n!}{k!(n-k)!}. \qquad \text{(EQ 155)}$$

OpenGL evaluators. OpenGL provides basic functions for calculating Bezier curves. Specifically, it uses *glMap1f()* to set up the interval (e.g., $0 \leq t \leq 1$), number of values (e.g., *3* for *xyz* or *4* for *xyzw*) to go from one control point to the next, degree of the equation (e.g., *4* for cubics), and control points (an array of points). Then, instead of calculating curve points and using *glVertex()* to specify the coordinates, we use *glEvaluCoord1()* to specify the coordinates at specified *t*'s, and the Bezier curve is calculated by the OpenGL system, as shown in Example *J5_4_Bezier.java*. A snapshot is in Fig. 5.5.

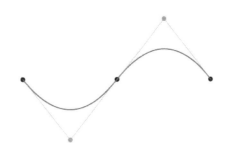

Fig. 5.5 Bezier curve

/* use OpenGL evaluators for Bezier curve */

```
import net.java.games.jogl.GL;
import net.java.games.jogl.GLDrawable;

public class J5_4_Bezier extends J5_3_Hermite {

   double ctrlpts[] =
                {0.0, -1.0, -0.5, -1.0, 1.0, -1.0,
                  -1.0, -1.0, 1.0, 1.0, 0.05, 1.0};

   public void drawSphere() {

      int i;
```

```
// specify Bezier curve vertex with:
//      0<=t<=1, 3 values (x,y,z), and 4-1 degrees
gl.glMap1d(GL.GL_MAP1_VERTEX_3, 0, 1, 3, 4, ctrlpts);
gl.glEnable(GL.GL_MAP1_VERTEX_3);

gl.glDisable(GL.GL_LIGHTING);

gl.glLineWidth(3);
gl.glColor4f(1f, 1f, 1f, 1f);

gl.glBegin(GL.GL_LINE_STRIP);

for (i = 0; i<=30; i++) {
  gl.glEvalCoord1d(i/30.0); // use OpenGL evaluator
}

gl.glEnd();

// Highlight the control points
gl.glPointSize(4);
gl.glBegin(GL.GL_POINTS);
gl.glColor4f(1f, 1f, 0f, 1f);
 gl.glVertex3d(ctrlpts[0], ctrlpts[1], ctrlpts[2]);
gl.glVertex3d(ctrlpts[3], ctrlpts[4], ctrlpts[5]);
gl.glVertex3d(ctrlpts[6], ctrlpts[7], ctrlpts[8]);
gl.glVertex3d(ctrlpts[9], ctrlpts[10], ctrlpts[11]);
gl.glEnd();

// draw the convex hull as transparent
gl.glEnable(GL.GL_BLEND);
gl.glDepthMask(true);
gl.glBlendFunc(GL.GL_SRC_ALPHA,
               GL.GL_ONE_MINUS_SRC_ALPHA);

gl.glBegin(GL.GL_TRIANGLES);
gl.glColor4f(0.9f, 0.9f, 0.9f, 0.3f);
gl.glVertex3d(ctrlpts[0], ctrlpts[1], ctrlpts[2]);
gl.glVertex3d(ctrlpts[3], ctrlpts[4], ctrlpts[5]);
gl.glVertex3d(ctrlpts[9], ctrlpts[10], ctrlpts[11]);

gl.glColor4f(0.9f, 0.0f, 0.0f, 0.3f);
gl.glVertex3d(ctrlpts[0], ctrlpts[1], ctrlpts[2]);
gl.glVertex3d(ctrlpts[9], ctrlpts[10], ctrlpts[11]);
gl.glVertex3d(ctrlpts[6], ctrlpts[7], ctrlpts[8]);

gl.glColor4f(0.0f, 0.9f, 0.0f, 0.3f);
gl.glVertex3d(ctrlpts[0], ctrlpts[1], ctrlpts[2]);
gl.glVertex3d(ctrlpts[6], ctrlpts[7], ctrlpts[8]);
```

```
gl.glVertex3d(ctrlpts[3], ctrlpts[4], ctrlpts[5]);

gl.glColor4f(0.0f, 0.0f, 0.9f, 0.3f);
gl.glVertex3d(ctrlpts[3], ctrlpts[4], ctrlpts[5]);
gl.glVertex3d(ctrlpts[6], ctrlpts[7], ctrlpts[8]);
gl.glVertex3d(ctrlpts[9], ctrlpts[10], ctrlpts[11]);

gl.glEnd();

gl.glDepthMask(false);

// for the background texture
gl.glBindTexture(GL.GL_TEXTURE_2D, STARS_TEX[0]);

}


public static void main(String[] args) {
  J5_4_Bezier f = new J5_4_Bezier();

  f.setTitle("JOGL J5_4_Bezier");
  f.setSize(WIDTH, HEIGHT);
  f.setVisible(true);
}
}
```

5.4.4 Natural Splines

A spline is constructed from cubic curves with C^2 continuity. A natural cubic spline goes through all its control points. For $n+1$ control points, there are n cubic curves (segments). As in Equation 121 on page 203, a cubic curve equation has four parameters that define the curve. Therefore we need *4* constraints to decide the four parameters. For n cubic curves, we need *4n* constraints.

How many constraints we have already for a natural cubic spline? Well, for all cubic curves (segments) in a natural cubic spline, the two end points are known. There are n curves, therefore *2n* end points. Because the curves are connected with C^2 continuity, the first and second derivatives at the joints are equal. There are *n-1* joints, so there are *2n-2* constraint equations for the first derivatives and the second derivatives. Altogether we have *4n-2* constraints, but we need *4n* constraints in order to specify all curve segments of the natural cubic spline. We can add two assumptions such as the tangent vectors of the two end points of the spline.

Natural spline curves are calculated by solving a set of $4n$ equations, which is time consuming. Also, changing one constraint (such as moving a control point) will result in changing the shape of all different segments, so all of the curve segments need to be calculated again. We call this global control. We would prefer a curve with local control, so changing a constraint only affects the curve locally. Hermite and Bezier curves are local control curves, but they only support C^1 continuity. In the next section, we introduce B-spline, which satisfies local control as well as C^2 continuity.

5.4.5 B-splines

A B-spline curve is a set of connected cubic curves based on control points that lie outside each of the curves. For $n+1$ control points, there are $n-2$ cubic curves (segments) on a B-spline:

$Q_3(t)$ is defined by $C_0C_1C_2C_3$,
$Q_4(t)$ is defined by $C_1C_2C_3C_4$,

...,
$Q_n(t)$ is defined by $C_{n-3}C_{n-2}C_{n-1}C_n$.

The cubic B-spline equation for $Q_i(t)$ is as follows:

$$p_i(t) = B_0(t)C_{i-3} + B_1(t)C_{i-2} + B_2(t)C_{i-3} + B_3(t)C_i \qquad \text{(EQ 156)}$$

where the blending functions, which are also called the *basis functions* because the B in B-spline stands for "basis", are

$$B_0(t) = \frac{1}{6}(1-t)^3, \qquad \text{(EQ 157)}$$

$$B_1(t) = \frac{1}{6}(3t^3 - 6t^2 + 4), \qquad \text{(EQ 158)}$$

$$B_2(t) = \frac{1}{6}(-3t^3 + 3t^2 + 3t + 1), \qquad \text{(EQ 159)}$$

$$\text{and } B_3(t) = \frac{1}{6}t^3. \qquad \text{(EQ 160)}$$

As Bezier curves, the sum of the B-spline's blending functions is everywhere unity and each function is everywhere nonnegative, as shown in Fig. 5.6. That is, a B-spline curve segment is just a weighted average of the four control points and is contained in the convex hull of the four control points.

For two consecutive curve segments on a B-spline, their connection point is called a *knot*, which has corresponding knot value $t=1$ on the first segment and $t=0$ on the second segment. This type of B-spline is called *Uniform B-spline*, whose knot values are in equal unit value. We have $p_i(1)$ and $p_{i+1}(0)$:

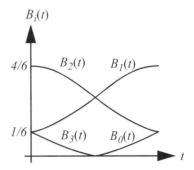

Fig. 5.6 B-spline blending functions

$$p_i(1) = 0C_{i-3} + \frac{1}{6}C_{i-2} + \frac{2}{3}C_{i-1} + \frac{1}{6}C_i, \qquad \text{(EQ 161)}$$

$$p_{i+1}(0) = \frac{1}{6}C_{i-2} + \frac{2}{3}C_{i-1} + \frac{1}{6}C_i + 0C_{i+1}. \qquad \text{(EQ 162)}$$

So the two end points meet at the knot:

$$p_i(1) = p_{i+1}(0) = \frac{1}{6}C_{i-2} + \frac{2}{3}C_{i-1} + \frac{1}{6}C_i. \qquad \text{(EQ 163)}$$

That is, the knot is constrained by three control points as in Equation 163, while a B-spline curve segment is constrained by four control points wherever not on the knots. This is also obvious from Fig. 5.6.

We can calculate the first derivatives at the knots,

$$p'_i(1) = 0C_{i-3} + \left(-\frac{1}{2}\right)C_{i-2} + 0C_{i-1} + \frac{1}{2}C_i \qquad \text{(EQ 164)}$$

$$p'_{i+1}(0) = \left(-\frac{1}{2}\right)C_{i-2} + 0C_{i-1} + \frac{1}{2}C_i + 0C_{i+1} \qquad \text{(EQ 165)}$$

So the two end points' tangent vectors are equal. We can further calculate the second derivatives and see that B-splines are C^2 continuity at their knots, which is the same as natural cubic splines. Unlike natural cubic splines, B-splines do not go through the control points, and moving one control point to a different position affects only four curve segments at most. That is, B-spline curves are local-control, while natural cubic spline curves are global-control. If we use a control point twice in the equations (e.g., $C_i = C_{i+1}$), then the curves are pulled closer to this point. Using a control point three times will result in a line segment.

We can write B-spline equation in matrix form:

$$p_i(t) = \begin{bmatrix} t^3 & t^2 & t & 1 \end{bmatrix} \frac{1}{6} \begin{bmatrix} -1 & 3 & -3 & 1 \\ 3 & -6 & 3 & 0 \\ -3 & 0 & 3 & 0 \\ 1 & 4 & 1 & 0 \end{bmatrix} \begin{bmatrix} C_{i-3} \\ C_{i-2} \\ C_{i-1} \\ C_i \end{bmatrix} \qquad \text{(EQ 166)}$$

That is,

$$p_i(t) = TM_{Bs}C \qquad \text{(EQ 167)}$$

where M_{Bs} is called the B-spline matrix, and C represents the corresponding boundary constraints. Each curve is defined on its own domain ($0 \le t \le 1$). We can adjust the parameters so that the parameter domains for the various curve segments are sequential: $t_i \le t \le t_{i+1}$, $t_{i+1} - t_i = 1$, and $3 \le i \le n$. Here the knots are spaced at unit intervals of parameter t, and the B-splines are called Uniform B-splines. If t is not spaced evenly, we have Non-uniform B-splines, which is discussed in the next section.

B-splines of general degree. B-splines can be easily extended into higher degrees. Given $n+1$ control point positions, we can blend them to produce the following:

$$p(t) = \sum_{k=0}^{n} C_k B_{k,d}(t), \qquad \text{(EQ 168)}$$

where the blending functions are $(d\text{-}1)$ degree polynomials where $2 \leq d \leq n+1$:

$$B_{k,1}(t) = \begin{cases} 1, \text{ when} & t_i \leq t < t_{i+1} \\ 0, \text{ otherwise} \end{cases}, \qquad \text{(EQ 169)}$$

and $B_{k,d}(t) = \dfrac{t - t_k}{t_{k+d-1} - t_k} B_{k,d-1}(t) + \dfrac{t_{k+d} - t}{t_{k+d} - t_{k+1}} B_{k+1,d-1}(t).$ **(EQ 170)**

For an arbitrary n and d, we need knot value $t = 0$ up to $t = n + d$ to calculate the blending functions. In other words, we need a knot vector of $n + d$ values. For a cubic Uniform B-spline with 4 control points, $n = 4$ and $d = 4$, so we need to provide a uniform knot vector of 8 values: [0 1 2 3 4 5 6 7]. So the cubic Uniform B-spline we discussed above is just a special case here.

5.4.6 Non-uniform B-splines

If the parameter interval between successive knot values are not uniform, we have a knot vector, for example, [0 0 1 3 4 7 7]. The number of repeating knot values is the *multiplicity* of the curve. With such a knot vector, the blending function will be calculated resulting in different equations by Equation 169 and Equation 170. The multiplicity also reduces the continuity of the curve at the repeating knots by the number of repeating knot values, and the curve segments are shrunk into a point for the repeating knots. This is the primary advantage of Non-uniform B-splines.

If the continuity is reduced to C^0 with multiplicity 3, the curve interpolates a control point. For example, for a cubic B-spline with 4 control points, if the knot vector is [0 0 0 0 1 1 1 1], the curve goes through the first and the last control points, which is a Bezier curve. So a Bezier curve is a special case of a B-spline. For multiple curve segments with multiplicity 4, the curve segments can be dissected into pieces.

5.4.7 NURBS

3D models are transformed by MODELVIEW and PROJECTION matrices in homogeneous coordinates. If we apply perspective projection to the control points and then generate the curve using the above (non-rational) Hermite, Bezier, or B-spline equations, the generated curves change their shapes. In other words, they are variant under perspective projection. This problem can be solved by using rational curve equations, which can be considered as curves in homogeneous coordinates projected into 3D coordinates. We extend a curve in homogeneous coordinates as:

$$Q_h(t) = (x(t), y(t), z(t), w(t)).$$
(EQ 171)

Then, a rational curve in 3D coordinates is as:

$$Q(t) = \left(\frac{x(t)}{w(t)}, \frac{y(t)}{w(t)}, \frac{z(t)}{w(t)} \right).$$
(EQ 172)

If the rational equations are Non-uniform B-splines, they are called *NURBS* (Non-uniform Rational B-splines):

$$p(t) = \frac{\displaystyle\sum_{k=0}^{n} \omega_k C_k B_{k,d}(t)}{\displaystyle\sum_{k=0}^{n} \omega_k B_{k,d}(t)}.$$
(EQ 173)

where ω_k are user-specified weight factors for the control points. When all the weight factors are set to 1, the rational form is reduced to non-rational form, so non-rational equations are special cases of rational equations.

In addition to being invariant under perspective transformation, NURBS can be used to obtain various conics by choosing specific weight factors and control points. The GLU library provides NURBS functions built on top of the OpenGL evaluator commands for both NURBS curves and surfaces.

5.5 Bi-cubic Surfaces

As discussed before, cubic Hermite, Bezier, and B-spline curve equations are

$$p(t) \; = \; TM_h P, \qquad\qquad\qquad \text{(EQ 174)}$$

$$p(t) \; = \; TM_b C, \qquad\qquad\qquad \text{(EQ 175)}$$

$$\text{and } p(t) \; = \; TM_{Bs} C_{Bs} \text{ for one segment.} \qquad \text{(EQ 176)}$$

Their differences here are really their matrices and constraint parameters. For a curve, if its constraints are themselves variables, the curve can be considered moving in 3D and changing its shape according to the variations of the constraints, and sweeping out a curved surface. If the constraints are themselves cubic curves, we have bi-cubic surfaces.

5.5.1 Hermite Surfaces

Let us assume that s and t are independent parameters, and our original Hermite curve equation with variable s has its constraints of variable t. We have bi-cubic Hermite surface equation as follows:

$$p(s, t) = SM_h \begin{bmatrix} p(0, t) \\ P(1, t) \\ \dfrac{\partial}{\partial s}p(0, t) \\ \dfrac{\partial}{\partial s}p(1, t) \end{bmatrix} = SM_h \begin{bmatrix} TM_h \begin{bmatrix} p(0, 0) \\ P(0, 1) \\ \dfrac{\partial}{\partial t}p(0, 0) \\ \dfrac{\partial}{\partial t}p(0, 1) \end{bmatrix} \\[2em] TM_h \begin{bmatrix} p(1, 0) \\ P(1, 1) \\ \dfrac{\partial}{\partial t}p(1, 0) \\ \dfrac{\partial}{\partial t}p(1, 1) \end{bmatrix} \\[2em] TM_h \begin{bmatrix} \dfrac{\partial}{\partial s}p(0, 0) \\ \dfrac{\partial}{\partial s}P(0, 1) \\ \dfrac{\partial^2}{\partial s\partial t}p(0, 0) \\ \dfrac{\partial^2}{\partial s\partial t}p(0, 1) \end{bmatrix} \\[2em] TM_h \begin{bmatrix} \dfrac{\partial}{\partial s}p(1, 0) \\ \dfrac{\partial}{\partial s}P(1, 1) \\ \dfrac{\partial^2}{\partial s\partial t}p(1, 0) \\ \dfrac{\partial^2}{\partial s\partial t}p(1, 1) \end{bmatrix} \end{bmatrix}. \qquad \textbf{(EQ 177)}$$

Because matrix expression can be reversed under transposition: $MN = N^T M^T$, we have the following

$$p(s, t) = SM_h \begin{bmatrix} p(0, 0) & P(0, 1) & \frac{\partial}{\partial t}p(0, 0) & \frac{\partial}{\partial t}p(0, 1) \\ p(1, 0) & P(1, 1) & \frac{\partial}{\partial t}p(1, 0) & \frac{\partial}{\partial t}p(1, 1) \\ \frac{\partial}{\partial s}p(0, 0) & \frac{\partial}{\partial s}P(0, 1) & \frac{\partial^2}{\partial s\partial t}p(0, 0) & \frac{\partial^2}{\partial s\partial t}p(0, 1) \\ \frac{\partial}{\partial s}p(1, 0) & \frac{\partial}{\partial s}P(1, 1) & \frac{\partial^2}{\partial s\partial t}p(1, 0) & \frac{\partial^2}{\partial s\partial t}p(1, 1) \end{bmatrix} M_h^T T^T \qquad \text{(EQ 178)}$$

That is,

$$p(s, t) = SM_h P_h M_h^T T^T \qquad \text{(EQ 179)}$$

Therefore, for a Hermite bi-cubic surface, we need to specify 16 constraints for an x, y, or z parametric equation, respectively. There are 4 end points on the surface patch, 8 tangent vectors in s or t directions at the 4 end points, and 4 "twists" at the 4 end points, which you can think to be the rate of a tangent vector in s direction twists (changes) along the t direction, or vice versa. Just like Hermite curves, Hermite surface patches can be connected with C^1 or G^1 continuity. We just need to specify the connecting end points' tangent vectors and twists equal or proportional.

For lighting or other purposes, the normal at any point (s, t) on the surface can be calculated by the cross-product of the s and t tangent vectors:

$$\frac{\partial}{\partial s}Q(s, t) \times \frac{\partial}{\partial t}Q(s, t) \qquad \text{(EQ 180)}$$

5.5.2 Bezier Surfaces

Bi-cubic Bezier surfaces can be derived the same way as above:

$$p(s, t) = SM_b CM_b^T T^T,$$ (EQ 181)

where the control points (as shown in Fig. 5.7) are

$$C = \begin{bmatrix} C_{00} & C_{01} & C_{02} & C_{03} \\ C_{10} & C_{11} & C_{12} & C_{13} \\ C_{20} & C_{21} & C_{22} & C_{23} \\ C_{30} & C_{31} & C_{32} & C_{33} \end{bmatrix}.$$ (EQ 182)

As their corresponding curves, Bezier surfaces are C^1 or G^1 continuity. Also, Bezier surfaces can be easily extended into higher degrees, and OpenGL implements two-dimensional evaluators for Bezier surfaces of general degree, as discussed below.

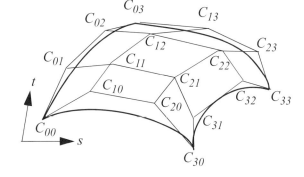

Fig. 5.7 Bi-cubic Bezier surface control points

Bezier surfaces of general degree. Given $(n + 1)(m + 1)$ control point positions C_{ij}, where $0 \le i \le n$ and $0 \le j \le m$, we can blend them to produce the following:

$$p(s, t) = \sum_{i=0}^{n} \sum_{j=0}^{m} C_{ij} B_{i, n}(s) B_{j, m}(t),$$ (EQ 183)

where the blending functions are the Bernstein polynomials discussed in Equation 154 and Equation 155 on page 211.

OpenGL two-dimensional evaluators. OpenGL provides basic functions for calculating Bezier surfaces of general degree. Specifically, it uses *glMap2f()* to set up the interval (e.g., $0 \leq s,t \leq 1$), number of values in *s* or *t* directions to skip to the next value (e.g., *3* for *xyz* or *4* for *xyzw* in *s* direction, and *12* for *xyz* or *16* or *xyzw* in *t* direction), degree of the equation (e.g., *4* for cubics), and control points (an array of points). Then, instead of calculating curve points and using *glVertex()* to specify the coordinates, we use *glEvaluCoord2(s, t)* to specify the coordinates at specified position, and the Bezier surface is calculated by the OpenGL system, as shown in Example *J5_5_BezierSurface.java*. A snapshot is in Fig. 5.8.

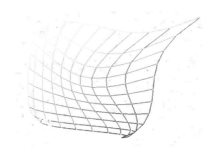

Fig. 5.8 Bezier surfaces

In OpenGL, *glMap*()* is also used to interpolate colors, normals, and texture coordinates.

/* draw a Bezier surface using 2D evaluators */

```
import net.java.games.jogl.GL;

public class J5_5_BezierSurface extends J5_4_Bezier {
    double ctrlpts[] = { // C00, C01, C02, C03
                         -1.0, -1.0, 1, -1.0, -0.75, -1.0,
                         -1.0, 0.75, 1.0, -1.0, 1, -1.0,
                         // C10, C11, C12, C13
                         -0.75, -1.0, -1, -0.75, -0.75, 0,
                         -0.75, 0.75, -5.0, -0.75, 1, 1.0,
                         // C20, C21, C22, C23
                         0.75, -1.0, 1, 0.75, -0.75, 0,
                         0.75, 0.75, 1.0, 0.75, 1, -1.0,
                         // C30, C31, C32, C33
                         1, -1.0, -1, 1, -0.75, 1.0,
                         1, 0.75, -1.0, 1, 1, 1.0,
    };

    public void drawSphere() {
        int i, j;
```

```
// define and invoke 2D evaluator
gl.glMap2d(GL.GL_MAP2_VERTEX_3, 0, 1, 3, 4,
            0, 1, 12, 4, ctrlpts);
gl.glEnable(GL.GL_MAP2_VERTEX_3);

gl.glDisable(GL.GL_LIGHTING);
for (j = 0; j<=10; j++) {
  gl.glBegin(GL.GL_LINE_STRIP);
  for (i = 0; i<=10; i++) {
    gl.glColor3f(i/10f, j/10f, 1f);
    // use OpenGL evaluator
    gl.glEvalCoord2d(i/10.0, j/10.0);
  }
  gl.glEnd();
  gl.glBegin(GL.GL_LINE_STRIP);
  for (i = 0; i<=10; i++) {
    gl.glColor3f(i/10f, j/10f, 1f);
    // use OpenGL evaluator
    gl.glEvalCoord2d(j/10.0, i/10.0);
  }
  gl.glEnd();
}

// Highlight the knots: white
gl.glColor3f(1, 1, 1);
gl.glBegin(GL.GL_POINTS);
for (j = 0; j<=10; j++) {
  for (i = 0; i<=10; i++) {
    gl.glEvalCoord2d(i/10.0, j/10.0);
  }
}
gl.glEnd();

// for the background texture
gl.glBindTexture(GL.GL_TEXTURE_2D, STARS_TEX[0]);
}


public static void main(String[] args) {
  J5_5_BezierSurface f = new J5_5_BezierSurface();

  f.setTitle("JOGL J5_5_BezierSurface");
  f.setSize(WIDTH, HEIGHT);
  f.setVisible(true);
}
}
```

5.5.3 B-spline Surfaces

Bi-cubic B-spline surfaces can be derived the same way as above, respectively:

$$p(s,\ t)\ =\ SM_{BS}C_{BS}M_{BS}^{T}T^{T}.$$

(EQ 184)

As their corresponding curves, Bezier surfaces are C^{1} or G^{1} continuity, and B-spline surfaces are C^{2} or G^{2} continuity.

The GLU library provides a set of NURBS functions built on OpenGL evaluator commands that includes lighting and texture mapping functions, which is convenient for applications involving NURBS curves and surfaces.

5.6 Review Questions

1. Check out glPolygonMode() and draw models in points, lines, and surfaces in J5_1_Quadrics.java.

2. Please specify the names of the 3D models that are available in GLUT and GLU.

3. What are the models available for texture mapping in GLUT and GLU?

4. Prove that the sum of the Bezier blending functions is everywhere unity and each function is everywhere nonnegative.

5. Prove that the sum of the B-spline blending functions is everywhere unity and each function is everywhere nonnegative.

6. Compare Bezier and B-spline curves. Please list their properties separately. Then, discuss their similarities and differences.

7. Which of the following is wrong:

a. Bezier curves are C^{2} continuity   b. A natural cubic spline is C^{1} continuity
c. B-splines are C^{2} continuity   d. Hermite curves are C^{1} continuity

8. Compared with B-spline, which of the following is true:

a. Natural spline is simpler to calculate   b. Bezier curves are global control
c. Hermite curve interpolates its end points   d. They are all C^{2} curves with segments

9. Which of the following is true about B-spline:

    a. Using the same control points multiple times is the same as increasing multiplicity
    b. All B-splines are invariant under perspective transformation
    c. Conics can be generated using certain B-splines
    d. Increasing multiplicity will reduce the curve into line segments

10. How many constraints are there for a bi-cubic Hermite surface patch? How many control points are there for a bi-cubic B-spline surface patch?

5.7 Programming Assignments

1. Check out glPolygonMode() and draw models in points, lines, and surfaces in J5_1_Quadrics.java.

2. As mentioned in the text, we can create a sphere on a display through subdivision, through a sphere's equation, or through a rotation of a circle. There are many ways to store a 3D model and display it. Explain in detail what are exactly saved in the computer for a sphere model and the algorithms used to display the model. Implement the algorithms accordingly.

3. A superellipsoid is represented as follows. Please draw the 3D model at ($a = 0, 1, 2, 3$) and ($b = 0, 1, 2, 3$) with different combinations:

$$x = r_x(\cos\phi)^a(\cos\theta)^b, \quad 0 \le \phi \le \pi, \qquad \text{(EQ 185)}$$

$$y = r_y(\cos\phi)^a(\sin\theta)^b, \quad 0 \le \theta \le 2\pi, \qquad \text{(EQ 186)}$$

$$\text{and } z = r_z(\sin\phi)^a. \qquad \text{(EQ 187)}$$

4. Draw two Hermite curves with C^1 continuity. Build an interactive system so that the constraints are interactively specified.

5. Draw a uniform non-rational B-spline with multiple control points. Again, the control points are interactively specified.

6. Draw a non-uniform non-rational B-spline, and demonstrate its difference and advantage over Uniform Non-rational B-spline.

7. Draw a B-spline curve surface with 4 patches. Allow the control points to be interactively specified. Learn GLU NURBS functions and use them to draw a surface.

6
Programming in Java3D

Chapter Objectives:

- Briefly introduce scene graph structure and Java3D programming

6.1 Introduction

Java3D is another API by Sun Microsystems that provides 3D graphics capabilities to Java applications. It is built on OpenGL and therefore has higher level of abstractions and architectures than OpenGL/JOGL. Java3D programmers work with high-level constructs, called *scene graphs*, for creating and manipulating 3D geometric objects. The details of rendering are handled automatically. Java3D programs can be stand-alone applications as well as applets in browsers that have been extended to support Java3D. A comprehensive tutorial, advanced books, and other information are available at http://java.sun.com/products/java-media/3D/collateral/

In this chapter, we provide a shortcut to scene graph structure and Java3D programming.

6.2 Scene Graph

A 3D virtual environment, or universe, is constructed by graphics models and their relations. A group of graphics models and their relations can be represented by an abstract tree structure, called scene graph, where nodes are models and link arcs

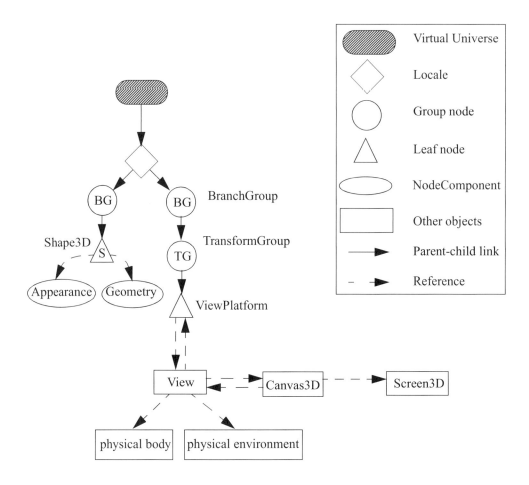

Fig. 6.1 Scene graph and its notations

represent relations. A Java3D virtual universe is created from a scene graph, as shown in Fig. 6.1.

The *nodes* in the scene graph are the objects or the instances of Java3D classes. The *arcs* represent the two kinds of relationships between nodes: parent-child or reference. A *Group node* can have any number of children but only one parent. A *Leaf node* has no children. A *Reference* associates a NodeComponent with a Leaf node. A *NodeComponent* specifies the geometry, appearance, texture, or material properties of a Leaf node (Shape3D object). A NodeComponent is not part of the scene graph tree and may be referenced by several Leaf nodes. All other objects following reference links are not part of the scene graph tree either. All nodes in the scene graph are accessible following solid arcs from the *Locale object*, which is the root. The arcs of a tree have no cycles, therefore there is only one path from the root to a leaf, which is called a *scene graph path*. Each scene graph path completely specifies the state information of its leaf. That is, the transformations and visual attributes of a leaf object depend only on its scene graph path. The scene graph, NodeComponents, references, and other objects all together form a virtual universe.

In Fig. 6.1, there are two scene graph branches. The branch on the right is for setting up viewing transformations, which is mostly the same for many different applications and is called a view branch. The branch on the left is for building up 3D objects and their attributes and relations in the virtual universe. Sometimes we call the object branch the scene graph and ignore the view branch, because the object branch is the major part in building and manipulating a virtual universe.

6.2.1 Setting Up Working Environment

To install and run Java3D, we need to install Java Development Kit first. In addition, a Java IDE is also preferred to speed up coding. At the beginning of this book, we have installed Java, JOGL, and Eclipse or JBuilder IDE. Now, we need to download and install Java3D SDK from:
http://java.sun.com/products/java-media/3D/download.html

For Windows platform, we should download the Java3D for Windows (OpenGL Version) SDK for the JDK (includes Runtime). We should install Java3D in the JDK that our IDE uses. If necessary, we can install multiple times into different version of JDKs that we use for different IDEs, such as JBuilder, which comes with its own JDK. Once we install the downloaded software, we are ready to edit and execute our sample programs.

After downloading Java3D SDK, you may download Java3D API specification as well, which includes online references to all Java3D objects as well as basic concepts and example programs. After going through this introduction, you may extend your knowledge on Java3D and use the online material to implement many more applications quickly.

Example Java3D_0.java in the following constructs a simple virtual universe as in Fig. 6.1 except that, for simplicity purposes, it uses a ColorCube object to replace the Shape3D leaf object and its appearance and geometry NodeComponents. ColorCube is designed to make a testbed easy. The result is as shown in Fig. 6.2. Here we only see the front face of the ColorCube object.

Fig. 6.2 Draw a color cube [*See* **Color Plate 7**]

/* draw a cube in Java3D topdown approach */

```java
import java.awt.*;
import java.awt.event.*;
import javax.media.j3d.*;
import com.sun.j3d.utils.geometry.ColorCube;
import javax.vecmath.Vector3f;
import com.sun.j3d.utils.universe.*;


public class Java3D_0 extends Frame {

  Java3D_0() {

    //1. Create a drawing area canvas3D
    setLayout(new BorderLayout());
    GraphicsConfiguration gc =
       SimpleUniverse.getPreferredConfiguration();
    Canvas3D canvas3D = new Canvas3D(gc);
    add(canvas3D);

    // Quite window with disposal
    addWindowListener(new WindowAdapter()
      {public void windowClosing(WindowEvent e)
        {dispose(); System.exit(0);}
      }
    );

    //2. Construct ViewBranch topdown
    BranchGroup viewBG = createVB(canvas3D);
```

```
//3. Construct sceneGraph: a color cube
BranchGroup objBG = new BranchGroup();
objBG.addChild(new ColorCube(0.2));

//4. Go live under locale in the virtualUniverse
VirtualUniverse universe = new VirtualUniverse();
Locale locale = new Locale(universe);
locale.addBranchGraph(viewBG);
locale.addBranchGraph(objBG);
}

BranchGroup createVB(Canvas3D canvas3D) {

//5. Initialize view branch
BranchGroup viewBG = new BranchGroup();
TransformGroup viewTG = new TransformGroup();
ViewPlatform myViewPlatform = new ViewPlatform();
viewBG.addChild(viewTG);
viewTG.addChild(myViewPlatform);

//6. Move the view branch to view object at origin
Vector3f transV = new Vector3f(0f, 0f, 2.4f);
Transform3D translate = new Transform3D();
translate.setTranslation(transV);
viewTG.setTransform(translate);

//7. Construct view for myViewPlatform
View view = new View();
view.addCanvas3D(canvas3D);
view.setPhysicalBody(new PhysicalBody());
view.setPhysicalEnvironment(new PhysicalEnvironment());
view.attachViewPlatform(myViewPlatform);

return (viewBG);
}


public static void main(String args[]) {

Java3D_0 frame = new Java3D_0();

frame.setSize(500,500);
frame.setVisible(true);
}
}
```

6.2.2 Drawing a ColorCube Object

The above Example *Java3D_0.java* is a Java application that draws a colored cube using Java3D. Our future examples are built on top of this first example. Here we explain the exmaple in detail. We only need to understand the following:

1. We create <u>canvas3D</u> that corresponds to the default display device with a Screen3D object implied.

2. With <u>canvas3D</u>, we construct the view branch under the BranchGroup node, <u>viewBG</u>, which will be a child under <u>locale</u>. The detail of creating the view branch will be discussed later in this section.

3. We create the object branch under <u>objBG</u>, which is a ColorCube object under the group node.

4. We create <u>universe</u> and its associated <u>locale</u>, and add the view branch and the object branch to form the virtual universe completely. Whenever a branch is attached to the Locale object, all the branch's nodes are considered to be *live*. When an object is live, it's parameters cannot be changed unless through special means that we will discuss later.

5. Here in the subroutine we initialize the view branch. Under the BranchGroup <u>viewBG</u>, we have TransformGroup <u>viewTG</u>. Under <u>viewTG</u>, we have <u>myViewPlatform</u>, which a View object (<u>view</u>) corresponding to <u>canvas3D</u> will be attached to.

6. The purpose of <u>viewTG</u> is to move the viewpoint along positive z axis to look at the origin in perspective projection. Here we translate <u>myViewPlatform</u> along positive z axis, which sets the viewpoint to be centered at $(0, 0, 2.41)$ looking in the negative z direction toward the origin, and the view plane at the origin is a square from $(-1, -1, 0)$ to $(1, 1, 0)$.

7. We construct the View object <u>view</u> and attach it with <u>myViewPlatform</u>. The View object contains all default parameters needed in rendering a 3D scene from one viewpoint as specified above. The technical details are ignored in this introduction. The PhysicalBody object contains a specification of the user's head. The PhysicalEnvironment object is used to set up input devices (sensors) for head-tracking and other uses in immersive virtual environment.

In summary, we construct a virtual universe as shown in Fig. 6.1. The object branch specifies a ColorCube object from (-0.2, -0.2, -0.2) to (0.2, 0.2, 0.2). The view branch specifies a perspective projection with a viewpoint at (0, 0, 2.41) and view plane cross section at the origin from (-1, -1, 0) to (1, 1, 0). Each scene graph path, as we can see now, is like a series of OpenGL commands for setting up viewing or drawing a hierachical scene. The details of rendering are handled automatically by the Java3D runtime system. The Java3D renderer is capable of optimizing and rendering in parallel. Therefore, in Java3D, we build a virtual universe with hierachical structure, which is composed of nodes or instances of Java3D classes, in a scene graph tree structure.

6.3 The SimpleUniverse

Because the view branch is mostly the same for many different applications, Java3D provides a SimpleUniverse class that can be used to construct the view branch automatically, as shown in Fig. 6.3. This way we can simplify the code dramatically and focus on generating object scene graph. However, we lost the flexibility of modifying and controlling View, ViewPlatform, PhysicalBody, and PhysicalEnvironment directly, which are useful under special applications. Here we ignore them for simplicity purposes, because we can use SimpleUniverse to construct a testbed with all default components in a virtual universe. We focus our attention on generating a scene graph with more contents and controls here.

Example *Java3D_1_Hello.java* generates the same result as *Java3D_0.java*, as shown in Fig. 6.2 below. The difference is that here it uses the SimpleUniverse object simpleU to construct a virtual universe, including the Locale object and the view branch, which simplifies the code significantly.

/*draw a cube in Java3D topdown approach */

```
import java.awt.*;
import java.awt.GraphicsConfiguration;
import com.sun.j3d.utils.universe.*;
import com.sun.j3d.utils.geometry.*;
import javax.media.j3d.*;
import java.awt.event.*;
```

```java
// renders a single cube.
public class Java3D_1_Hello extends Frame {

  Java3D_1_Hello() {

    //1. Create a drawing area canvas3D
    setLayout(new BorderLayout());

    GraphicsConfiguration gc =
        SimpleUniverse.getPreferredConfiguration();

    Canvas3D canvas3D = new Canvas3D(gc);
    add(canvas3D);

    //2. Create a simple universe with standard view branch
    SimpleUniverse simpleU = new SimpleUniverse(canvas3D);

    //3. Move the ViewPlatform back to view object at origin
    simpleU.getViewingPlatform().setNominalViewingTransform();

    //4. Construct sceneGraph: object branch group
    BranchGroup objBG = createSG();

    //5. Go live under simpleUniverse
    simpleU.addBranchGraph(objBG);

    // exit windows with proper disposal
    addWindowListener(new WindowAdapter() {
      public void windowClosing(WindowEvent e) {
        dispose();
        System.exit(0);
      }
    }
    );
  }


  BranchGroup createSG() {
    BranchGroup objBG = new BranchGroup();

    objBG.addChild(new ColorCube(0.2));
    return (objBG);
  }


  public static void main(String[] args) {

    Java3D_1_Hello frame = new Java3D_1_Hello();
```

```
        frame.setSize(500, 500);
        frame.setVisible(true);
    }
}
```

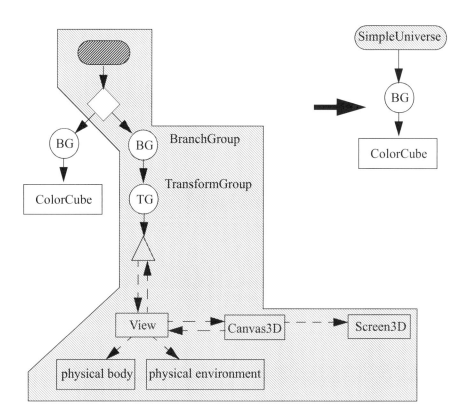

Fig. 6.3 **A SimpleUniverse generates a view branch automatically**

In the above, the method *setNominalViewingTransform()* sets the viewpoint at 2.41 meters. The default viewing volume and projection are the same as the previous example.

6.4 Transformation

In the following, we add a TransformGroup node as shown in Fig. 6.4a, which is named objTransform in the program. Here the transformation includes a rotation around *y* axis, and then a translation along *x* axis. The result is shown in Fig. 6.4b. As we mentioned earlier, a scene graph path determines the leaf object's state completely. Here, the ColorCube object will be transformed by the matrix built in objTransform and then sent to the display.

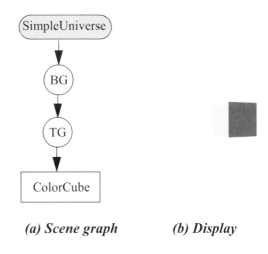

(a) Scene graph   *(b) Display*

Fig. 6.4 A transformation group node [*See Color Plate 7*]

BranchGroup objects can be *compiled*, as the method calls *objRoot.compile()* in Example *Java3D_2_Transform.java* below. Compiling a BranchGroup object converts the object and its descendants to a more efficient form for the Java3D renderer. Compiling is recommended as the last step before making it live at the highest level of a BranchGroup object, which is right under the Locale object.

/* draw a cube with transformation */

```
import com.sun.j3d.utils.geometry.*;
import javax.media.j3d.*;
import javax.vecmath.Vector3f;


public class Java3D_2_Transform extends Java3D_1_Hello {

  // Construct sceneGraph: object branch group
  BranchGroup createSG() {

    // translate object has composite transformation matrix
    Transform3D rotate = new Transform3D();
```

```
Transform3D translate = new Transform3D();
rotate.rotY(Math.PI/8);

// translate object actually saves a matrix expression
Vector3f transV = new Vector3f(0.4f, 0f, 0f);
translate.setTranslation(transV);

translate.mul(rotate); // final matrix: T*R

TransformGroup objTransform = new TransformGroup(
    translate);
objTransform.addChild(new ColorCube(0.2));

BranchGroup objRoot = new BranchGroup();
objRoot.addChild(objTransform);

// Let Java3D perform optimizations on this scene graph.
objRoot.compile();

return objRoot;
} // end of CreateSceneGraph method


public static void main(String[] args) {

    Java3D_2_Transform frame = new Java3D_2_Transform();

    frame.setSize(999, 999);
    frame.setVisible(true);
  }
}
```

6.5 *Multiple Scene Graph Branches*

In the following, we add another BranchGroup, as shown in Fig. 6.5a. The result is shown in Fig. 6.5b. Here a ColorCube object is rotated around *y* axis, and then translated along positive *x* axis, while another ColorCube object is rotated around *x* axis, and then translated along negative *x* axis. The code is shown in Example *Java3D_3_Multiple.java*.

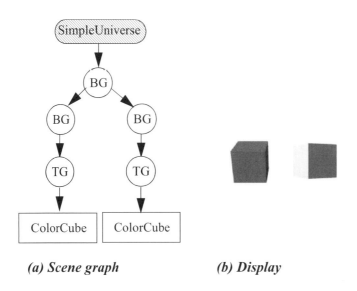

(a) Scene graph   *(b) Display*

Fig. 6.5 Multiple scene graph branches [*See* Color Plate 7]

As we mentioned before, a valid scene graph does not form a cycle, and each scene graph path determines the state of its leaf object completely. To draw two ColorCube objects exactly as in Fig. 6.5, we can form many different structures. For example, we can have the two TransformGroup nodes go directly under the root BranchGroup node; we can have the two BranchGroup nodes go directly under the Locale object, so each node is an independent root. A good hierachical structure design will be easier for understanding and implementation.

/* draw two cubes with transformations */

```
import com.sun.j3d.utils.geometry.*;
import javax.media.j3d.*;
import javax.vecmath.Vector3f;


public class Java3D_3_Multiple extends Java3D_2_Transform {

  BranchGroup createSG() {
```

```
  //1. construct two scene graphs
  BranchGroup objRoot1 = createSG1();
  BranchGroup objRoot2 = createSG2();

  BranchGroup objRoot = new BranchGroup();
  objRoot.addChild(objRoot1);
  objRoot.addChild(objRoot2);

  return objRoot;
}


BranchGroup createSG2() {

  Transform3D rotate = new Transform3D();
  Transform3D translate = new Transform3D();
  rotate.rotY(Math.PI/8);

  //2. translate and rotate matrices are mult. together
  Vector3f transV = new Vector3f(0.4f, 0f, 0f);
  translate.setTranslation(transV);
  translate.mul(rotate);

  TransformGroup objTransform = new TransformGroup(
      translate);
  objTransform.addChild(new ColorCube(0.2));

  BranchGroup objRoot = new BranchGroup();
  objRoot.addChild(objTransform);
  return objRoot;
}


BranchGroup createSG1() {

  Transform3D rotate = new Transform3D();
  Transform3D translate = new Transform3D();
  rotate.rotX(Math.PI/8);

  Vector3f transV = new Vector3f(-0.4f, 0f, 0f);
  translate.setTranslation(transV);
  translate.mul(rotate);

  TransformGroup objTransform = new TransformGroup(
      translate);
  objTransform.addChild(new ColorCube(0.2));

  BranchGroup objRoot = new BranchGroup();
  objRoot.addChild(objTransform);
```

```
      return objRoot;
    }


  public static void main(String[] args) {
    Java3D_3_Multiple frame = new Java3D_3_Multiple();
    frame.setSize(999, 999);
    frame.setVisible(true);
  }
}
```

6.6 Animation

Once a node is made live or compiled, the Java3D rendering system converts it to a more efficient internal representation so its values are fixed. In order to create animations, we need the capability to change values in a scene graph object after it becomes live. The list of values that can be modified is called the *capabilities* of the object. Each node has a set of capability bits. The values of these bits determine what capabilities exist for the node. The capabilities must be set before the node is either compiled or gone live.

As shown in Fig. 6.6, a behavior node is in reference to the transformation group node to modify its transformation and is added as a leaf child to it. Here the default transformation being modified is rotation around y axis by an interpolation of repeating values in an infinite loop. Example *Java3D_4_Animate.java* creates a scene graph as shown in Fig. 6.6, and an animation sequence is shown in Fig. 6.7.

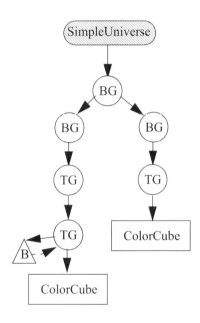

Fig. 6.6 A behavior object that modifies a transformation

Fig. 6.7 Animate a color cube [*See* Color Plate 7]

/* draw a cube with animation */

```
import com.sun.j3d.utils.geometry.*;
import javax.media.j3d.*;
import javax.vecmath.Vector3f;


public class Java3D_4_Animate extends Java3D_3_Multiple {

  BranchGroup createSG1() {

    Transform3D rotate = new Transform3D();
    Transform3D translate = new Transform3D();

    rotate.rotX(Math.PI/8);

    Vector3f transV = new Vector3f(-0.4f, 0f, 0f);
    translate.setTranslation(transV);

    translate.mul(rotate);

    TransformGroup objTransform = new TransformGroup(
        translate);

    BranchGroup objRoot = new BranchGroup();
    objRoot.addChild(objTransform);

    //1. Node closer to leaf object takes effect first
```

```
// Here objSpin transformation happens first,
//    then objTransform
TransformGroup objSpin = new TransformGroup();
objTransform.addChild(objSpin);
objSpin.addChild(new ColorCube(0.2));

//2. setCapability allows live change, and the default
//    change is rot on Y axis
objSpin.setCapability(TransformGroup.
                    ALLOW_TRANSFORM_WRITE);

//3. Alpha provides a variable value of 0-1 for
// the angle of rotation; -1 means infinite loop
// 5000 means in 5 second alpha goes from 0 to 1
Alpha a = new Alpha(-1, 5000);

//4. rotator is a behavior node in reference to ojbSpin
// i.e., rotator links ojbSpin to alpha for rotation
RotationInterpolator rotator = new RotationInterpolator(
    a, objSpin);

//5. Bounding sphere specifies a region in which a
// behavior is active. Here a sphere centered at the
// origin with radius of 100 is created.
BoundingSphere bounds = new BoundingSphere();
rotator.setSchedulingBounds(bounds);

//6. rotator (behavior node) is child of objSpin (TG)
objSpin.addChild(rotator);

return objRoot;
}


public static void main(String[] args) {

    Java3D_4_Animate frame = new Java3D_4_Animate();

    frame.setSize(999, 999);
    frame.setVisible(true);
}

}
```

Example *Java3D_4_Animate.java* animates a colored cube in Java3D. Here we explain some details in the code:

1. We create two transformation nodes, objTransform and objSpin, and objSpin is a child of objTransform. As in OpenGL, because objSpin is closer to the colored cube, it takes effect first. As we will see, objSpin is a dynamic rotation around y axis. After that, objTransform will rotate the colored cube on x axis and then translate it along negative x axis. The result is an animation and a snapshot is shown in Fig. 6.7.

2. Here we setCapability so we can modify the transformation matrix after objSpin becomes live. The default that we can write into the matrix is a rotation around y axis.

3. Here an Alpha object a is used to create a time varying value of 0 to 1 for controlling the angle of rotation. In *Alpha a = new Alpha(-1, 5000),* -1 means infinite loop and 5000 means in 5 seconds alpha goes from 0 to 1.

4. A RotationInterpolator object rotator is a behavior object that links a with objectSpin to change objSpin to a specific angle according to the current value of a. Because the value of a changes over time, the rotation changes as well. The default value of RotationInterpolator object is rotating around y axis from 0 to 360 degrees, and the colored cube will rotate 360 degrees every 5 second. You can check out RotationInterpolator Class to find out how to set up rotation around other axes.

5. Because behaviors are time consuming, for efficiency purposes, Java3D allows programmers to specify a spatial boundary, called a *scheduling region*, for a behavior to function. A behavior is not active unless the shape object is inside or intersects a Behavior object's scheduling region. Here Bounding sphere specifies a region in which a behavior is active, which is a sphere centered at the origin with radius of 1 as default.

6. The behavior object rotator is set to be one of the children of objSpin, as shown in the scene graph in Fig. 6.6.

6.7 *Primitives*

In general, we define a shape through a Shape3D object and its NodeComponent objects, as in Fig. 6.8. The Geometry node component defines the object's geometry, such as vertices and per-vertex colors. The Appearance node component defines the object's attributes, material color, texture, and other information that is not defined in geometry. For simplicity, we have only used the ColorCube class to define 3D objects, which have predefined geometry and appearance already. Here we introduce more basic primitives in Java3D, and construct a virtual universe in *Java3D_5_Primitives.java*, as in Fig. 6.9.

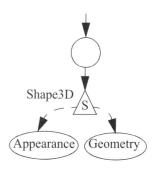

Fig. 6.8 **Shape3D**

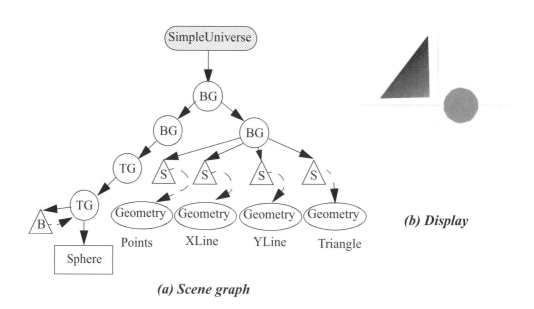

(a) Scene graph

(b) Display

Fig. 6.9 **Shapes and their geometries and appearances [*See* Color Plate 7]**

The Java3D geometric utility classes create box, cone, cylinder, and sphere geometric primitives. Here a primitive object has pre-specified geometry, but the appearance can be specified, which has more flexibility than ColorCube. Each primitive class is actually composed of one or more Shape3D objects with their own Geometry node components, and in this example the Shape3D objects share one Appearance node component specified with the primitive. In our example in the left branch of the scene graph, we specify a sphere, and its default Appearance is white. In the right branch of the scene graph, we specify several Shape3D objects (points, lines, and triangles) with only their Geometry (coordinates and colors). The points and lines may not be obvious or visible in the display, but they exist.

/* draw multiple primitives */

```java
import com.sun.j3d.utils.geometry.*;
import javax.media.j3d.*;
import javax.vecmath.*;


public class Java3D_5_Primitives extends Java3D_4_Animate {

    Color3f red = new Color3f(1.0f, 0.0f, 0.0f);
    Color3f green = new Color3f(0.0f, 1.0f, 0.0f);
    Color3f blue = new Color3f(0.0f, 0.0f, 1.0f);
    Color3f white = new Color3f(1.0f, 1.0f, 1.0f);

  //Create sphere (cone, etc) rotating around y axis
  BranchGroup createSG1() {

    Transform3D rotate = new Transform3D();
    Transform3D translate = new Transform3D();
    rotate.rotX(Math.PI/8);

    Vector3f transV = new Vector3f(0.4f, 0f, 0f);
    translate.setTranslation(transV);
    translate.mul(rotate);

    TransformGroup objTransform = new TransformGroup(
        translate);
    TransformGroup objSpin = new TransformGroup();
    BranchGroup objRoot = new BranchGroup();
    objRoot.addChild(objSpin);

    objSpin.addChild(objTransform);
```

```
        //1. draw a sphere, cone, box, or cylinder
        Appearance app = new Appearance();
        Sphere sphere = new Sphere(0.2f);
        sphere.setAppearance(app);
        objTransform.addChild(sphere);

//      Cone cone = new Cone(0.2f, 0.2f);
//      cone.setAppearance(app);
//      objSpin.addChild(cone);

//      Box box = new Box(0.2f, 0.2f, 0.2f, app);
//      box.setAppearance(app);
//      objSpin.addChild(box);

//      Cylinder cylinder = new Cylinder(0.2f, 0.2f);
//      cylinder.setAppearance(app);
//      objSpin.addChild(cylinder);


        objSpin.setCapability(TransformGroup.
                                ALLOW_TRANSFORM_WRITE);

        Alpha a = new Alpha(-1, 5000);
        RotationInterpolator rotator =
            new RotationInterpolator(a, objSpin);
        BoundingSphere bounds - new BoundingSphere();

        rotator.setSchedulingBounds(bounds);
        objSpin.addChild(rotator);

        return objRoot;
    }


    // primitive points, lines, triangles, etc.
    BranchGroup createSG2() {

        BranchGroup axisBG = new BranchGroup();

        //2. Create two points, may not be obviously visible
        PointArray points =
            new PointArray(2, PointArray.COORDINATES);
        axisBG.addChild(new Shape3D(points));

        points.setCoordinate(0, new Point3f(.5f, .5f, 0));
        points.setCoordinate(1, new Point3f(-.5f, -.5f, 0));

        //3. Create line for X axis
        LineArray xLine =
```

```
        new LineArray(2, LineArray.COORDINATES
                      |LineArray.COLOR_3);
    axisBG.addChild(new Shape3D(xLine));

    xLine.setCoordinate(0, new Point3f(-1.0f, 0.0f, 0.0f));
    xLine.setCoordinate(1, new Point3f(1.0f, 0.0f, 0.0f));
    xLine.setColor(0, red);
    xLine.setColor(1, green);

    //4. Create line for Y axis
    LineArray yLine =
        new LineArray(2, LineArray.COORDINATES
                      |LineArray.COLOR_3);
    axisBG.addChild(new Shape3D(yLine));

    yLine.setCoordinate(0, new Point3f(0.0f, -1.0f, 0.0f));
    yLine.setCoordinate(1, new Point3f(0.0f, 1.0f, 0.0f));
    yLine.setColor(0, white);
    yLine.setColor(1, blue);

    //5. Create a triangle
    TriangleArray triangle =
        new TriangleArray(3, TriangleArray.COORDINATES
                          |TriangleArray.COLOR_3);
    axisBG.addChild(new Shape3D(triangle));

    triangle.setCoordinate(0, new Point3f(-.9f, .1f, -.5f));
    triangle.setCoordinate(1, new Point3f(-.1f, .1f, .0f));
    triangle.setCoordinate(2, new Point3f(-.1f, .7f, .5f));

    triangle.setColor(0, red);
    triangle.setColor(1, green);
    triangle.setColor(2, blue);

    return axisBG;
  }


  public static void main(String[] args) {

    Java3D_5_Primitives frame = new Java3D_5_Primitives();

    frame.setSize(999, 999);
    frame.setVisible(true);
  }
}
```

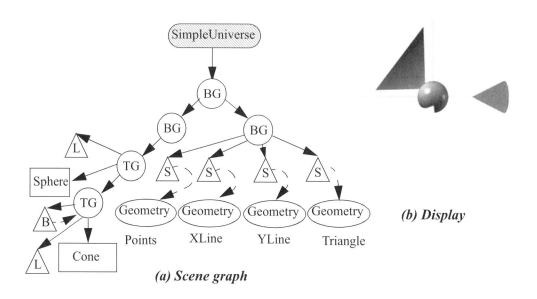

(a) Scene graph

(b) Display

Fig. 6.10 Shapes and their appearances with light sources [*See* Color Plate 7]

6.8 Appearance

As we discussed earlier, Appearance class specifies attributes, material properties, textures, etc. As shown in Fig. 6.10a, here we implement a cone with coloring attribute (red), and a sphere with material properties (whitish) that work with light sources. There are two light sources in the environment. One light source is specified as a directional light facing the origin after transformation, is a sibling of the cone with the same color, and moves with the cone. The other light source is a white fixed point light source, which, according to its scene graph path, does not go through any transformation. The result is as shown in Fig. 6.10b.

/* draw objects with Appearance - light sources */

```
import com.sun.j3d.utils.geometry.*;
import javax.media.j3d.*;
import javax.vecmath.*;
```

```
public class Java3D_6_Appearance extends
    Java3D_5_Primitives {

  static Color3f redish = new Color3f(0.9f, 0.3f, 0.3f);
  static Color3f whitish = new Color3f(0.8f, 0.8f, 0.8f);
  static Color3f blackish = new Color3f(0.2f, 0.2f, 0.2f);
  static Color3f black = new Color3f(0f, 0f, 0f);

  // primitive sphere (cone, etc) rotate around y axis
  BranchGroup createSG1() {

    TransformGroup objSpin = new TransformGroup();
    BranchGroup objRoot = new BranchGroup();
    objRoot.addChild(objSpin);

    //1.  set material attributes 4 the app. of an sphere
    Appearance app1 = new Appearance();
    Material mat = new Material();
    mat.setAmbientColor(blackish);
    mat.setDiffuseColor(whitish);
    mat.setEmissiveColor(black);
    mat.setShininess(200);
    app1.setMaterial(mat);

    // sphere at origin
    Sphere sphere =
      new Sphere(0.2f, Primitive.GENERATE_NORMALS, 80, app1);
    sphere.setAppearance(app1);
    objSpin.addChild(sphere);

    //2. specify a cone rotating around the sphere
    Transform3D rotate = new Transform3D();
    Transform3D translate = new Transform3D();
    rotate.rotZ(Math.PI/2);

    Vector3f transV = new Vector3f(0.7f, 0f, 0f);
    translate.setTranslation(transV);
    translate.mul(rotate);

    TransformGroup objTransform =
      new TransformGroup(translate);
    // objTransform is a child of objSpin
    objSpin.addChild(objTransform);
    // cone is a child of objTransform
    Cone cone = new Cone(0.2f, 0.4f);
    objTransform.addChild(cone);
```

```java
//3. Set coloring attributes for appearance of a cone
Appearance app = new Appearance();
app.setColoringAttributes(
    new ColoringAttributes(redish, 1));
cone.setAppearance(app);

//4. Specify a light source that goes with the cone
BoundingSphere lightbounds = new BoundingSphere();
Vector3f light1Direction = new Vector3f(0f, 1f, 0.0f);
// facing origin as cone
DirectionalLight light1 = new DirectionalLight(
    redish, light1Direction);
light1.setInfluencingBounds(lightbounds);
// cone is a sibling, they go through same transform.
objTransform.addChild(light1);


//5. Specify another light source
PointLight light2 = new PointLight();
light2.setPosition(-1, 1, 1);
light2.setInfluencingBounds(lightbounds);
light2.setEnable(true);
objRoot.addChild(light2);

objSpin.setCapability(TransformGroup.
                      ALLOW_TRANSFORM_WRITE);

Alpha a = new Alpha(-1, 5000);
RotationInterpolator rotator =
    new RotationInterpolator(a, objSpin);
BoundingSphere bounds = new BoundingSphere();
rotator.setSchedulingBounds(bounds);
objSpin.addChild(rotator);

return objRoot;
    }


  public static void main(String[] args) {
    Java3D_6_Appearance frame = new Java3D_6_Appearance();
    frame.setSize(999, 999);
    frame.setVisible(true);
  }
}
```

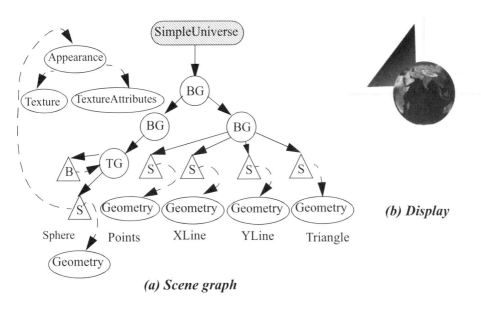

(a) Scene graph

(b) Display

Fig. 6.11 Texture mapping [*See* Color Plate 7]

6.9 *Texture Mapping*

Because texture mapping involves many options, here we go through the basic steps to make texture mapping available quickly. We just need to implement the following steps:

1. Prepare texture images: choose an image as a texture map. The image has to satisfy dimensions of power of 2 on the width and height as required by OpenGL texture mapping. A TextureLoader object loads JPEG, GIF, and other file formats.

2. Load the texture: once a TextureLoader object loads an image, the image can be used to "get texture" so the image is in texture representation.

3. Set the texture in Appearance bundle: Texture object is set in an appearance bundle referenced by the visual object.

4. Specify TextureCoordinates of Geometry: the programmer is allowed to specify the placement of the texture on the geometry through the texture coordinates. Texture coordinate specifications are made per geometry vertex. Each texture coordinate specifies a point of the texture to be applied to the vertex. When we create 3D objects, Java3D allows generating texture coordinates automatically.

Example *Java3D_7_Texture.java* demonstrates Java3D's texture capability. As shown in Fig. 6.11a, a Sphere object is specified. The sphere will be animated by its parent's behavior. At creation its geometry includes 3D coordinates and texture coordinates as well. Its texture map (image) and other attributes are specified with the Appearance node. TextureAttributes can be specified to define how the texture is applied to the Shape object, which we use default in this example.

/* Java3D texture mapping */

```
import javax.media.j3d.*;
import com.sun.j3d.utils.geometry.*;
import javax.media.j3d.*;
import com.sun.j3d.utils.image.TextureLoader;


public class Java3D_7_Texture extends Java3D_6_Appearance {

  BranchGroup createSG1() {

    TransformGroup objSpin = new TransformGroup();
    BranchGroup objRoot = new BranchGroup();

    objRoot.addChild(objSpin);

    //set material attributes 4 the app. of an sphere
    Appearance app = new Appearance();

    // Create Texture object
    TextureLoader loader =
        new TextureLoader("EARTH1.JPG", this);

    Texture earth = loader.getTexture();

    // Attach Texture object to Appearance object
    app.setTexture(earth);
```

```
// Create a sphere with texture
Sphere sphere =
    new Sphere(0.4f,Primitive.GENERATE_TEXTURE_COORDS,
               50,app);
objSpin.addChild(sphere);

objSpin.setCapability(TransformGroup.
                      ALLOW_TRANSFORM_WRITE);

Alpha a = new Alpha(-1, 5000);
RotationInterpolator rotator =
    new RotationInterpolator(a, objSpin);

BoundingSphere bounds = new BoundingSphere();
rotator.setSchedulingBounds(bounds);

objSpin.addChild(rotator);

return objRoot;
}


public static void main(String[] args) {
    Java3D_7_Texture frame = new Java3D_7_Texture();

    frame.setSize(999, 999);
    frame.setVisible(true);
}
}
```

6.10 Files and Loaders

In order to reuse constructed models and to transmit virtual universe across the Internet and on different platforms, 3D graphics files are created to save models, scenes, worlds, and animations. The relationships in an ordinary high-level 3D graphics tool are shown in Fig. 6.12. A 3D graphics tool is built on top of other 3D graphics tools or a low-level graphics library. Therefore, at the bottom of any graphics tool is a low-level graphics library. Low-level graphics libraries such as OpenGL or Direct3D are the rendering tools that actually draw 3D models into the display.

3D authoring tools are modeling tools that provide users with convenient methods to create, view, modify, and save models and virtual worlds, such as 3DStudio Max (3DS) and Alias Wavefront (OBJ). They free us from constructing complicated virtual universes and dealing with detailed specifications of 3D graphics file format definitions, which make our 3D virtual world construction job much easier. 3D authoring tools usually have good user interfaces, which provide rich object editing tools (such as object extruding, splitting, and cutting, etc.) and flexible manipulation approaches. Using these tools, you can construct complicated 3D models conveniently even without knowing the 3D file formats.

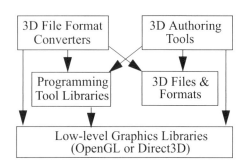

Fig. 6.12 Relationships in 3D graphics tool

3D graphics file formats are storage methods for virtual universes. Due to the complexities of a virtual universe, 3D file formats include many specifications about how 3D models, scenes, and hierarchies are stored. In addition, different applications include different attributes and activities and thus may require different file formats. Over the years, many different authoring tools are developed, and their corresponding 3D graphics file formats are in use today. DFX, VRML, 3DS, MAX, RAW, LightWave, POV, and NFF are probably the most commonly used formats.

Java3D has many loaders that are able to load virtual universes constructed from 3D modeling tools that are saved in 3D files. New loaders are in development and we can write custom loaders as well. The Java3D loaders define the interface for the loading mechanism, and users can develop file loader classes with the same interface as other loader classes. There are some loaders available at http://java3d.j3d.org/utilities/loaders.html. For a current loader class and its usage, please check the Java3D home page.

6.11 Summary

Java3D is a comprehensive high-level 3D graphics API. In this chapter, we only covered the basic concept and some examples. Many important components in Java3D are not discussed here, such as advanced objects, rendering effects, and interaction. Our purpose is to build a scene graph structure concept in your knowledge, and demonstrate what a high-level graphics programming tool can bring. From here, you can build a hierachical virtual universe and expand into many virtual environment related applications.

There are some other similar tools that exist as well, such as WorldToolKit and Vega. In the next chapter, we explain many graphics related tools and their applications, which are built on the basic graphics principle and programming we have covered so far.

6.12 Review Questions

1. Compare JOGL with Java3D; which of the following is appropriate:

    a. they are just two different 3D APIs with similar capabilities
    b. Java3D is a lower level programming environment
    c. JOGL is a runtime infrastructure for virtual objects and environments
    d. Java3D manipulates scene graphs in a hierarchy for a virtual world that JOGL doesn't perceive

2. Java3D is a fast runtime environment. Please provide three application examples where you would choose Java3D instead of JOGL.

3. Construct a scene graph for building a generalized solar system as in Chapter 4 with transparencies and texture.

4. VRML is a text based modeling language that is interpreted dynamically from the source files. A VRML browser can be implemented using Java3D. Please find a VRML file of about 100 lines of specifications and construct/sketch a scene graph from the VRML file.

6.13 Programming Assignments

1. Build a generalized solar system in Java3D. Compare the source code of this with JOGL implementation. What are the advantages and drawbacks of using Java3D?

2. Extend the above program to allow transparency and texture mapping, so the earth will be covered with earth texture, and the cones as light fields will be transparent.

3. Java3D works with an Internet browser. Try to set up and run your generalized solar system on a Web browser. Post a URL on your work.

4. Find a file loader online that would allow you to load and save a 3D model. Then, save your generalized solar system as a file. After that, download several models online and display them.

5. X3D is a scene description language in a text file format. There is a loader available for the X3D format at http://java3d.j3d.org/utilities/loaders.html. This loader also is capable of loading the majority of the VRML 97 specification, too. Please download it and use it to display some X3D and VRML models.

7

Advanced Topics

Chapter Objectives:

- Wrap up basic computer graphics principles and programming
- Briefly introduce some advanced graphics concepts and methods

7.1 Introduction

We have covered basic graphics principles and OpenGL programming. A graphics system includes a graphics library and its supporting hardware. Most of the OpenGL library functions are implemented in hardware, which would otherwise be very slow. Some advanced graphics functions built on top of the basic library functions, such as drawing curves and curved surfaces, are also part of the OpenGL library or the OpenGL Utility library (GLU). GLU is considered part of the OpenGL system to facilitate complex model construction and rendering.

On top of a graphics library, many graphics methods and tools (namely high-level graphics packages) are developed for certain capabilities or applications. For example, mathematics on curve and surface descriptions are used to construct curved shapes, constructive solid geometry (CSG) methods are used to assemble geometric models through logical operations, recursive functions are used to generate fractal images, visualization methods are developed to understand certain types of data, simulation methods are developed to animate certain processes, etc. In this chapter, we wrap up the book by briefly introducing some advanced graphics concepts.

7.2 Graphics Libraries

A *low-level graphics library* or package is a software interface to graphics hardware. All graphics tools or applications are built on top of a certain low-level graphics library. High-level graphics tools are usually easier to learn and use. An introductory computer graphics course mainly discusses the implementations and applications of low-level graphics library functions. A graphics programmer understands how to program in at least one graphics library. OpenGL, Direct3D, and PHIGS are well-known low-level graphics libraries. *OpenGL* and Direct3D are currently the most widely adopted 3D graphics APIs in research and applications.

A *high-level graphics library*, which is often called a *3D programming tool library* (e.g., OpenInventor), provides the means for application programs to handle scene constructions, 3D file imports and exports, object manipulations, and display. It is an API toolkit built on top of a low-level graphics library. Most high-level graphics libraries are categorized as animation, simulation, or virtual reality tools.

7.3 Visualization

Visualization employs graphics to make pictures that give us insight into the abstract data and symbols. The pictures may directly portray the description of the data or completely present the content of the data in an innovative form. Users, when presented with a new computed result or some other collection of online data, want to see and understand the meaning as quickly as possible. They often prefer understanding through observing an image or 3D animation rather than from reading abstract numbers and symbols.

7.3.1 Interactive Visualization and Computational Steering

Interactive visualization allows visualizing the results or presentations interactively in different perspectives (e.g., angles, magnitude, layers, levels of detail, etc.), and thus helps the user to better understand the results on the fly. Interactive visualization systems are most effective when the results of models or simulations have multiple or dynamic forms, layers, or levels of detail, which help users interact with visual presentations and understand the different aspects of the results.

For scientific computation and visualization, the integration of computation, visualization, and control into one tool is highly desirable, because it allows users to interactively "steer" the computation. At the beginning of the computation, before any result is generated, a few important pieces of feedback will significantly help in choosing correct parameters and initial values. Users can visualize some intermediate results and key factors to steer the computation in the right direction. With *computational steering*, users are able to modify parameters in their systems as the computation progresses and avoid errors or uninteresting output after long tedious computation. Computational steering is an important method for adjusting uncertain parameters, moving the simulation in the right direction, and fine tuning the results.

7.3.2 Data Visualization: Dimensions and Data Types

A visualization technique is applicable to certain data types (discrete, continual, point, scalar, or vector) and dimensions (1D, 2D, 3D, and multiple: *N*-D). *Scatter Data* represent data as discrete points on a line (1D), plane (2D), or in space (3D). We may use different colors, shapes, sizes, and other attributes to represent the points in higher dimensions beyond 3D, or use a function or a representation to transform the high dimensional data into 2D/3D. *Scalar Data* have scalar values in addition to dimension values. The scalar value is actually a special additional dimension that we pay more attention to. 2D diagrams like histograms, bar charts, or pie charts are 1D scalar data visualization methods. Both histograms and bar charts have one coordinate as the dimension scale and another as the value scale. Histograms usually have scalar values in confined ranges, while bar charts do not carry this information. Pie charts use a slice area in a pie to represent a percentage. 2D contours (iso-lines in a map) of constant values, 2D images (pixels of *x-y* points and color values), and 3D surfaces (pixels of *x-y* points and height values) are 2D scalar data visualization methods. Volume and iso-surface rendering methods are for 3D scalar data. A *voxel* (volume pixel) is a 3D scalar datum with (x, y, z) coordinates and an intensity or color value. *Vector Data* include directions in addition to scalar and dimension values. We use line segments, arrows, streamlines, and animations to present the directions.

Volume rendering or visualization is a method for extracting meaningful information from a set of 2D scalar data. A sequence of 2D image slices of human body can be reconstructed into a 3D volume model and visualized for diagnostic purposes or for planning of treatment or surgery. For example, a set of volumetric data such as a deck of Magnetic Resonance Imaging (MRI) slices or Computed Tomography (CT) can be blended into a 2D X-ray image by firing rays through the volume and blending the voxels along the rays. This is a rather costly operation and the blending methods vary. The concept of volume rendering is also to extract the contours from given data slices. An iso-surface is a 3D constant intensity surface represented by triangle strips or higher-order surface patches within a volume. For example, the voxels on the surface of bones in a deck of MRI slices appear to have the same intensity value.

From the study of turbulence or plasmas to the design of new wings or jet nozzles, flow visualization motivates much of the research effort in scientific visualization. Flow data are mostly 3D vectors or tensors of high dimensions. The main challenge of flow visualization is to find ways of visualizing multivariate data sets. Colors, arrows, particles, line convolutions, textures, surfaces, and volumes are used to represent different aspects of fluid flows (velocities, pressures, streamlines, streaklines, vortices, etc.)

The visual presentation and examination of large data sets from physical and natural sciences often require the integration of terabyte or gigabyte distributed scientific databases with visualization. Genetic algorithms, radar range images, materials simulations, and atmospheric and oceanographic measurements are among the areas that generate large multidimensional multivariate data sets. The data vary with different geometries, sampling rates, and error characteristics. The display and interpretation of the data sets employ statistical analyses and other techniques in conjunction with visualization.

The field of *information visualization* includes visualizing retrieved information from large document collections (e.g., digital libraries), the Internet, and text databases. Information is completely abstract. We need to map the data into a physical space that will represent relationships contained in the information faithfully and efficiently. This could enable the observers to use their innate abilities to understand through spatial relationships the correlations in the library. Finding a good spatial representation of the information at hand is one of the most challenging tasks in information visualization.

Many forms and choices exist for the visualization of 2D or 3D data sets, which are relatively easy to conceive and understand. For data sets that are more than 3D, visualization methods are challenging research topics. For example, the Linked micromap plots are developed to display spatially indexed data that integrate geographical and statistical summaries (http://www.netgraphi.com/cancer4/).

7.3.3 Parallel Coordinates

The *parallel coordinates* method represents d-dimensional data as values on d coordinates parallel to the x-axis equally spaced along the y-axis (Fig. 7.1, or the other way around, rotating 90 degrees). Each d-dimensional datum corresponds to the line segments between the parallel coordinates connecting the corresponding values. That is, each polygonal line of $(d-1)$ segments in the parallel coordinates represents a point in d-dimensional space. Parallel coordinates provide a

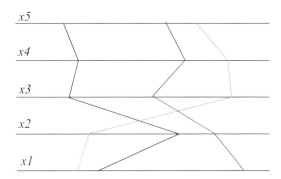

Fig. 7.1 **Parallel coordinates: an example**

means to visualize higher order geometries in an easily recognizable 2D representation. It also helps find the patterns, trends, and correlations in the data set.

The purpose of using parallel coordinates is to find certain features in the data set through visualization. Consider a series of points on a straight line in Cartesian coordinates: $y=mx+b$. If we display these points in parallel coordinates, the points on a line in Cartesian coordinates become line segments. These line segments intersect at a point. This point in the parallel coordinates is called the *dual* of the line in the Cartesian coordinates. The point~line duality extends to conic sections. An ellipse in Cartesian coordinates maps into a hyperbola in parallel coordinates, and vice versa. Rotations in Cartesian coordinates become translations in parallel coordinates, and vice versa.

Clustering is easily isolated and visualized in parallel coordinates. An individual parallel coordinate axis represents a 1D projection of the data set. Thus, separation between or among sets of data on one axis represents a view of the data of isolated clusters. The *brushing* technique is to interactively separate a cluster of data by painting it with a unique color. The brushed color becomes an attribute of the cluster. Different clusters can be brushed with different colors, and relations among clusters can then be visually detected. Heavily plotted areas can be blended with color mixes and transparencies. Animation of the colored clusters through time allows visualization of the data evolution history.

The grand tour method is used to search for patterns in the high-dimensional data by looking at the data from different angles. That is, to project the data into all possible *d*-planes through generalized rotations. The purpose of the grand tour animation is to look for unusual configurations of the data that may reflect some structure from a specific angle. The rotation, projection, and animation methods vary depending on specific assumptions. There are visualization tools that include parallel coordinates and grand tours:

ExplorN (ftp://www.galaxy.gmu.edu/pub/software/ExplorN_v1.tar), CrystalVision (ftp://www.galaxy.gmu.edu/pub/software/CrystalVisionDemo.exe), and XGobi (http://www.research.att.com/areas/stat/xgobi/).

7.4 Modeling and Rendering

Modeling is a process of constructing a virtual 3D graphics object (computer model, or model) from a real object or an imaginary entity. Creating graphics models requires a significant amount of time and effort. Modeling tools make creating and constructing complex 3D models fast and easy. A graphics model includes geometrical descriptions (particles, vertices, polygons, etc.) as well as associated graphics attributes (colors, shadings, transparencies, materials, etc.), which can be saved in a file using a standard (3D model) file format. Modeling tools help create virtual objects and environments for CAD (computer-aided design), visualization, virtual reality, simulation, education, training, and entertainment.

Rendering is a process of creating images from graphics models. 3D graphics models are saved in computer memory or hard-disk files. The term *rasterization* and *scan-conversion* are used to refer to low-level image generation or drawing. All modeling tools provide certain drawing capabilities to visualize the models generated. However, in addition to simply drawing (scan-converting) geometric objects, rendering tools often include lighting, shading, texture mapping, color blending, ray tracing, radiosity, and other advanced graphics capabilities. For example, the *RenderMan* Toolkit includes photorealistic modeling and rendering of particle systems, hair, and many other objects with advanced graphics functions such as ray tracing, volume display, motion blur, depth-of-field, and so forth. Many powerful graphics tools include modeling, rendering, animation, and other functions in one package.

Basic modeling and rendering methods were discussed in previous chapters. Here we introduce some advanced modeling and rendering techniques.

7.4.1 Sweep Representations

We can create a 3D volume by sweeping a 2D area along a linear path normal to the area. *Sweeping* is implemented in most graphics modeling tools. The generated model contains many vertices that may be eliminated. Algorithms are developed to simplify models and measure the similarity between models. A model can also be represented with multiple levels of detail for use with fast animations and high-resolution rendering interchangeably.

7.4.2 Instances

In a hierachical model, there are parts that are exactly the same. For example, all four wheels of a car can be the same model. Instead of saving four copies of the model, we save just one primitive model and three *instances*, which are really pointers to the same primitive. If we modify the primitive, we know that the primitive and the instances are identically changed.

7.4.3 Constructive Solid Geometry

Constructive Solid Geometry (CSG) is a solid modeling method. A set of solid primitives such as cubes, cylinders, spheres, and cones are combined by union, difference, and intersection to construct a more complex solid model. In CSG, a solid model is stored as a tree with operators at the internal nodes and solid primitives at the leaves. The tree is processed in the depth-first search with a corresponding sequence of operations and, finally, rendering. CSG is a modeling method that is often used to create new and complex mechanical parts.

7.4.4 Procedural Models

Procedural models describe objects by procedures instead of using a list of primitives. Fractal models, grammar-based models, particle system models, and physically-based models are all procedural models. Procedural models can interact with external events to modify themselves. Also, very small changes in specifications can result in drastic changes of form.

7.4.5 Fractals

A *fractal* is a geometric shape that is substantially and recursively self-similar. Theoretically, only infinitely recursive processes are true fractals. Fractal models have been developed to render plants, clouds, fluid, music, and more. For example, a grammar model can be used to generate self-similar tree branches: T -> T | T[T] | (T)T | (T)[T] | (T)T[T], where square brackets denote a right branch and parentheses denote a left branch. We may choose a different angle, thickness, and length for the branch at a depth in the recursion with flowers or leaves at the end of the recursions.

7.4.6 Particle Systems

Particle systems are used to model and render irregular fuzzy objects such as dust, fire, and smoke. A set of particles are employed to represent an object. Each individual particle generated evolves and disappears in space, all at different times depending on its individual animation. In general, a particle system and its particles have very similar parameters, but with different values:

- Position (including orientation in 3D space and center location x, y, and z)
- Movement (including velocity, rotation, acceleration, etc.)
- Color (RGB) and transparency (alpha)
- Shape (point, line, fractal, sphere, cube, rectangle, etc.)
- Volume, density, and mass
- Lifetime (only for particles)
- Blur head and rear pointers (only for particles)

The position, shape, and size of a particle system determine the initial positions of the particles and their range of movement. The movements of the particles are restricted within the range defined by their associated particle system. The shape of a particle system can be a point, line segment, fractal, sphere, box, or cylinder. The movement of a particle system is affected by internal or external forces, and the results of the rotations and accelerations of the particles as a whole. A particle system may change its shape, size, color, transparency, or some other attributes. The lifetime defines how long a particle will be active. A particle has both a head position and a tail position. The head position is animated and the tail position follows along for motion blur.

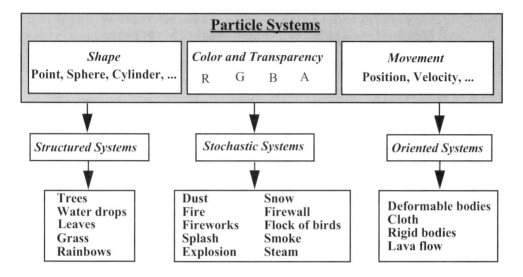

Fig. 7.2 Applications of particle systems in computer graphics

In general, particle systems are first initialized with each particle having an original position, velocity, color, transparency, shape, size, mass, and lifetime. After the initialization, for each calculation and rendering frame, some parameters of the particles are updated using a rule base, and the resulting particle systems are rendered. Fig. 7.2 summarizes the applications that employ particle systems. Structured particle systems are often used to model trees, water drops, leaves, grass, rainbows, and clouds. Stochastic particle systems are often used to model fireworks, explosions, snow, and so forth. Oriented particle systems are often used to model deformable and rigid bodies such as cloth, lava flow, etc.

7.4.7 Image-based Modeling and Rendering

Image-based modeling or rendering uses images or photographs to replace geometric models. This technique achieves shorter modeling times, faster rendering speeds, and unprecedented levels of photorealism. It also addresses different approaches to turn images into models and then back into renderings, including movie maps, panoramas, image warping, light fields, and 3D scanning.

It has been observed that the rendering process can be accelerated significantly by reusing the images to approximate the new frames instead of rendering them from the geometric model directly. The rendering error introduced by the approximation, which determines whether or not an image must be refreshed, can be calculated by comparing the image to the object's geometry.

Given the view position and direction, we can use a texture image mapped onto a polygon with transparent background to replace a complex model such as a tree, building, or human avatar. The polygon is called a *billboard* or *poster* if it is always perpendicular to the viewpoint.

We can integrate image-based rendering and model-based rendering in one application. For example, we can use images to render avatar body parts and employ geometrical transformations to move and shape the parts. A human-like avatar geometric model consists of joints and body segments. The 3D positions of these joints, governed by the movement mechanism or pre-generated motion data, uniquely define the avatar's gesture at a moment. The entire animation process is used to find the joint coordinates of each frame in terms of animation time.

If we project every segment of the 3D avatar separately onto the projection plane, the synthesis of these projected 2D images will be the final image of the 3D avatar we actually see on the screen, provided the segment depth values are taken into account appropriately. Therefore, avatar walking can be simulated by the appropriate transformations of the avatar segment images. From this point of view, the avatar's walking is the same as its segments' movements in the 3D space. Here, the basic idea is to reuse the snapshot segment images over several frames rather than rendering the avatar for each frame from the geometric model directly. The complicated human-like 3D avatar model is used only for capturing body segment images when they need to be updated. The subsequent animation frames are dynamically generated through 2D transformations and synthesis of the snapshot segment images.

7.5 *Animation and Simulation*

Computer *animation* is achieved by refreshing the screen display with a sequence of images at more than 24 frames per second. *Keyframe* animation is achieved by using pre-calculated keyframe images and in-between images, which may take a significant amount of time, and then displaying (playing back) the sequence of generated images in real time. Keyframe animation is often used for visual effects in films and TV commercials, where no interactions or unpredictable changes are necessary. Interactive animation, on the other hand, is achieved by calculating, generating, and displaying the images simultaneously on the fly. When we talk about *real-time animation*, we mean the virtual animation occurring in the same time frames as real world behavior. However, for graphics researchers, real-time animation often simply implies the animation is smooth or interactive. Real-time animation is often used in virtual environments for education, training, and 3D games. Many modeling and rendering tools are also animation tools, which are often associated with simulation.

Simulation, on the other hand, is a software system we construct, execute, and experiment with to understand the behavior of the real world or imaginary system, which often means a process of generating certain natural phenomena through scientific computation. The simulation results may be large data sets of atomic activities (positions, velocities, pressures, and other parameters of atoms) or fluid behaviors (volume of vectors and pressures). Computer simulation allows scientists to generate the atomic behavior of certain nanostructured materials for understanding material structure and durability and to find new compounds with superior quality. Simulation integrated with visualization can help pilots learn to fly and aid automobile designers in testing the integrity of the passenger compartment during crashes. For many computational scientists, simulation may not be related to any visualization at all. However, for many graphics researchers, simulation often simply means animation. Today, graphical simulation, or simply simulation, is an animation of a certain process or behavior that is often generated through scientific computation and modeling. Here we emphasize an integration of simulation and animation — the simulated results are used to generate graphics models and control animation behaviors. It is far easier, cheaper, and safer to experiment with a model through simulation than with a real entity. In fact, in many situations, such as training space-shuttle pilots and studying molecular dynamics, modeling and simulation are the only feasible methods to achieve the goals. *Real-time simulation* is an overloaded term. To computational scientists, it often means the simulation time is the actual time in which the physical process (under simulation) should occur. In automatic control, it means the output response time is fast enough for automatic feedback and control. In graphics, it often means that the simulation is animated at an interactive rate of human perception. The emphasis in graphics is more on responsiveness and smooth animation rather than strictly accurate timing of the physical process. In many simulation-for-training applications, the emphasis is on generating realistic behavior for interactive training environments rather than strictly scientific or physical computation.

7.5.1 Physics-based Modeling and Simulation: Triangular Polyhedra

A *polyhedron* is an arbitrary 3D shape whose surface is a collection of flat polygons. A *regular* polyhedron is one whose faces and vertices all look the same. There are only five regular polyhedra: the *tetrahedron* — 4 faces with three equilateral triangles at a vertex; the *cube* — 6 faces with three squares at a vertex; the *octahedron* — 8 faces with four equilateral triangles at a vertex; the *dodecahedron* — 12 faces with three pentagons at a vertex; and the *icosahedron* — 20 faces with five equilateral triangles at a vertex. The regular polyhedron models can be found in many books and graphics packages. However, the complex polyhedron model requires effort to be constructed.

Physics-based modeling (also called physically-based modeling) is a modeling method that employs physics laws to construct models. Here, we use the physics-based modeling method to construct some polyhedra. Given an arbitrary number n, we construct a triangular polyhedron model of n vertices such that the distance from each vertex to the origin equals one, and the distances between the neighboring vertices are as far distant as possible. Let's assume that the radius of the polyhedron is one. The method includes the following steps:

1. Generate n arbitrary vertices *vtx[i]* in 3D space for $i=0$ to $n-1$. Each vertex is an imaginary object with mass M.

2. Normalize the vertices so that the distance from each vertex to the origin is one. The vertices can be viewed as vectors. A normalized vector has unit length.

3. Establish a physical relation between each pair of vertices by connecting them with an imaginary spring. The spring is at rest when the distance between the vertices is two, which is the farthest distance on a sphere of unit radius. Otherwise, the spring will apply an attracting or repelling force on the two vertices. According to Hooke's law, the spring force on vertex i from all vertices j is

```
f[i].x = f[i].y = f[i].z = 0;

for (j = 0; j < n; j++) if (i != j) {
  f[i].x = f[i].x + K*(direction.x*2 - vtx[i].x + vtx[j].x);
  f[i].y = f[i].y + K*(direction.y*2 - vtx[i].y + vtx[j].y);
```

```
    f[i].z = f[i].z + K*(direction.z*2 - vtx[i].z + vtx[j].z);
}
```

where K is the spring coefficient and *direction* is a unit vector along vertex i and j. Because x, y, and z components are basically the same and independent, in the rest of the discussion we only present the x component.

As we know, a spring will bounce back and forth forever if there is no damping force. Therefore, we add an air friction force proportional to the vertex's velocity. The vertices will eventually converge to stable coordinates after a number of iterations:

```
    f[i].x = f[i].x - K1*dv[i].x;
    // K1 is the velocity damping coefficient
```

4. Calculate the new coordinates of the vertices after a short period DT according to the physics relation: for each vertex,

```
    ddv[i].x = f[i].x/M;
    // the acceleration

    dv[i].x = dv[i].x + ddv[i].x*DT;
    // the new velocity and

    vtx[i].x = vtx[i].x + dv[i].x*DT;
    // the new position.
```

5. Repeat Steps 2 to 4 until a satisfactory condition is reached. Draw the current polyhedron. A satisfactory condition can be, for example, that each vertex velocity is smaller than some criterion.

The samples and source code for the above modeling method are at http://graphics.gmu.edu/polyhedra/.

In the program, we can construct and display an equilateral triangle, a tetrahedron, an octahedron, or an icosahedron (Fig. 7.3) by simply specifying 3, 4,

Fig. 7.3 An icosahedron [*See* **Color Plate 8**]

6, or 12 vertices, respectively. We can also construct many specific irregular polyhedra. From the above example, we know that we can achieve many different shapes by specifying different physics relations among the vertices and the origin. This method is totally different from the traditional methods used to construct polyhedron models. Instead of using mathematical relations to find out the exact vertex coordinates, it relies on physics relations to dynamically construct the models. The construction process is a simulation of the designed physics relations. Many complex models could be constructed easily this way. Today, physics-based modeling is employed in some advanced graphics modeling tools for constructing certain 3D models.

7.5.2 Real-Time Animation and Simulation: A Spider Web

The display refresh rate is the rate of reading from the frame buffer and sending the pixels to the display by the video controller. A refresh rate at 60 (frames per second) is smoother than one at 30, and 120 is marginally better than 60. However, if the image frame rate is much lower, the animation could be jittery. Sometimes, it is an easy-to-be-rendered model that takes time to be constructed. Sometimes, it is an easy-to-be-constructed model that takes time to be rendered. To achieve smooth animation, we need high-performance algorithms as well as graphics hardware to efficiently carry out modeling, simulation, and graphics rendering. Graphical simulation, or simply simulation, animates certain processes or behaviors generated through scientific computation and modeling. A *simulation model* is a physics or math description of the simulated entity or system. Simulation can be used to achieve a static graphics model like a polyhedron, or dynamic behavior like a waving spider web. In the above example of modeling polyhedra, the simulation model describes the physical relationships among the vertices. The simulated results are used to generate the graphics models and control the animation behavior. That is, the simulation model describes the graphics model, and the graphics model is the simulation result.

A real-time simulation is a simulation where the time is the actual time in which the physical process (under simulation) occurs. Many real-time simulation systems are *event-driven*, in which the evolution of the simulation is determined by the complexity of both the computation and the graphics rendering. A real-time simulation can be synchronized with a wall clock, so that the simulation proceeds accurately on the physical time scale we perceive. The simulation will appear at the same speed on different computing platforms. The method is as follows. A variable (lastTime) is used to record the last time the simulation updated its state. Each time the simulation begins to update its state, it reads the computer's clock to get the current time (currentTime) and subtract lastTime from currentTime to determine the period between the current time and the last time when the state was updated. This period, the time slice passed — together with the simulation's old state — determines the simulation's new state. At the same time, lastTime will be updated to currentTime.

Real-time simulation often employs a wide range of physical laws that are functions of time. To retain numerical stability and to limit the numerical offset error, many activities cannot be calculated with a time slice bigger than a threshold. However, varying time slices between states can be so large that the numerical computation of the physics-based model diverges. Our solution to this problem is as follows. Let's assume that DT satisfies numerical stability and at simulation state m the time slice is DT_m. When DT_m is larger than DT, DT_m can be divided into a number of $DT\underline{s}$ and the physical phenomena can be simulated DT_m/DT times. The residue of the time division can be added to the next simulation period.

As an example, we simulate a spider walking on a web in real time synchronized with the wall clock. Again, we use springs to construct the simulation model. The data structure for the web is as in Fig. 7.4. The modeling method mainly includes the following steps:

1. Generate *4* vertex arrays *a[i]*, *b[i]*, *c[i]*, *and d[i]* in 3D space for *i=0* to *n-1*. Each vertex is an imaginary object with mass *M*.

2. Fix the end points of the vertex arrays.

3. Rotate the web into an orientation of your choice. The vector *down* is a fixed direction pointing toward the ground after the rotation.

4. Establish a physical relationship between neighboring vertices by connecting them with a spring line, as

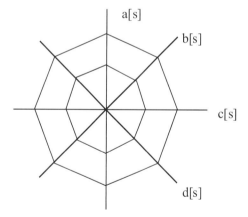

Fig. 7.4 A spider-web data structure

in Fig. 7.4. The spring is at rest when the distance between the vertices is zero. Otherwise, the spring will apply an attracting force on the two neighboring vertices. According to Hooke's law, the spring force *Fa[i]* on vertex *a[i]* includes 4 components (in x, y, and z direction, respectively; here we only show the force in x direction):

```
Fa[i].x = K*(a[i+1].x - a[i].x) + K*(a[i-1].x - a[i].x);
// the force generated by
// the 2 springs along the diagonal line

Fa[i].x = Fa[i].x + K1*(b[i].x-a[i].x)+
          K1*(d[S-1-i].x-a[i].x);
// the force generated by
// the 2 springs along the circle line

Fa[i].x = Fa[i].x - K2*da[i].x;
// the air damping force according to
// the velocity of a[i]

Fa[i].x = Fa[i].x + gravity*down.x;
// the gravity force so the web will be
// drawn towards the ground

If (spider is at a[i])
    Fa[i].x = Fa[i].x + spiderWeight*down.x;
// the spider's weight. The spider is
// moving around on the web
```

5. Calculate the new coordinates of the vertices after a period

```
DTm = period() + (DTm % DT);
```

where *period()* returns the clock time passed since last time we updated the vertices, and *(DTm % DT)* is the remainder time from the last simulation. We repeat the following simulation *(DTm/DT)* times (except the acceleration, which only calculates once):

```
dda[i].x = fa[i].x/M;
// the acceleration

da[i].x = da[i].x + dda[i].x*DT;
// the new velocity and

a[i] = a[i]+da[i]*DT;
// the new position
```

6. Draw the current spider and web.

7. Move the spider. Repeat Steps 3 to 7.

Fig. 7.5 is a snapshot of the simulation result: a spider walking on the web. We may have multiple spiders in the environment as well. The samples and source code for the above modeling method are on line at http:// graphics.gmu.edu/spider/.

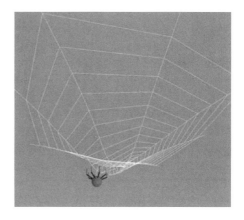

Fig. 7.5 A simulation of a spider web [*See* Color Plate 8]

7.5.3 The Efficiency of Modeling and Simulation

Fortunately, in the above example the simulation and graphics rendering are both fast enough on an ordinary PC to achieve the web and spider behavior in real time. More often than not, the simulation efficiency and the physical and visual realism are contradictory to the point that we cannot achieve both. To achieve real time, we sacrifice the physical realism and/or the visual quality by simplifying the complex physics-based model and/or the graphics rendering method. The 3D graphics rendering speed is often the bottleneck of real-time simulation. The bottom line is that the associated processing loads must not reduce the system update rate below what we consider to be real time (24 frames per second). We can improve the simulation efficiency by changing the software or hardware, or both, to accommodate real time. A real-time graphics simulation pipeline is a loop that includes the following major processes:

1. Handle user input (keyboard, mouse, external sensors, VR trackers, etc.);

2. Calculate the new state of the simulation model;

3. Preprocess 3D objects (collision detection, clipping/culling, organization, etc.);

4. Render the virtual world. Repeat Steps 1 to 4.

Software methods. For Step 2, we can simplify the simulation model to the point that it satisfies the minimum requirements, or use a simpler model that achieves the partial requirements. For Step 3, where there are different algorithms that provide collision detection and other graphics preprocessing functions, we can choose the most efficient algorithms. For Step 4, we have different rendering methods that will significantly change the efficiency. For example, we can use polygons instead of curved surfaces, shaded polygons instead of texture mapped polygons, flat polygons instead of shaded polygons, wire-frame objects instead of polygonal objects, etc. Choosing graphics rendering methods to improve efficiency often requires more understanding of the graphics system.

Hardware methods. Many low-level graphics functions are implemented in the hardware on a graphics card. In fact, without a graphics card, no graphical simulation can be in real time. However, not all graphics cards are the same. Some functions are expensive to implement in hardware. The prices on the graphics cards are different. Therefore, it is important to know what graphics functions are necessary and to purchase the card that comes with the necessary functions. For example, if a simulation application requires large-number polygon rendering, we may choose a specially configured intensive-polygon-rendering hardware. If a simulation requires frequent texture mapping, we will need texture mapping hardware. Texture mapping would be extremely slow if there were no hardware support. Some high-performance graphics cards, such as Intense3D Wildcat 5110, have very large dedicated texture memory and frame buffers for hardware texture mapping. Hardware makes it possible to achieve advanced graphics effects such as lighting, texture mapping, volume rendering, antialiasing, and scene accumulation in real time.

7.6 Virtual Reality

Virtual Reality (VR) extends 3D graphics world to include stereoscopic, acoustic, haptic, tactile, and other feedbacks to create a sense of immersion. A 3D image is like an ordinary picture we see, but a stereo image gives a strong sense of depth in 3D. It is generated by providing two slightly different views (images) of the same object to our two eyes separately. The head-mounted device (HMD), the ImmersaDesk/CAVE, and the VREX stereo projectors are different kinds of display devices for stereo images. A HMD has two separate display channels/screens to cover our two eyes. An ImmersaDesk or CAVE has only one channel like an ordinary display screen, except that it displays two different images alternatively for our two eyes. Lightweight liquid crystal shutter glasses are worn by viewers. These glasses activate each eye in succession. The glasses are kept synchronized with the two images through an infrared emitter. CAVE is the predecessor of ImmersaDesk, which is more expensive and has multiple display screens surrounding the viewers. An ImmersaDesk can be considered to be a one-wall CAVE. VREX's stereo projectors generate two images at the same time that can be viewed through lightweight, inexpensive polarized glasses.

7.6.1 Hardware and Software

The key hardware technologies in achieving VR are real-time graphics, stereo displays/views, tracking sensors, sound machines, and haptic devices. Real-time graphics (computer) and stereo displays (HMD, ImmersaDesk, CAVE, or VREX projectors) allow us to view stereoscopic scene and animation, and provide us a sense of immersion. Tracking sensors, which get the position and orientation of the viewer's head, hands, body parts, or other inputs, will enable us to manipulate models and navigate in the virtual environment. Sound machines provide a sense of locations and orientations of certain objects and activities in the environment. Like sound machines, haptic devices vibrate and touch a user's body, generating another feedback from the virtual environment in addition to stereoscopic view and 3D sound, enhancing the sense of immersion.

Some VR software tools are available that recognize well-defined commercial tracking sensors, sound machines, and haptic devices, in addition to functions in developing 3D virtual environment. Sense8's WorldToolKit and World_Up are cross-platform software development system for building real-time integrated 3D applications. WorldToolKit also supports network-based distributed simulations, CAVE-like immersive display options, and many interface devices, such as HMDs, trackers, and navigation controllers. Lincom's VrTool is an OpenInventor-based toolkit to provide a rapid prototyping capability to enable VR users to quickly get their application running with the minimum amount of effort. MultiGen-Paradigm's Vega is a real-time visual and audio simulation software tool that includes stereo imaging. MR (Minimal Reality) Toolkit by the graphics group at University of Alberta is a set of software tools for the production of virtual reality systems and other forms of three-dimensional user interfaces.

7.6.2 Non-immersive Systems

Often non-immersive 3D graphics systems are also called VR systems by some people. Users can change the viewpoint and navigate in the virtual world through input devices interactively. VRML (Virtual Reality Modeling Language) is a

Web-based 3D modeling and animation language – a subset of OpenInventor. Java3D, similar to VRML, is also a Web-based graphics tool to assemble and manipulate predefined geometric models. DIVE (Distributed Interactive Virtual Environment) is an Internet-based multi-user VR system where participants navigate in 3D space and see, meet and interact with other users and applications. Alice is a scripting and prototyping environment for 3D object behavior. By writing simple scripts, Alice users can control object appearance and behavior, and while the scripts are executing, objects respond to user input via mouse and keyboard.

7.6.3 Basic VR System Properties

In an immersive VR system, users wear head-mounted devices (HMD) or special glasses to view stereoscopic images. The viewpoint usually follows the viewer's head movement in real time. In a non-immersive VR, which is usually a lot cheaper, users usually do not wear any device, and the viewpoint does not follow the user's head movement. Users navigate in the virtual world through input devices interactively and the image is usually a first-person view. In a VR system, navigation allows a user to move around and to view virtual objects and places, and interaction provides an active way for a user to control the appearance and behavior of objects. 3D navigation, probably with interaction, stereoscopes, and visualization, is the main property of a VR system, immersive or not.

Simulation is another property of a VR system. Simulations integrate scientific results and rules to control, display, and animate virtual objects, behaviors, and environments. Without simulation, the virtual world will not be able to describe and represent real world phenomena correctly. Different VR applications may simulate different objects, phenomena, behaviors, and environments, mostly in real time. These properties make the VR technology able to be applied in various areas such as data visualization, training, surgery, scientific studying, science learning, and game playing.

7.6.4 VR Tools

A VR system often simulates certain real-world activities in various areas, such as training, education, and entertainment. A VR system always repeats the following processing steps:

1. Handle user inputs from various devices — keyboard, mouse, VR trackers, sensors, voice recognition systems, etc.

2. Calculate the new state of the objects and the environment according to the simulation models.

3. Preprocess 3D objects including collision detection, levels of detail, clipping/culling, etc.

4. Render the virtual world.

In order to achieve the above process, the software in the VR system has to be able to create a virtual world, handle various events from input devices, control the appearances and behaviors of the 3D objects, render the virtual world and display it on the display devices. In Step 2, different VR applications may use different simulation models. No matter what application a VR system implements, the software to handle the other three steps, a high-level graphics library called a VR tool (or VR toolkit), is always needed. Therefore, VR tools, which are built on a low-level graphics library, are usually independent of the applications.

7.6.5 VR Simulation Tools

A VR system is usually a VR application implemented on top of a VR tool, which provides an API for the VR application to manipulate the objects according to the simulation models. VR tools are likely to be device dependent, built on low-level basic graphics libraries with interfaces to sensory devices. Some VR tools, such as MR Toolkit, OpenInventor, and WorldToolkit, only provide APIs embedded in certain programming languages for VR developers. It requires more knowledge and programming skills to employ these toolkits, but they provide more flexibility in application implementations. Others, such as Alice and WorldUp (often called VR simulation tools), provide graphical user interfaces (GUIs) for the developers to build applications. Developers achieve virtual worlds and simulations by typing, clicking, and dragging through GUIs. Sometimes simple script languages are used to construct simulation processes. VR simulation tools allow developing a VR system quicker and easier, but the application developed is an independent fixed module that cannot be modified or integrated in a user-developed program. A VR simulation tool, which is part of VR tools, is generally developed on top of another VR tool, so it is one level higher than the basic VR tools in software levels.

7.6.6 Basic Functions in VR Tool

In addition to a simulation loop and basic graphics functions, a VR tool usually provides the following functions as well:

- **Import** that loads 3D objects or worlds from files on the hard disk into computer internal memory as data structures (called scene graphs) for manipulation and rendering. The 3D virtual world is usually generated with a 3D modeling tool.

- **Stereo display** that allows two different projections of the VR environment to appear in our two eyes. For different display devices, such as HMD, CAVE, and Workbench, the display channels and operating mechanisms are different. A VR tool should support different display devices as well.

- **Event handling** that accepts and processes user interaction and control. Various input from users and external devices are generated in the form of events. The event handling must be fast enough to guarantee the system to run in real time.

- **Audio and haptic output** that generates sounds through the computer speaker or headphone and signals to drive the haptic devices.

- **Collision detection** that prevents two objects to collide with each other and to touch or pick up virtual objects. Collision detection is a time-consuming operation, so most VR tools provide collision Enable/Disable switching functions for VR applications to turn it on/off if necessary.

- **Level of detail (LOD)** that optimizes the rendering detail for faster display and animation. To provide LOD, a VR tool should save multiple different models for one object. VR tool will choose a corresponding model to render according to the distance between the viewpoint and the object.

- **User interface** that accepts user inputs for data and status managements.

7.6.7 Characteristics of VR

We have briefly introduced VR. What does a high-end VR offer data visualization that conventional technologies do not? Although a number of items could be cited, here is a list of those that are important:

- **Immersion**, which implies realism, multisensory coverage, and freedom from distractions. Immersion is more an ultimate goal than a complete virtue due to the hardware limitations. For data visualization, immersion should provide a user with an increased ability to identify patterns, anomalies, and trends in data that is visualized.

- **Multisensory**, which allows user input and system feedback to users in different sensory channels in addition to traditional hand (mouse/keyboard) input and visual (screen display) feedback. For data visualization, multisensory allows multimodal manipulation and perception of abstract information in data.

- **Presence**, which is more subjective – a feel of being in the environment, probably with other realistic, sociable, and interactive objects and people. Presence can contribute to the "naturalness" of the environment in which a user works and the ease with which the user interacts with that environment. Clearly, the "quality" of the virtual reality—as measured by display fidelity, sensory richness, and real-time behavior—is critical to a sense of presence.

- **Navigation**, which permits users to move around and investigate virtual objects and places not only by 3D traversal, but through multisensory interactions and presence. Navigation motivate users to "visualize" and investigate data in multiple perspectives that goes beyond traditional 3D graphics.

- **Multi-modal displays**, which "displays" the VR contents through auditory, haptic, vestibular, olfactory, and gustatory senses in addition to the visual sense. The mapping of information onto more than one sensory modality may well increase the "human bandwidth" for understanding complex, multi-variate data. Lacking a theory of multisensory perception and processing of information, the critical issue is determining what data "best" maps onto what sensory input channel. Virtual reality offers the opportunity to explore this interesting frontier to find a means of enabling users to effectively work with more and more complex information.

7.7 Graphics on the Internet: Web3D

The Internet has been the most dynamic new technology in the past decade. Many Web-based 3D modeling, rendering, and animation tools have emerged. It is not difficult to foresee that Web3D will be the future of education, visualization, advertising, shopping, communication, and entertainment. Currently, most Web3D tools are individual plug-ins for a general Web browser. Most of the tools are built on OpenGL or Direct3D, such as X3D (VRML) browser and the Java3D programming environment. Here, after a brief introduction to VRML and X3D, we discuss Java3D in detail to integrate with Java and JOGL programming.

7.7.1 Virtual Reality Modeling Language (VRML)

VRML is a scene description language that presents 3D objects and environments over the Internet. It is also a file format that defines the layout and content of a 3D world. VRML worlds usually have the file extension *.wrl* or *.wrl.gz* as opposed to *.html*. When a Web browser sees a file with the *.wrl* file extension, it launches the VRML engine, which is usually a plug-in viewer. A VRML file containing complex interactive 3D worlds is similar to an ordinary HTML page in size.

7.7.2 X3D

X3D is new open file format standard for 3D graphics and interactive simulation based on VRML. It provides an XML-encoded scene graph and scene authoring interface. The XML encoding enables 3D to be incorporated into Web services and distributed environments (including mobile computing devices), and facilitates cross-platform 3D data transfer between applications. X3D is VRML Backwards Compatible and preserves VRML97 content and developments.

7.7.3 Java3D

Java3D by Sun Microsystems, which was introduced in the previous chapter, is a scene-graph based 3D API that runs on multiple platforms, which can be deployed over the Internet. Unlike JOGL, which is a low-level OpenGL graphics library, Java3D was developed earlier on top of Direct3D or OpenGL with a scene-graph strecture. 3D graphics can be easily integrated with Java applications and applets. VRML and other 3D files can be loaded into the Java3D environment, which are controlled and manipulated according to the program and user interactions.

On top of lower graphics libraries, many new Web-based 3D API engines similar to Java3D have been developed by individuals and companies. VRML, X3D, Java, Java3D, Streaming Media, and dynamic database are evolving technologies that will enable a new kind of 3D hypermedia Web site.

7.8 3D File Formats

In order to reuse constructed models and to transmit virtual worlds across the Internet and on different platforms, 3D graphics files are created to save models, scenes, worlds, and animations. However, graphics developers have created many different 3D graphics file formats for different applications. Here, we discuss some popular 3D graphics file formats, programming tool libraries that understand different formats, authoring tools that create virtual worlds and save them in graphics files, and format conversion tools that transform files from one format into another. We hope to provide a panoramic view of 3D virtual world technologies to facilitate 3D modeling, reuse, programming, and virtual world construction.

The relationships in an ordinary high-level 3D graphics tool are shown in Fig. 7.6. A 3D graphics tool is built on top of other 3D graphics tools or a low-level graphics library. Therefore, at the bottom of any graphics tool is a low-level graphics library. Low-level graphics libraries such as OpenGL or Direct3D are the rendering tools that actually draw 3D models into the display. 3D models can also be stored and transmitted as 3D graphics files. 3D authoring tools

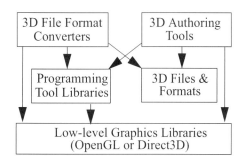

Fig. 7.6 Relationships in 3D graphics tools

are modeling tools that provide users with convenient methods to create, view, modify, and save models and virtual worlds. In general, a 3D authoring tool includes a 3D browser. 3D browsers or viewers are graphics tools that read, analyze, and convert 3D graphics files into the tools' internal formats, and then display the converted worlds to the user. 3D graphics viewers, authoring tools, and format converters may access 3D files directly, or go through programming tool library functions.

7.8.1 3D File Formats

There are different names for virtual worlds or environments. A virtual world is a scene database, which is composed of hierarchical 3D scenes, for example, as in VRML. A 3D scene is an ordered collection of nodes that include 3D models, attributes, animations, and so forth. 3D graphics file formats are storage methods for virtual worlds. Due to the complexities of virtual worlds, 3D file formats include many specifications about how 3D models, scenes, and hierarchies are stored. In addition, different applications include different attributes and activities and thus may require different file formats. Over the years, many different 3D graphics file formats have been developed that are in use today. DFX, VRML, 3DS, MAX, RAW, LightWave, POV, and NFF are probably the most commonly used formats.

7.8.2 3D Programming Tool Libraries

3D programming tool libraries provide powerful and easy-to-use functions for programs to handle 3D file imports and exports, model and scene constructions, and virtual world manipulations and display. They are also called high-level graphics libraries, built on top of low-level graphics libraries, but they are really primitive functions for higher-level graphics applications. They make sophisticated 3D file formats and virtual world hierarchies easy to handle and thus reduce application developers' programming efforts. Many high-level graphics tools are built on top of certain programming tool libraries. Usually, a 3D programming tool library supports one 3D file format by providing a series of functions that an application program can call to store, import, parse, and manipulate 3D models or scenes. If we develop our own 3D applications, we save much time and effort by using a 3D programming tool library. In general, for the same file format, commercial products with customer service are much more reliable than freeware tools.

7.8.3 3D Authoring Tools

3D graphics authoring tools, which in general are modeling tools, free us from constructing complicated objects, worlds, and dealing with complicated specifications of 3D graphics file format definitions and make our 3D world construction job much easier. 3D authoring tools usually have good user interfaces, which provide rich object editing tools (such as object extruding, splitting, and cutting, etc.) and flexible manipulation approaches. Using these tools, you can construct complicated 3D models conveniently even without knowing the 3D file formats.

7.8.4 3D File Format Converters

There are many 3D file formats in use. Every 3D file-format has its specific details. People have created and are still creating huge amounts of 3D models and 3D scenes with different 3D graphics file formats. Without knowing clearly the 3D file format specifications, is it possible — or is there a shortcut for us — to use these different formatted 3D resources and import (reuse) them into our own 3D worlds? Fortunately, the answer is yes. We can employ the 3D graphics file format conversion tools. By the way, many 3D authoring tools also provide certain 3D file format conversion functions.

Some attributes and properties of the 3D models or scenes may be lost during the format converting. This is because some specifications of a 3D file format can't be translated into another 3D file format; the converters just throw these specifications away. So we should not anticipate that all the details of the 3D models or scenes will be fully translated from one 3D file format to another. Here we briefly introduce a couple of commonly used tools. A detailed list of the tools is provided later.

7.8.5 Built-in and Plug-in VRML Exporters

X3D/VRML is the standard 3D file format on the Web. Many 3D file converters can convert different file formats to VRML format. Many 3D authoring tools have the capability to import 3D models from some other file formats and export 3D scenes to VRML file format. Here is a list of authoring tools that support VRML export: Alias/Wavefront's Maya, AutoCAD's Mechanical Desktop, Bentley MicroStation, CAD Studio, Kinetix's VRML Exporter (a free plug-in for 3D Studio MAX), Lightwave, Poser, and SolidWorks.

7.8.6 Independent 3D File Format Converters

Some independent 3D file format conversion tools, such as Crossroads 3D and 3DWinOGL, are free. Others are commercial products with reliable technique supports, such as Interchange and NuGraf.

7.9 3D Graphics Software Tools

Today, 3D graphics tools, or simply 3D tools, facilitate powerful visual technologies, including visualization, modeling, rendering, animation, simulation, and virtual reality. These visual technologies enable new methods in research, engineering, medicine, and entertainment. Scientists in different disciplines realize the power of 3D graphics but are also bewildered by the complex implementations of a graphics system and numerous 3D tools. If we choose a wrong 3D tool for an application, we likely end up with unsatisfactory results. Hopefully, if we know what basic functions many graphics tools provide, we can understand and employ some graphics tools without spending much precious time on learning all the details that may not be applicable.

7.9.1 Low-Level Graphics Libraries

OpenGL, Direct3D, PHIGS, and GKS-3D are well-known low-level graphics libraries. As we know, Java is a rapidly growing language and many universities have already adopted it as the programming platform. Released by Sun Microsystems in June 2003, the recent OpenGL binding with Java, JOGL, provides students, scientists, and engineers a new venue of graphics learning, research, and applications. The examples in this book are developed in JOGL.

Direct3D is the de facto standard 3D graphics API for Windows platform. It has an OpenGL-comparable feature set. It is mainly used in PC games. Both Direct3D and OpenGL are mostly supported by hardware graphics card vendors.

PHIGS and GKS-3D are earlier international standards that were defined in the 1980s. Some high-level graphics packages had been developed on PHIGS or GSK-3D.

7.9.2 Visualization

AVS, IRIS Explorer, Data Explorer, MATLAB, PV-WAVE, Khoros, and Vtk are multiple purpose visualization commercial products that satisfy most of the visualization needs. AVS has applications in many scientific areas, including engineering analysis, CFD, medical imaging, and GIS (Geographic Information Systems). It is built on top of OpenGL and runs on multiple platforms. IRIS Explorer includes visual programming environment for 3D data visualization, animation, and manipulation. IRIS Explorer modules can be plugged together, which enables users to interactively analyze collections of data and visualize the results. IRIS Explorer is built on top of OpenInventor, an interactive 3D object scene management, manipulation, and animation tool. OpenInventor was used as the basis for the Virtual Reality Modeling Language (VRML). The rendering engine for IRIS Explorer and OpenInventor are OpenGL. IBM's Data Explorer (DX) is a general-purpose software package for data visualization and analysis. OpenDX is the open source software version of the DX Product. DX is also built on top of OpenGL and runs on multiple platforms. MATLAB was originally developed to provide easy access to matrix software. Today, it is a powerful simulation and visualization tool used in a variety of application areas including signal and image processing, control system design, financial engineering, and medical research. PV-WAVE integrates charting, volume visualization, image processing, advanced numerical analysis, and many other functions. Khoros is a software integration, simulation, and visual programming environment that includes image processing and visualization. Vtk is a graphics tool that supports a variety of visualization and modeling functions on multiple platforms. In Vtk, applications can be written directly in C++ or in Tcl (an interpretive language).

Volumizer, 3DVIEWNIX, ANALYZE, and VolVis are 3D imaging and volume rendering tools. Volume rendering is a method of extracting meaningful information from a set of volumetric data. For example, a sequence of 2D image slices of the human body can be drawn (namely rendered) in 3D volume and visualized for diagnostic purposes or for planning of surgery.

StarCD, FAST, pV3, FIELDVIEW, EnSight, and Visual3 are CFD (Computational Fluid Dynamics) visualization tools. Fluid flow is a rich area for visualization applications. Many CFD tools integrate interactive visualization with scientific computation of turbulence or plasmas for the design of new wings or jet nozzles, the prediction of atmosphere and ocean activities, and the understanding of material behaviors.

NCAR, Vis5D, FERRET, Gnuplot, and SciAn are software tools for visual presentation and examination of data sets from physical and natural sciences, often requiring the integration of terabyte or gigabyte distributed scientific databases with visualization. The integration of multi-disciplinary data and information (e.g., atmospheric, oceanographic, and geographic) into visualization systems will help and support cross-disciplinary explorations and communications.

7.9.3 Modeling and Rendering

Modeling tools make creating and constructing complex 3D models easy and simple. A graphics model includes geometrical descriptions (particles, vertices, polygons, etc.) as well as associated graphics attributes (colors, shadings, transparencies, materials, etc.), which can be saved in a file using certain standard 3D model file formats. Modeling tools help create virtual objects and environments for CAD (computer-aided design), visualization, education, training, and entertainment. For examples, MultigenPro is a powerful modeling tool for 3D objects and terrain generation/editing, AutoCAD and MicroStation are popular for 2D/3D mechanical designing and drawing, and Rhino3D is for freeform curve surface objects. There are numerous powerful modeling tools around.

All modeling tools provide certain drawing capabilities to visualize the models generated. However, in addition to simply drawing (scan-converting) geometric objects, rendering tools often include lighting, shading, texture mapping, color blending, ray tracing, radiosity, and other advanced graphics capabilities. For example, RenderMan Toolkit includes photorealistic modeling and rendering of particle system, hair, and many other objects with advanced graphics functions such as ray tracing, volume display, motion blur, depth-of-field, and so forth. Some successful rendering tools were free (originally developed by excellent researchers at their earlier career or school years), such as POVRay, LightScape, Rayshade, Radiance, and BMRT. POVRay is a popular ray tracing package across multiple platforms that provides a set of geometric primitives and many surface and texture effects. LightScape employs radiosity and ray tracing to produce realistic digital images and scenes. Rayshade is an extensible system for creating ray-traced images that includes a rich set of primitives, CSG (constructive solid geometry) functions, and texture tools. Radiance is a rendering package for the analysis and visualization of lighting in design. It is employed by architects and engineers to predict illumination, visual quality and appearance of design spaces, and by researchers to evaluate new lighting technologies. BMRT (Blue Moon Rendering Tools) is a RenderMan-compliant ray tracing and radiosity rendering package. The package contains visual tools to help users create RenderMan Input Bytestream (RIB) input files. Today, some of these tools are getting obsolete due to lack of support and continuation.

Many powerful commercial graphics tools include modeling, rendering, animation, and other functions in one package, such as Alias|Wavefront's Studio series and Maya, SoftImage, 3DStudioMax, LightWave, and TrueSpace. It takes serious course training to use these tools. Alias|Wavefront's Studio series provides extensive tools for industrial design, automotive styling, and technical surfacing. Its Maya is a powerful and productive 3D software for character animation that has been used to create visual effects in some of the hottest film releases, including *A Bug's Life* and *Titanic*. SoftImage3D provides advanced modeling and animation features such as NURBS, skin, and particle system that are excellent for special effects and have been employed in many computer games and films, including animations in *Deep Impact* and *Airforce One*. 3DStudioMax is a very popular 3D modeling, animation, and rendering package on Windows platform for game development. Its open plug-in architecture makes it an ideal platform for third-party developers. LightWave is another powerful tool that has been successfully used in many TV feature movies, games, and commercials. TrueSpace is yet another popular and powerful 3D modeling, animation, and rendering package on Windows platforms.

7.9.4 Animation and Simulation

Many modeling and rendering tools, such as 3DStudioMax, Maya, and MultigenPro, are also animation tools. Animation is closely related to and   associated with simulation. Vega is MultiGen-Paradigm's software environment for real-time visual and audio simulation, virtual reality, and general visualization applications. It provides the basis for building, editing, and running sophisticated applications quickly and easily. It simplifies development of complex applications such as flight simulation, simulation-based design, virtual reality, interactive entertainment, broadcast video, CAD, and architectural walk-through. EON Studio is a comprehensive tool box for creating and deploying interactive real-time 3D simulations on the Windows platforms. Popular application areas include marketing and sales tools, product development, simulation based training, architectural studies, and community planning.   Activeworlds is a collection of networked virtual environments for interactive shopping, gaming, and chatting. It's a networked virtual environment that provides a range of user, client, server, and development applications. WorldUp is a 3D modeling, rendering, and simulation tool good at creating various VR worlds. 20-sim is a modeling and simulation program for electrical, mechanical, and hydraulic systems or any combination of these systems. VisSim/Comm is a Windows-based modeling and simulation program for end-to-end communication systems at the signal or physical level. It provides solutions for analog, digital, and mixed-mode communication system designs. SIMUL8 is a visual discrete event simulation tool. It provides performance measures and insights into how machines and people will perform in different combinations. Mathematica is an integrated environment that provides technical computing, simulation, and communication. Its numeric and symbolic computation abilities, graphical simulation, and intuitive programming language are combined with a full-featured document processing system. As we discussed earlier, MATLAB, Khoros, and many other tools contain modeling and simulation functions.

7.9.5 Virtual Reality

Some VR software tools are available that recognize well-defined commercial tracking sensors, sound machines, and haptic devices, in addition to functioning as developing and rendering stereo virtual environments. Java3D is an extension to Java for displaying 3D graphics, and it includes methods for stereo virtual environment. Sense8's WorldToolKit and World_Up are cross-platform software development systems for building real-time integrated 3D applications. Lincom's VrTool is an OpenInventor-based toolkit to provide a rapid prototyping capability to enable VR users to quickly get their application running with the minimum amount of effort. MultiGen-Paradigm's Vega is a real-time visual and audio simulation software tool that includes stereo imaging. MR (Minimal Reality) Toolkit is a set of software tools for the production of virtual reality systems and other forms of three-dimensional user interfaces.

7.9.6 Web3D

VRML is a scene description language that presents 3D objects and environments over the Internet. It is also a file format that defines the layout and content of a 3D world. VRML worlds usually have the file extension .wrl or .wrl.gz as opposed to .html. When a Web browser sees a file with the .wrl file extension, it launches the VRML engine, which is usually a plug-in viewer. A VRML file containing complex interactive 3D worlds is similar to an ordinary HTML page in size. VRML was first specified in 1994 from simplifying the OpenInventor file format by SGI. The current version is VRML97 (ISO/IEC 14772-1:1997). Since 1997, VRML was mostly stopped due to the debut of X3D, which is VRML compatible.

X3D is a newer Open Standard XML-enabled 3D file format to enable Web3D. It has a rich set of features for use in visualization, CAD, simulation, and Web-based virtual environment. According to Web3D Consortium (http://www.web3d.org), X3D is a considerably more mature and refined standard than its VRML predecessor.

Xj3D is an emerging API of the Web3D Consortium focused on creating a toolkit for VRML97 and X3D content written completely in Java. This toolkit has the capability to import X3D and VRML content as well as to create a fully-fledged browser. Web standards or file specifications, such as X3D (http://www.web3d.org) or VRML, can then be executed in existing browsers (http://www.web3d.org/applications/tools /viewers_and_browsers/).

Java3D by Sun Microsystems, Inc. has been employed to develop web-based 3D animations. Java3D, however, is not actively supported. Instead, JOGL (Java for OpenGL) is under development.

On top of the lower graphics libraries, many new Web-based 3D API engines similar to Java3D have been developed by individuals and companies. XML, X3D, VRML, Java3D, streaming media, and dynamic database are evolving technologies that will enable a new kind of 3D hypermedia Website in the future if not now.

7.9.7 3D File Format Converters

There are 3D model and scene file format converting tools available, such as PolyTrans, Crossroads, 3DWin, InterChange, Amapi3D, PolyForm, VIEW3D, and Materialize3D. Some attributes and parameters unique to certain formats will be lost or omitted for simplicity in the conversions.

PolyTrans imports and exports about 24 different file formats. Each import converter basically simulates a specific animation/rendering program, allowing it to translate the external scene database to the internal PolyTrans scene database format. Once imported, the scene can be manipulated and/or examined with the PolyTrans graphical user interface then exported to another format. NuGraf, a companion of PolyTrans, includes a rendering software that allows all the supported import 3D formats to be rendered and contains all the functionality of PolyTrans. PolyTrans converts formats among Alias Triangle, Apple 3D Metafile, 3DS, Lightwave, NuGraf BDF, OpenFlight, SoftImage, StereoLithography, Strata StudioPro, TrueSpace, and Wavefront. Crossroads is a freeware that converts formats among 3D Studio (3DS), AutoCAD (DXF), POVRay, RAW Triangle, TrueSpace, VRML, Wavefront, and WorldToolkit. 3DWin is another freeware that includes 3DS (*.3ds, *.prj, *.asc), Imagine (*.iob, *.obj), Lightwave (*.iwo, *.iws), Autodesk (*.dxf), POV-Ray (*.pob, *.pov), Alias/Wavefront (*.obj), SoftFX (*.sce), RenderWare (*.rwx), VRML (*.wrl), Dirext 3D (*.x), and Real 3D (*.rpl, *.obj). InterChange includes 3DS, MLI, Alias, BRender, CAD-3D, Coryphaeus, GDS, Imagine, LightWave, Movie BYU, Haines NFF, PLG, Prisms, Pro/E, QuickDraw 3D, RenderMorphics, Sculpt, Sense8 NFF, Stereolithography, Swivel, Symbolics, TrueSpace, Vertigo, Vista DEM, VideoScape, Wavefront, Inventor, Alias, and VRML files. Amapi3D is an interactive 3D modeler and converter for PC and Mac that creates and converts models for a range of applications. It provides 3D file format converting functions including imports: AutoCAD DXF, IGES, VRML, 3DMF (Mac), Illustrator, 3DS, Softimage, Amapi,

Immersion MicroScribe-3D, and PICT (Mac); and exports: AutoCAD DXF, 3DS, Renderman RIB, 3DGF, Illustrator, RayDream, IGES, LightWave, FACT (Mac), 3DMF, VRML, Artlantis Render, STL, TrueSpace, POVRay, Softimage, PICT, HPGL, 3DMF (Mac), and Amapi. PolyForm converts over 20 3D file formats including 3DS, DXF, TrueSpace, Wavefront, LightWave3D, Imagine, Sculpt 4D, Caligari, Vista Pro DEM, Scenery Animator DEM, Color PostScript, and EPS. VIEW3D is a 3DS file viewer that can render 3DS files in OpenGL then output them as C programs in OpenGL language, thus you can include them in your own OpenGL applications. Materialize3D is a 3D model converter, material and texture editor, and polygon processor. It has an easy-to-use interface that allows you to process any polygons you desire regardless of model object hierarchies, create vertex normals, reverse polygon ordering, project textures, and add or modify materials and textures. It has imports: 3DS, AutoCAD, and Direct3D X; and exports: POV-ray, AutoCAD, and Direct3D X.

Index